S0-BBJ-542

"**Sex in Human Loving** will give you a more valid *Everything You Always Wanted to Know About Sex* and collaterally, yourself."
—*The Kirkus Reviews*

"Don't mistake it for a sex manual...breezy, colloquial and loaded with one-liners."
—*Publishers' Weekly*

"Berne's bantering returns a degree of amused sanity to a favorite sport and preoccupation of humanity." —*Sacramento Bee*

"...astounding insight...the true genius of the great man that was Eric Berne comes through." —David Reuben, M.D., author of
Everything You Always Wanted to Know About Sex But Were Afraid to Ask

SEX IN HUMAN LOVING
was originally published by
Simon and Schuster.

Books by Eric Berne, M.D.

Games People Play
A Layman's Guide to Psychiatry and Psychoanalysis
The Mind in Action
Principles of Group Treatment
Sex in Human Loving*
The Structure and Dynamics of Organizations and Groups
Transactional Analysis in Psychotherapy
What Do You Say After You Say Hello?

*Published by POCKET BOOKS

SEX
in Human Loving

Eric
Berne, M.D.

PUBLISHED BY POCKET BOOKS NEW YORK

SEX IN HUMAN LOVING

Simon and Schuster edition published 1970
POCKET BOOK edition published August, 1971
8th printing.......................March, 1975

L

This POCKET BOOK edition includes every word contained
in the original, higher-priced edition. It is printed from
brand-new plates made from completely reset, clear, easy-to-
read type. POCKET BOOK editions are published by POCKET
BOOKS, a division of Simon & Schuster, Inc., 630 Fifth
Avenue, New York, N.Y. 10020. Trademarks registered
in the United States and other countries.

Standard Book Number: 671-78986-4.
Library of Congress Catalog Card Number: 77-130466.
Front cover design by Terry McKee
Printed in the U.S.A.

To All Those
Who Have Been My Friends
for Still These Many Years . . . in Love,
Appreciation, and Gratitude

CONTENTS

5 / SEXUAL GAMES

6 / SEX AND WELL-BEING OR PREVENTIVE INTIMACY

PART III: AFTERPLAY

7 / QUESTIONS

8 / A MAN OF THE WORLD

APPENDIX: THE CLASSIFICATION OF HUMAN RELATIONSHIPS

TABLE OF FIGURES

FOREWORD

This book is based on the Jake Gimbel Sex Psychology lectures which I was privileged to give at the University of California in April and May of 1966. Dr. Salvatore P. Lucia, Professor of Medicine and Preventive Medicine at San Francisco Medical Center, was on the selection committee, and I believe it was mainly through his influence that I was chosen for this honor. I am grateful to him and to the other members of the committee for giving me such an opportunity. About 600 people attended and overflowed into the aisles and the back of the auditorium, each from a different background and with a different way of approaching the subject. The original program read as follows:

THE 1966 JAKE GIMBEL SEX PSYCHOLOGY
LECTURES UNDER THE AUSPICES OF THE
COMMITTEE FOR ARTS AND LECTURES,
UNIVERSITY OF CALIFORNIA,
SAN FRANCISCO MEDICAL CENTER

SEX IN HUMAN LIVING

APRIL 6 Talking About Sex
APRIL 13 Forms of Human Relationship
APRIL 20 Sex and Well-Being
APRIL 27 Sexual Games

The above four lectures will be given at 8:30 P.M. in the Medical Sciences Auditorium, San Francisco Medical Center.

MAY 23   Language and Lovers

>   The above lecture will be given in the Field
>   House, University of California at Santa Cruz.
>   All interested persons are cordially invited to
>   attend.

Although "all interested persons" were invited to attend,
the audience consisted mainly of students, faculty, professional people and their co-workers. Dr. Lucia was a most
gracious and diplomatic chairman, and my assistant, Miss
Pamela Blum, ably assisted in the platform arrangements.
Meanwhile, Dr. Lucia's secretary, Marjorie Hunt, arranged
to preserve the lectures on tape, and Miss Olga Aiello
typed them out for me. Without this service, of course,
the lectures would have been lost forever, since I had no
text and my notes consisted only of topic headings.

But primarily I am grateful to the late Jake Gimbel for
making such a series of lectures possible in the first place.
When he died in 1943, he left a substantial trust for this
purpose, to alternate between Stanford University and the
University of California. Since then, the Lectureship has
been held by a list of distinguished authorities. They have
set a standard which is such a difficult challenge that it has
taken me four years to attempt to meet it by placing my
thoughts in writing before the public, and it is with some
diffidence that I do so even now.

There has been a considerable emergence and spread of
sexual knowledge since these lectures were given. In 1967
began the publication of the monthly journal *Medical Aspects of Human Sexuality,*[1] the most reasonable, reliable,
and respectable periodical of its kind. It has much less of
the slightly sensational and disapproving attitude of its
most illustrious predecessor, the old *Zeitschrift für Sexual-
wissenschaft* wherein the pioneers of psychoanalysis published some of their early papers, and which was a prime
source for Havelock Ellis and students of the "psycho-
pathology" of sex of that era. During the same four-year
period, the Sex Information and Education Council of the
United States[2] emerged into prominence under the leader-

ship of Dr. Mary Calderone, of New York. The impeccable qualifications and manner of Dr. Calderone have undoubtedly contributed to the wide acceptance of her work, particularly in promoting sex education in the schoolroom. A third force in emergent sexual knowledge is the classified advertisement columns of the *Berkeley Barb* or *Tribe* and other underground papers, which reveal the prevalence and variety of departures from the official vis-à-vis position in sexual intercourse much more poignantly than Kinsey and his associates did, although less romantically perhaps than Havelock Ellis' writings. A fourth influence which has made itself felt in a significant way during the past two or three years is the legal relaxations: the acceptance of homosexual consent liaisons in England, and of pornography in Denmark, for example. Best of all is the recent conjunction of sex with healthy wit and humor (as opposed to morbid, distasteful, or derogatory jokes), as in the satirical *Official Sex Manual,*[3] and the sexy picture parodies in *Evergreen* magazine. The current advanced position is that sex is reasonably decent and is here to stay, so we had best face it. This is in distinction to the rightist position that sex is nastier than anything, and the radical position that nothing is nasty so that sex will not suffer if it is thrown into the pot with violence and garbage.

All of these influences, including the underground papers (which have to be repudiated by everyone else for reasons of "respectability"), come into fullest flower in the writings of Dr. Eugene Schoenfeld, who forthrightly enlightens the public in a weekly column under the name of Dr. Hip Pocrates.[4] (He has now retired from this activity.)

The greatest change which has taken place during this period, however, is not an educational one but a practical one. The fuller impact of "the pill" on American life is marked by the emergence or resurgence of the "emancipated woman," with her claim for full sexual equality. The manuscript of this book was combed by several of them for signs of "male chauvinism." Some of the examples they found were pretty hairy, so I made appropriate changes in the final draft. In other instances, where I felt "female chauvinism" was rearing its head, I have stood my ground, and allowed them to have their say in footnotes, where they are represented by the initials EW, with my replies on occasion labeled EB. In fairness to EW, I should say that I have not included their many approving and enthusiastic comments.

What I have done in this book is tell it like I think it is, which entails the use of colloquialisms, imagery, and case reports. Anyone is at liberty to keep it out of the hands of their children under sixteen, or under eighteen, or under twenty-one (or under forty, for that matter), if they feel a need to. I will gladly receive the documentation of anyone who wishes to correct any error I have made in facts. As to matters of opinion, I cannot conscientiously defer to someone else unless he or she has listened to more or to more cogent sexual histories than I have during the past thirty years. I imagine that there are some pimps and prostitutes who know more about sex in general, and some scientists who know more about particular aspects of it, than an experienced and interested psychiatrist does. On the whole, I think that there is as much science as art in what I have put down, and any disputation should be supported by an appropriate body of evidence.

A lot of what is written here was not said in the lectures, or was said in a different way. For one thing, I have learned a lot since 1966, and for another, lecturing is different from writing. Thus it was necessary to edit, change, cut, rearrange, and add to the lectures, to bring them up to date and make them more readable. In order to do this most effectively, I have adopted the device of writing as though I were writing for an audience of one. In other places I have referred to a writer called Cyprian St. Cyr, who is the purported author of a work entitled *Letters to My Wife's Maid*. These letters are supposed to have been written while St. Cyr was traveling with his wife to faraway places, and are for the purpose of preparing the young lady in question to venture out into the world alone when she leaves her present employment. That is a suitable context for the present work, which is therefore written in the spirit of St. Cyr's "Letters," while still endeavoring to maintain the tone of the original lectures as well. In line with this, the previous order of programming, as given above, has been abandoned, along with the original title of the series.*

Because of the many changes which have been made, it is only fair to say that neither the Jake Gimbel Trust nor the University of California is responsible for any of the opinions expressed. That responsibility is solely my own.

I want to thank the members of the San Francisco Transactional Analysis Seminar for spending several evenings listening while I read the manuscript to them, and for the many valuable suggestions and constructive and destructive criticisms they made, and also those who read the whole manuscript at their own leisure and did likewise. These include, emancipated or square, Bertha Joung, Al and Pam Levin, Arden Rose, Valerie Venger, Nadja and Valerio Giusi, and Rick Berne.

CARMEL, CALIFORNIA
APRIL, 1970.

NOTES AND REFERENCES

1. *Medical Aspects of Human Sexuality*, edited by The-odore Bawer, M.D., and David M. Reed, Ph.D., and a board of consulting editors. Published monthly at 18 East 48 Street, New York, N.Y. 10017.

2. SIECUS, 1855 Broadway, New York, N.Y. 10023.

3. *The Official Sex Manual*, by Gerald Sussman. G. P. Putnam's Sons, New York, 1965.

4. *Dear Doctor Hip Pocrates*, by Eugene Schoenfeld. Grove Press, New York, 1969.

---

* The "official" title of this book, for those who prefer to think of sex in a more academic way, is "Cerebral and Behavioral Correlates of Coupling in Higher Primate Communities."

Sex
in # Human
Loving

INTRODUCTION: TALKING ABOUT SEX

A

SEX IS WET

Sex is not an easy subject to write about, mainly because it is wet. In fact it is more than wet, it is slippery. Anyone who ignores that is going to feel a little sticky talking about it. I knew a poet once who wrote about it beautifully, but without impact, and I said to her, "I think it's a mistake to use dry words to talk about wet feelings." So she started to use wet words, and then I said, "Wet words aren't good enough either. You have to use words that people's minds will slip on." She liked that, and in return told me that a pregnant woman sitting by a window thought of a black snake. I didn't understand that, not being a woman, but it sounded right. It sounded better than the pregnant woman who was very proper in her speech, and said that she was hoping to have a good flow of milk so she could raise a bust-fed baby. That one reminded me of the joke about the lady from Boston who always apologized when she talked about "chamber" music or "cocktail" parties, and who reported one day that a friend of hers had fallen over a precipeepee.

To start off with, I think we should review our vocabulary and decide which words will most clearly and comfortably say what we are talking about.

1

B

SOME COLD DRY WORDS

The words that people use for sex start with *conjugation,* which is what lower organisms do, and *copulation,* which is for higher animals. *Sexual intercourse* is for people. Scientists call it co'-i-tis, although if it makes them nervous they sometimes call it co-igh'-tus, but *co'-i-tus* is what it is. *Sexual union* is something you can talk about in front of an audience, but only on Sunday. In fact you can talk about any of these except sexual intercourse. You are not supposed to talk about that; instead you must communicate. Communication may be very difficult, and it gives some people, including me, a headache, so just plain talking is better if you can get away with it. Even listening to other people communicate can give you a headache sometimes, especially if they don't know what they're communicating about or whom they're communicating with. In short, communication may cause trouble, and most people who indulge in it should learn to talk to each other sooner or later if they want to get along. The worst kind of communication is called a continuing dialogue, which may give the participants not only a headache but often chronic stomach trouble as well. Sometimes, however, people in a continuing dialogue start talking to each other, and then everything gets better. A cynical friend of mine, Dr. Horseley, tells overeducated couples who are not getting along to stop communicating and start talking.

The trouble with all the words above is that they seem cold and dry and sterile even though they are not. Conjugation sounds like making a fire by rubbing two eggs together. Copulation sounds wet but slightly repulsive, while coitus just sounds sticky, like walking through molasses in a pair of sneakers. Sexual intercourse is an okay phrase to use in public or in writing, although it sounds too sensible to be much fun. For variety's sake, the sex act is a convenient synonym.

The words used for the results of all these activities are not much better. Sexual satisfaction is instead of a good steak for a man, or instead of a cheese soufflé for a woman. Sexual outlets are like the faucets of an aluminum coffee urn or the tap on the bottom of a boiler that you turn on once a month to drain out the sludge. Climax started off as a decent enough word, but it has been so overworked on the newsstands that it now sounds like the moment when two toasted marshmallows finally get stuck to each other. Orgasm, I think, is the best word to use in writing.

Lawyers have words of their own, but they don't help much. Their favorites are cohabitation, sexual relations, and adultery, all of which are charges or accusations. Lawyers have no interest whatsoever in whether sex is any fun. They are only interested in "establishing" it or "proving" it so that someone will have to pay for it. You pay just as much if it wasn't any fun as if it was the greatest thrill you ever had. There is no deduction for dreariness and no premium for ecstasy. Lawyers also have other words that are called crimes against nature, although nature has never filed any complaints. There is no such word in the legal vocabulary as decent exposure. All exposure is deemed indecent until proven otherwise. This seems contrary to the constitutional provision that says a man is innocent until proven guilty, or decent until proven indecent. Some of the biggest fights between lawyers are over the word *obscenity,* and we will talk about that later.

The real trouble with all these words and phrases is that they evade the issue, which is lust and pleasure and intoxication, and that is why they sound cold and dry and sterile.

C

SOME WARM DAMP WORDS

Mating sounds warm, and fertile; it has a great future ahead of it, but it lacks presence. Perhaps the most human and least vulgar of all sexual terms is *making love*. It has a warm, damp, fertile ring to it, and also a promise of something more enduring than the act itself. Nobody knows what happens after sunrise to the people who copulate or have coitus or sexual intercourse. But people who make love are the most likely to have breakfast together, and that is why most young ladies prefer the term to all the others. Unfortunately, perhaps, it seems to be slightly less popular among men, even men who are willing to face their women at the breakfast table.

To *come* is another warm damp word. What it lacks in drama it makes up in coziness. Some people, oddly enough, say *go* instead.

D

OBSCENE WORDS

It is perfectly possible, and I think desirable, to talk about obscenities without being obscene. For example, we can write four of the commonest sexual obscenities backward or sideways as *cuff, swerk, kirp,* and *tunc,* without misleading or offending anyone.

Cuff is the only word in the English language that gives the full feeling, excitement, slipperiness, and aroma of the sexual act. Its lascivious "f" sound also helps to give it a realistic punch. The synonyms mentioned in the previous section carefully avoid the idea of excitement and lust, and even more carefully avoid one of the most primitive and powerful elements in sex, which is smell. Cuff takes in all of these, just as a child does, because it starts off as a child's word.

Oddly enough, it is not, as is commonly supposed, an Anglo-Saxon word. It got into English from Scotland in the 1500's[1] and most probably came from an old Dutch or German word, *ficken,* which means to beat, very much like the Arabic *dok,* which means to pound like a pestle in a mortar. Thrusting or pounding is one of the most important elements in sexual intercourse, as we shall see. Equally important is what Arabic sexologists call *hez,* which means an exhilarating, lascivious, free-swinging movement of the female pelvis. It is just because cuff means *dok* and *hez* that it has such a thrust and swing.

Cuffing is something two people do together, where swerking is a more one-sided word. A very wise girl named Amaryllis once said to me, "I like cuffing, but I don't want a boy who will swerk me just for the glory of it." Balling is something people do together too.*

There is no need to discuss kirp and tunc and their numerous synonyms, since they are all mere vulgarities that add little to our understanding. Penis, to most people, brings up a picture of something skinny and not very imposing, or, for those who have little boys in the house, cute. It will do for the organ in its flaccid state. For the more noble state of erection, I think *phallus* comes closer to the truth, even though it sounds artificial and lacking in juice. *Vagina* will serve for the female organ. It has the warmth, if not all the other qualities, of tunc. The main difficulty is with the external genitals of the female, called by anatomists the *vulva.* That is much too clinical a word for everyday use, but there is really no polite term for them, so we shall have to settle for the conventional *genitals.*

There are lots of other words that you can find in *Roget's Thesaurus,* in various dictionaries of slang,[2] and

---

* EW: Balling is a post-pill phenomenon. There is no feeling of exploitation, it implies mutual consent, an act carried out together, not done to someone but with someone. It is the wet-word equivalent of "making love," used with pride and joy.

in the Criminal Codes of various jurisdictions, but the
above list should be enough for everyday purposes.

E

THE NATURE OF OBSCENITY

I will now explain why I prefer to avoid the use
of obscenity. The word obscene itself means sort of repulsive. Obscenity is usually divided into two types—pornography and scatology. Pornography means writing about
harlots, and is properly applied to bedroom words, while
scatology applies to bathroom vulgarities. Some people
find both pornography and scatology offensive, while
others find one obscene but not the other. This all makes
it sound as though obscenity were a matter of artificial
rules, but that is not quite so. It has a much deeper psychological meaning than that.

Any word worth saying arouses an image in the speaker
—and also in the hearer. These images do not always present themselves clearly, but with a little care they can be
fished up from the deeps of the mind. The images for
most words are bland, poorly formed and shadowy, and
fade into an unknown background unless they are very
familiar. That is why they are so seldom noticed when the
speaker speaks. These may be called Adult or shadow
images. Other words are accompanied by images which
are more vivid and powerful. Those images are relics of
childhood, and are called Child or primal images.[3] Because they are so detailed and colorful, primal images
arouse emotional responses. Some of them are strikingly
beautiful, like the images people often see when they
smoke marijuana or take LSD. Others are repulsive, and
these are the ones we are concerned with here, since they
give us a psychological way of defining obscenity. A word
becomes obscene when the accompanying image is primal
and repulsive. It is so because the image and the reality
it stood for became vivid and repulsive in childhood, as is

commonly the case with odorous excretions during toilet training, and the image keeps that power in later years.[4] This definition of obscenity is not based on artificial rules made by oppressive and ignoble authorities to deprive the people of freedom of speech, but comes from the structure of the human nervous system and its profound psychology.

If obscenity is based on deep and universal psychological factors dating from childhood, then only childhood words should have such potency. If a language is learned later in life, say after the age of six, it can have no obscenities for the learner because he never heard its words in the primal years of life. Thus a proper Englishman may be able to say or read words like *merde, Scheiss, fourrer, vögeln, cul,* or *Schwanz* without embarrassment or diffidence because those words, although he may know very well what they mean, do not arouse any primal imagery, but maintain in his mind a more abstract quality. If the new language become deeply ingrained, however, and he starts thinking in it, certain of its words may gradually penetrate through to the primal layers, and thus become obscene.

Such observations indicate that the quality of obscenity is here to stay, but the particular words that arouse an obscene reaction are a matter of choice or chance. Basically it has to do with smell and taste, and also slippery touch. Obscene words are ones that become connected with slippery sensations in primal imagery. In special cases, the most inoffensive words can become farfetched obscenities as a result of experiences during the childhood period when these images are formed.

Thus a new generation can knock down old obscenities, but their offspring will create new ones, perhaps by turning a common word into an obscene one ("pig") or by pulling a rare phrase into common usage ("mother-cuffer"). It is conceivable that children could be raised completely free of obscenity reactions, but it does not seem likely because of the way the human nervous system is constructed. I think it would be very difficult to train out the relief most people feel when they get outdoors from the community latrine.

The shock value of obscene words, or their relief value,

if they are used for that purpose, or their erotic value, if they are used as stimulants, come from their aromatic quality as much as from their indecency. The strongest obscenities are those with the strongest fragrance—cuff, tunc, and tish; while the weakest are the scientific and literary words that are far removed from primal images and are completely deodorized. For the neurologist and psychologist, this is a fascinating phenomenon having to do with the whole structure of the brain and mind: the relationship between smell, visual imagery, words, social action, and emotional shock, relief, or stimulation.

Because of such psychological verities, a respect for the power of obscenity is not a quaint relic of an antique way of thinking. Rather it is one aspect of a way of life in which the most important quality is grace. Grace means graceful movements, and graceful moments of solitude or communion. This quality is well understood by dancers, rhetoricians, and students of Zen and other Oriental philosophies. It means speaking gracefully and making each hour a work of art. It requires an appearance and a demeanor that make each year better than the last. And finally, it means that a whole lifetime of friendships and enmities, intimacies and confrontations, comedies and tragedies, will have at least the possibility of ending up with some strain of wholeness and nobility running through it. For me class = grace = reticence, the avoidance of overstatement and disharmony, in speech as in ballet as in painting.

To encounter ugliness and look it in the face is different from embracing it. Each person has his own idea of beauty, so there is no way to define it by saying what it is. But at least it can be split off by saying what it is not. There is one, and I think only one, universal rule of esthetics, universal because it became an inherited biological trait in the evolution of the human race. Beauty can be in spite of bad smells, but not because of them. And everybody knows what a bad smell is. It is the smell of a stranger's tish, his unwanted intrusion with every breath we draw. With a friend, it is the opposite. As Amaryllis once put it, "A friend is one whose tish and tarfs don't stink, and the sound of whose sipp is a song to your ears. If a stranger tries to give you that kind of park, you give him a kick in the tootches." (Amaryllis has a slightly vulgar turn of mind, as shown by her use of the word stink.)

In view of all this, I believe that obscenity should not be imposed on others without their consent. For some, it is part of their life plan and adds to their joy. For others, free speech stops not only at yelling "Fire!" in a crowded theater, but also at crying vulgarities before children. Poetry is always more appealing. Menstruation is not very attractive as "monthlies," but becomes charming (to men at least) as "blood on the face of the moon," or in the French term "I have my flowers."

Whatever you want to say, you should say it, provided you can still remain pure by your own standards. It is only that purity is very important when so many things are polluted.

F

THE TRASH CAN

It is true that you can find out an awful lot about your neighbors by looking in their trash cans. A philosophical scavenger could develop a whole philosophy of life from what he finds in people's garbage: he can see what they throw away, how economical or wasteful they are, and what they feed their kids. And there are a lot of people in the world who would see in him the purveyor of ultimate rock-bottom truth. Look in the trash can and that's the real scoop on the human race, man! But it isn't. Archaeologists often happen on kitchen-middens and very little else, and from this they try to reconstruct what a society was like. There are some writers who follow the same plan, trying to reconstruct and judge our way of living by its garbage. But archaeologists get much further by uncovering a city like Pompeii than by studying any number of kitchen-middens. By seeing the whole city, they can judge better what went on among its people, the noble as well as the ignoble. The office and the library, the nursery and the rumpus room, contain more of the universal truth about people than the junky's pad. The sweat and the humanity of a nunnery is more worthwhile than the sweat and humanity of a brothel, since the nunnery appeals, however narrowly, to the upward aspirations of the human race, while the brothel, at least as described by pornophiles and pimp-lovers, is static, or if it moves at all, goes sideways or downward. And there is, after all, more humanity in a baby than in a tumor of the womb, and an embryo has more truth in it than a fibroid.

All of which is to say that obscene books are no more enlightening and no nearer the nitty-gritty than proper ones. Only Tolstoi could see what he saw in *War and Peace,* but any clever high school boy who was angry enough at his mother could have written de Sade's *Philosophy in a Bedroom,* including both the bedroom scenes and the philosophy.

————————

G

THE MOTHER-CUFFERS

In the extreme case, obscenity becomes a way of living. The pornographer, sentenced to life in the bedroom, and eternally seeking the promise of an orgasm, will never see the forests and the oceans and the sunshine. The scatologist, closeted in his odorous little cubicle, must paw through every happening to find the tish that he is bound and indentured to prove that everything turns into. Both are losers, for the pornographer will never find the magic, all-satisfying vagina that he is looking for, nor will the scatologist, standing amid the piles of feces he has laboriously accumulated, ever succeed in transmuting them into gold. The pornographer is better off, for he at least wins some passing pleasures, while there is only one prize that can come out of a bathroom, and that is a crock of ungold. True, crying obscenities does give relief to some people, but this only confirms the fact that such terms have a special psychological primacy.

The childlike theory that if you only say enough dirty words everything will come out all right just doesn't work on a five- or ten-year follow-up. Right from the beginning it is a loser's approach. After such a person says "tish" or "mother-cuffer" 100,000 times in the course of ten years (at a modest thirty times a day) he nearly always (in my clinical experience) finds that things have gotten worse instead of better, and then he can only scream, "Look how hard I've tried! Why does this always happen to me?" Which only proves that trying harder is not the answer, since things won't get any better if he says his favorite obscenity three hundred times a day.

It is not the theory itself that makes the loser, but the way it is practiced. A winner, working on the same assumption, would take two days off and run through the whole program, fifty thousand curses per day, and see if he got the desired result. If he didn't, he would find a new theory for success and move on to that, thereby saving ten years. That is the difference between a winner and a loser in life. Whether he is a winner or a loser is the most important thing for the course of a person's life as well as for its outcome, since that determines whether or not other people will trust him.

H

OBSCENITY FOR FUN

There are others who agree that uninvited obscenity is in most cases an assault and therefore reprehensible.[5] But there are two situations where it may be effective just because of its indecency, and thosse are in seduction and in fun.

In seduction, obscenity may be used as a sales talk.

Then it is corrupt in the same way that the Boy Scouts of America (supposedly based on the outdoor idealism of Sir Robert Baden-Powell) are corrupt in having a merit badge of Salesman. It is the art of making a fast buck intruding on the beauties of nature.*

Obscenity for fun is a satire on corruption, and satire is the surgical laughter that opens the festers of the body politic and the corpus of human relations. Hence obscenity for fun makes life less obscene. Rabelais is more scatological than most writers because he was trying to enjoy his scatological times. The dedication to my favorite edition of his works (Sir Thomas Urquhart's translation) reads:

> One inch of joy surmounts of grief a span,
> Because to laugh is proper to the man.

But satire is different from the obscenity of revolt: "I'm going to say these dirty words so I can watch the expression on your face to see if you're a square or if you stop loving me as a result, you pig."

In the same way, the humorous poems of the Restoration Rakes about the clap and the great pox, syphilis, which were virtually unavoidable and incurable for a rake of those days, are different from the self-pitying word-spitting of some modern writers on the same subject. Obscenities are mostly obnoxious when they are taken seriously by the person who says them or by the one who hears them. If they are said in fun, and not thrown in the face like old grapefruit rinds, the reader or listener can either join in the fun or else withdraw and say, "I am not amused."

Puns, jokes and limericks are the favorite ways of having fun with obscenity. Unfortunately the number of

---

* Amaryllis tells about a male acquaintance who successfully uses obscenity as a method of seduction. As soon as possible after meeting a likely female, he makes a more than ordinarily indecent proposal to her in explicit language. In this way he wins the favors of some women and loses the respect of many others, thus demonstrating both positively and negatively the unusual corruptive powers of obscene words.

possible puns that can be made on the six principal obscene words is limited, and they have all been made long, long ago. The number of possible obscene jokes is larger, but most of them come out of the attic too, since a hundred million college students have spent a hundred billion hours at a hundred thousand taverns in the past hundred years.[6] The principal field left open for originality nowadays is limericks.

One of the most amusing ways to make fun of obscenity and its censors is to use like-sounding made-up words in place of the real thing, after the manner of the *Official Sex Manual*,[7] which tells all about *erroneous zones*, the *vesuvious* and the *plethora*, "a tiny football-shaped object located near the *frunella*, just above the *pomander* tubes." During *coginus*, of course, the male's *vector* has to break the *hyphen*. But *Billy and Betty*, a novel by Twiggs Jameson, has a made-up vocabulary that is even better because the Jameson words sound closer to the originals and are great fun for real lovers to use. For example, those who can't find partners for *clamming* can always *automate* instead, and Jameson illustrates by example how to go about finalizing that way, whether you have an empty *pudarkus* or a full *glander*.

I

OBSCENITY AND LOVE

Perhaps a proper place for obscenity is in making love.[8] This is the primal scene, and that is why primal imagery, at least of the sexual kind, may have its value here. This does not include seduction or exploitation. It means love-making in which both parties have already given their consent, and more than that, in which each is actively interested in increasing the other's enjoyment. The primal images aroused need no longer be repudiated, but for some people come into full flower. They reinforce, and are reinforced by, the multitude of sensations that set them free: sight, sound, touch, smell, taste, and the warmth which the flushed skins radiate to each other. This is quite the opposite of using obscenity as an insult and a blasphemy, as shown in the following verse:

THE DIFFERENCE
She said "Cuff you!" and then saw red
When he went out and found instead
A lady whom he took to tea,
Who later said, "Oh, yes, cuff me!"

J

SEX EDUCATION, JUNIOR TYPE

Our purpose here is a serious one: sex education, or even inspiration. We have agreed on a preferred vocabulary, including some anagrams, and we have agreed to avoid obscenity whenever possible. Let us also agree that there is no reason to avoid fun, and we can then move on to consider various approaches to the main subject.

The most bothersome question about "sex education" is "How do you explain sex to your children?" The reason this is bothersome is that it is a rather futile question, and makes no more sense than "How do you explain history (or geometry, or cooking) to your children?" It takes several years of concerted teaching and homework to "explain" history or geometry, and even then very few children, or for that matter not all teachers, really "understand" them. Many parents end up saying to themselves (or to each other): "So you don't know how to explain sex to your children, you nincompoop!" or even worse: "Ha! I'm one parent who knows how to explain sex to his children!" What is really wrong is not the parents, but the idea that there is really such a thing as "sex" that can be "explained." There isn't, any more than there is something called "cooking" which can be "explained." (*La-*

rousse Gastronomique doesn't even try—it just gives some history.) It might be helpful to talk about the heat and aroma of the pot, but you don't make a good cook by drawing a picture of the gas plumbing, or by warning against poisonous mushrooms. There is no such thing as taking your son or daughter aside and saying: "I will now explain sex to you. A B C + D E F = G. Any questions? Good night, then. Time for bed." Aside from what?

In the case of young children, the first thing they usually ask is where babies come from. Since nobody really knows the answer to *that,* most parents feel called upon to explain about cuffing. They either evade the issue by calling in the friendly neighborhood bird-watcher, or face it by saying, "The man puts his goodie into the lady's goodie and plants a seed, etc., and that's how babies are made." The parent in most cases either looks jolly or keeps a stiff upper lip as he says this, partly because he knows it isn't the right answer and wishes somebody would tell him what is. The child, instead of listening to the information, asks himself the really important question: Why is father looking so jolly or keeping his upper lip so stiff? The kids on the street are much more natural about it and really *explain* it. Even if they explain it wrong, or some of their pupils maintain that nothing like that happens between *their* parents, they will all go away feeling that they have had a stimulating and instructive seminar. Everybody is serious, thoughtful, and argumentative, and nobody is jolly or keeping a stiff upper lip.

So much for junior sex education, age three to eleven. Intermediate sex education, age twelve to twenty, is not much better.

K

INTERMEDIATE SEX EDUCATION

Intermediate sex education is often offered in the form of books and lectures. You know that I think of every individual as being three different people: a Parent, who may be critical, sentimental, or nuturing; a rational, factual Adult; and a compliant, rebellious, or spontaneous Child.[9] Books and lectures about sex may be classified according to whether they come from the Parent (and even which Parent), the Adult, or the Child (and even what kind of a Child). Each book or lecture has its basic attitude toward the subject, and these for the most part fall into one of five classes.

1. *Sex is a Giant Squid.* It's all right in its place, which is the marriage chamber, where it's kept chained under the bed. But if you ever run into it anywhere else, watch out, or you'll get dragged under. What you have to watch out for is the opposite sex, who are going to do you in if you give them the slightest leeway. These dangers have been best summarized in the limerick about a young lady named Wilde, and anyone who knows that limerick knows all that is necessary about this monster.

> There was a young lady named Wilde
> Who kept herself quite undefiled
> By thinking of Jesus,
> Contagious diseases,
> And having an unwanted child.

The Giant Squid was invented by Father Parent, as it is written, although Mother knows about it too.[10]

2. *Sex is a Gift of the Angels.* It is a beautiful and sacred thing which should not be blasphemed by earthly considerations nor sullied by lustful thoughts. The Angels were invented by Mother Parent. Father knows about them, too, but he is a little skeptical since he has never met them personally.[11]

3. *Sex is a Triumph of Mechanical Engineering,* a kind of assembly line in which natural products go in at one end and babies come out at the other. Or it may be miniaturized into an assembly kit, as described in the

previous section: "Insert widget A into sprocket B and clamp down gudgeon C, and presto! there will be a baby on Christmas morning." This is a rational approach which states certain facts in correct Adult fashion, but it is not very inspiring. It may be true as far as it goes, but it is not the kind of truth that makes life better.[12]

4. *Sex is Naughty.* This is the approach taken when the rebellious Child gets the upper hand in a person of any age (most commonly in adolescence and over forty), and says: "You know, all these rules and prohibitions don't mean anything to me. I'm spilling my guts, using straight Anglo-Saxon words, and that proves I'm free." There are three things wrong with this. (a) The words aren't Anglo-Saxon. (b) It doesn't prove he's free. (c) It doesn't work. That is, ten years later, these people are no happier than most of the people around them. The Marquis de Sade is a good example.[13]

5. *Sex is Fun.* People who find that sex is fun don't usually talk about it very much. There is not much to say about fun except "That was fun," or "Wow!" This is a childlike approach like the one above, but certainly a more lovable and spontaneous Child.[14]

L

ADVANCED SEX EDUCATION

Advanced sex education is mainly slanted toward humorless collegians, wife-traders, Indian rajahs and maharajahs, and Arabian slaveholders, but many ordinary people can profit from it, too. It depends on whether you like to paint your own pictures or prefer the kind with numbered sections that tell you where to put each color.

The chief textbook for advanced sex education is the *Kama-Sutra* of Vatsayana, the founder of the Hindu, or Crafty, school of sex.[15] It dates from either 677 B.C. or

350 A.D. The companion volume is the *Ananga Ranga* of
Kalyanamalla, written about 1500.[16] Both of these give
subtle recipes for kissing, touching, skillful cuffing, leaving
tooth and nail marks in the right places, conning your
neighbor's wife, and salving your own conscience. They
are undoubtedly instructive, but they are also predatory,
and replace passion and creativity with technical virtuosity
and sometimes crookedness.

As my friend Dr. Horseley says, "There may be a
special thrill to learning the fine points of biting and
scratching and whoring, but it's even more fun if you think
of them yourself rather than getting them out of a book,
just as it's more fun finding your own wife rather than
getting her through a computer. On the other hand," he
adds somewhat sourly, "if you want to know the methods
used by prostitutes and paramours for extracting money
from men, you're undoubtedly better off reading these
books than trying to learn from your friendly neighborhood
prostitute or paramour, since the methods are the same
here and now as they were there and then."

"No point," agrees Amaryllis, "in ending up like the
sailor with false teeth who visited one of the girls and lost
them. That's the origin of the song 'The Gal That I Loved
Stole the Palate I Loved.'"

These books do have the virtue, however, of recom-
mending patience and gentleness, particularly with child
brides.

Next to the *Kama-Sutra* in hoary patina is the *Perfumed Garden* of Shaykh Nefzawi, spokesman for the
Arabian school of the 1400's.[17] This is a practical manual, giving many warnings against the deceits and treach-
eries of women, prescriptions for various sexual ailments
(including some for making Small Members Splendid),
and a set of reasonable positions for healthy couples.
Beyond that, the sheik also describes special positions for
special cases: fat couples, a small man and a tall woman,
and people suffering from various deformities. He pays due
deference to the superior knowledge and acrobatic ability
of the Indians, particularly the woman who can hold an
oil lamp aloft on the sole of her foot and keep it burning

during the whole procedure, but feels that many of their routines add more pain than pleasure to the act.

Nefzawi's long chapter on pederasty still remains to be translated, which is unfortunate, since this would no doubt throw some light on the fate of the slave boys and girls, ranging in age from four to ten, who are still imported by the planeload from the Sahara into the Arabian Peninsula.[18] (I myself have seen a two-year-old boy being trained in milder slavish arts in the Spanish Sahara.)

One more book deserves mention here, and that is Dr. Joseph Weckerle's *Golden Book of Love,* which describes 531 positions—more than the *Kama-Sutra,* the *Ananga Ranga,* and *The Perfumed Garden* combined, in this respect making those works obsolete, and probably *The Beharistan, The Gulistan,* and the seven erotic manuals of Ibn Kamal Pasha as well. But even Weckerle is only a European empiricist. Legman, using modern American computer methods, calculates that there are 3,780 possible positions.[19] Such a sophisticated approach almost makes Vatsayana look primitive, sort of the Grandma Moses of sexuality, but it is not really so.

But enough of the sexual sinks of India, Arabia and Vienna. Before we go on to consider the sexual education of healthy, red-blooded, clean-thinking American grown-ups, a word about "sex education" in school. It will take about twenty years to judge the effects of that, until a whole generation that has been exposed to it has a chance to grow up. The main thing is that it should not be taught by frigid people, with some dried-out members of the school board looking over their shoulders like kippered herring at a wake. In this situation, sex is like humor. Courses in humor, if they are given at all, should be given only by people who have laughed at least once in their lives—and enjoyed it.

M

ADULT SEX EDUCATION IN AMERICA

The United States has taken seriously the injunction "Make Love, Not War," and has evolved several indigenous schools of love-making, this by pure Yankee ingenuity, without any Federal or state funding, being one of the few fields in which research has proceeded independently of government support.

The first and most rigorous is the Sociology or Stopwatch School, whose slogan is "24–40 or fight," that is, twenty-four minutes and forty seconds for orgasm (or whatever figure the latest poll shows), the average time as determined by the sociologists quoted in the Sunday paper.[20] Although they pay lip service to variations, some disciples of this school imply that anyone who varies very much is either a failure, a kook, or a Communist—or all three.

Next comes the Woman's Journal of Standard Brands School, which gives the proper recipe for decorous middle-class lechery. You take your man out of the freezer and thaw him out, add a caress, place in a warm bed, and let simmer until a thin film forms over his eyeballs.[21] After that you are on your own and you can serve him or not, as you see fit. The recipes do not go into that part of it.

Then there is the Psychoanalytic or Bureau of Standards School. This is an officially recognized outfit that is the custodian of the International Standard Sex Life.[22] That is not the way Freud meant it to be,* but that is the way it has turned out. This school is the object of some fierce competition from the popular Communication Movement, founders of the School of Comparative Orgasms, whose members greet each other daily with: "How are you doing

---

* In fact one of Freud's most talented early followers expressly repudiates such judgments. (Karl Abraham, *Collected Papers.* Hogarth Press, London, 1948, p. 413.)

these days in interpersonal interaction in the area of orgasms?"[23] This is a polite way of asking, "Have you had one yet that matches the Standard Orgasm kept under glass in the U.S. Bureau of Standards next to the Standard Meter, the Standard Kilogram, and the now obsolete Standard Bowel Movement?" For these people, the Standard Orgasm has replaced the Holy Grail, and many a couple spend their lives chasing after it, crying "Tally ho! It slipped away from us again, dammit!"

N

A STANDARD SEXUAL VOCABULARY

Ideally, a complete sexual vocabulary should consist of four words. The Parental, or moral, aspect of the personality, acting as a kind of consultant, needs "Yes" and "No." The Adult, or rational and responsible organ, the one that sets up contracts and commitments with other people, also needs "Yes" and "No." The Child, or instinctual, aspect, the part that is actually going to take the trip, needs only one word to express his or her reaction: "Wow!" In rare cases, however, where the Parent or Adult aspect has made an error in judgment, the Child part may need "Ugh!" Anything beyond these four, Yes, No, Wow, and Ugh, means somebody is in trouble. Except for "Beautiful!" which may be kept in reserve. There are some who don't understand why and when people say "Wow!" and "Beautiful!" but for those who know the secret, there is nothing else to say.* So there are some for whom life is Yes and Wow, and others for whom it is No and Ow (or Ugh).

Having thus surveyed a few of the problems which arise

---

* Although "Wow!" has only recently come into common English usage as an expression of enthusiasm, the French have been using its equivalent for a long, long time in the form of "Ooh-la-la!"

in talking about sex, and finding solutions for some of them, let us proceed to talk about it and see whether we will fare any better than our predecessors. And remember that not only is many a true word spoken in jest, but truth is simply jokes stated seriously.

NOTES AND REFERENCES

1. Stone, Leo: "On the Principal Obscene Word of the English Language." *International Journal of Psychoanalysis* 35:30-56, 1954.

2. E.g., Partridge, E.: *A Dictionary of the Underworld.* Bonanza Books, New York, 1961.

3. Berne, E.: "Primal Images and Primal Judgments." *Psychiatric Quarterly* 29:634-658, 1955.

4. Cf. Ferenczi, S.: "On Obscene Words." In *Sex in Psychoanalysis.* Richard G. Badger, Boston, 1916.

5. Freud, S.: *Wit and Its Relation to the Unconscious.* In *The Basic Writings of Sigmund Freud.* Modern Library, New York, 1938, pp. 692-696.

6. Legman, G.: *Rationale of the Dirty Joke.* Grove Press, New York, 1968.

7. Sussman, G.: *The Official Sex Manual,* op. cit.

8. Symposium: "What Is the Significance of Crude Language During Sex Relations?" *Human Sexuality* 3:8-14, August, 1969.

9. Berne, E.: *Transactional Analysis in Psychotherapy.* Grove Press, New York, 1961.

10. The most horrifying description of sex as a Giant Squid is the very scholarly and very morbid work of Dr. Julius Rosenbaum, *The Plague of Lust.* Frederick Publications, Dallas, 1955.

11. One of the most popular sex manuals is also one of the most sentimental. Van de Velde, T. H.: *Ideal Marriage* (revised edition). Random House, New York, 1965.

12. The latest addition to this approach is the serious and well-documented clinical study of W. H. Masters and V. E.

Johnson, *Human Sexual Response*. Little, Brown and Company, Boston, 1966.

13. The Marquis de Sade is still the unsurpassed masthead of such literature. De Sade, D. A. F.: *Selected Works*. Grove Press, New York, 1966.

14. Legman's book, referred to above, is the most worthy example of the Sex Is Fun approach. It is interesting to contrast Legman's use of his broad and painstaking scholarship with Rosenbaum's misuse of his wide knowledge of the classics.

15. *Kama-Sutra of Vatsayana*. Translated by S. K. Mukherji, K.C. Acharya Oriental Agency, Calcutta, 1945.

16. *Ananga Ranga of Kalyanamalla*. Translated by T. Ray. Citadel Press, New York, 1964.

17. *Perfumed Garden of Shaykh Nefzawi*. Translated by Sir Richard Burton. G. P. Putnam's Sons, New York, 1964.

18. O'Callaghan, S.: *The Slave Trade Today*. Crown Publishers, New York, 1961. Includes the debate on this subject in the House of Lords (Hansard) Thursday, July 14, 1960. Burton has a long essay on the history of pederasty in Arabian countries and other regions of what he calls the Sotadic or pederastic zone (so called after Sotades, a scurrilous but rhythmic poet of ancient Greece). R. F. Burton: *Thousand Nights and a Night*. Privately printed for the Burton Club, n.d., Vol. 10 (probably 1886), pp. 205-254. There was even a hope among the debauched elements in Arabia that they would be supplied with "Wuldan" or beautiful boys in Paradise if they prayed regularly. In general, it appears from their literature and commerce that male Arabs regard their sexual partners as "supplies" rather than as people. For some more recent bloody examples, see *Musk, Hashish and Blood*, by Hector France (Printed for Subscribers Only, London & Paris, 1900).

19. Legman, G.: *Oragenitalism*. Julian Press, New York, 1969. It is hard to believe that anyone could write a monograph of 300 pages on this subject without being trivial, repetitive, or lubricious, but Legman has done it. For those who are interested, and are married, over 21, and live in a state where it is not a criminal offense (and have written permission from their parents?), this is probably the best

book on the subject, although I should say it is the only one I have looked through (because the publisher sent me a copy), so I may be doing some other author an injustice.

I have not seen Weckerle's book in German, and it has not yet been published in English.

20. Kinsey and his associates are the founders of the stopwatch school. (Kinsey, A. C., Pomeroy, W. B., and Martin, C. E.: *Sexual Behavior in the Human Male.* W. B. Saunders Company, Philadelphia, 1948, pp. 178-179.) This has been refined by Masters and Johnson by introducing tenths of a second in some of their measurements. Such measurements are useful to professionally trained people who can evaluate them properly, but they are easy for laymen, and even for non-medical social scientists, to misapply and misconstrue.

21. Almost every woman's magazine gives recipes for sex in the same tone as it gives recipes for apple pudding, except that they are less explicit and are surrounded by a halo of hush instead of mush.

22. Masters and Johnson claim, and have movies purporting to support it, that there is no separation between clitoral and vaginal orgasms as psychoanalysts have maintained.

23. There are now in this country a large number of organizations which promote "encounter groups" and "marathons" where orgasms are freely discussed and compared in the vocabulary peculiar to such groups, a classical example of which I have given in the text. Compare Maizlish, I. L.: "The Orgasm Game." *Transactional Analysis Bulletin* 4:75, October, 1965. Also Hartogs, R., and Fantel, H.: *Four-Letter Word Games: The Psychology of Obscenity.* M. Evans & Company, New York, 1967. These authors give further bibliography on the subject.

PART I

Sex
And
Sex
Organs

1

WHY
SEX IS
NECESSARY

A

INTRODUCTION

Life is a union of complex chemicals formed into strings, rings and spirals. The first and most important job of any living thing is to survive—that is, to prevent the intrusion of destruction from outside, and to keep the strings, rings and spirals working together. Unfortunately, all living things are exposed to danger. If they live through that, it is only to grow old sooner or later. Then the strings, rings, and spirals lose their bounce, and the organism gradually dies. Thus no living things can live forever as individuals, and in order to survive they have to reproduce themselves. If they do not do so in sufficient numbers to live through all the dangers, their kind will eventually become extinct, like the dinosaurs and dodos. So after ensuring its own survival, the most important thing an individual of any species can do is reproduce.*

---

* EW: Every individual? Not today, I don't believe.
  EB: Even when it's undesirable, it's still important.

27

It is well known that sex is one of the favorite ways of doing this, so next to staying alive, sex is the most important thing in the life of any sexy organism. In fact some animals, such as spiders, are even willing to sacrifice their lives for it.

Some humans do that, too, although it is something most people try to avoid. Thus sex is a means of survival. Protection is necessary for the survival of the individual's body, and sex is necessary for the survival of his genes. The body is mortal, but the genes can live forever if they are passed on from one body to another in the next generation. The genes are like a baton which is passed from one person to the next in a biological relay race which seems never-ending. But sometimes it ends in a whimper, as the poet said, and sometimes it threatens to explode.

B

WHAT IS SEX?

Sex is the result of evolution and the survival of the fittest, and human beings are at the top of the heap. People are more fun than anybody and human sex is the best (at least for humans), so as patriotic members of the human race we should all be proud of it. Anybody who isn't should go back where he came from, which is jellyfish.

Before sex, there were already two other methods of reproduction in the animal kingdom, or what was to become the animal kingdom. The lowest organisms (or at least we think they are the lowest, and so far they haven't objected) reproduce by binary fission. These are one-celled animalcules who keep eating until they are too big for their skins. Then they burst asunder, and there are two of them where there was one before. This sounds like a drag: "Here we go again!" or even "Why does this always happen to me?" rather than "Wow!" And it is certainly monotonous, because the two daughter cells are made of the same rings and spirals as their mother, so there is not much chance for originality. Even worse, since all the cells are the same, any overall change in the outside surroundings which destroys one of them is likely to destroy them all.

Conjugation is a slight improvement. It takes two to conjugate, and both must be one-celled organisms of the same species. They cuddle up to each other and trade some rings and spirals before they split. The result is that the daughters are mixtures, each a little different from the parents. This helps them survive, because a change in their surroundings may kill some of them, but others, being different, may go right on living. There are no males and females among such organisms, or at least it is difficult to tell them apart.

More congenial to humans is copulation, where the animals concerned are divided into two sexes. The male, in one way or another, usually gets to put his sperm into the female and fertilize her eggs. Since the sperm contains many different genes, and so does the egg, the result is like a folk dance, and in the course of trading off partners, many different combinations are possible. Thus except in the case of identical twins, each offspring is different from the others, which increases the chance that some of them will survive any changes in the music of the earthly sphere. There are some animals, like fish, which are divided into two sexes but don't get to copulate because the female lays her eggs in the water and the male discharges his sperm on them instead of inside her. Snails probably have more fun than anybody except people because they are hermaphrodites and both ends of them get to copulate at the same time.

Mating is the same as copulation but it sounds more romantic. Mating is a word used by bird-watchers, school-teachers, and pet-lovers. It means that the animals that copulate are supposed to have chosen their mates very carefully and to love them dearly, but this is not necessarily true.

Human mating is called sexual union, which, as already noted, is a phrase used mainly by clergymen. It means that there is, or should be, a spiritual element present which makes it even more beautiful than animal mating; but this is not necessarily true either. Nevertheless, such unions are usually spoken of as blessed, especially if they produce offspring.

In all the above words, there is a feeling that the purpose of the whole procedure is reproduction, but that is not always or even usually true as far as human beings are concerned. Mankind has made a great leap by splitting off the pleasures of sex from its biological purpose, and man is the only known form of life which can deliberately arrange to have sex without reproduction and reproduction without sex.

What we can say so far then is that sexual reproduction is an improvement over binary fission and conjugation. It is a way of mixing genes so as to provide a larger variety of offspring, giving a greater chance for survival under changing conditions in the outside world. Organisms seeking sexual partners tend to venture farther afield and take greater risks than those that are content with less glamorous methods of reproduction. And the more magnetic sex is, the farther the organism will wander in search of it, and the greater the risks it will take. Hence from a biological point of view sex and its pleasures are an excellent means for the production of a large variety of organisms living in a large variety of circumstances and for the evolution of more adaptable and adventurous forms of life.

C

BUT WHAT IS IT ALL ABOUT?

The explanation I have given so far might satisfy an inquiring snail, so that he would shuffle off sadder but wiser, but it doesn't help much for understanding the vibrations that pass between men and women in everyday life. So here is a list of some of the things that sex is about in human living, what it may be at times for almost everyone, and what it can be for almost anyone.

First, it is about fertilization: the quivering dive of the sperm into the fecund pool of the egg, which blasts a new life into throbbing flowerhood. But that can be done without sex by artificial insemination. (Did you know that there is a whole profession that spends its days squirting turkeys in this manner, so that these miserable birds are not only plucked and eaten, but cuckolded, syringed, and swindled into the bargain?)

Second, it is about impregnation—which may or may not be sexy, but it satisfies the woman's need to be filled with growing new life, and the man's need to fill her and change her body and her life through the power of his instrument.

Third, it may be about duty, for people who talk about it that way, and this is what they say: the duty of a woman to bear children for her husband, and the duty of a man to give them to his wife; the duty of a wife to yield to her husband's desires, and the duty of a husband to offer her what she could have as a maiden; and nowadays, the duty of a woman to give her man the orgasm she thinks he craves, and the duty of a man to give his woman the kind of orgasm she imagines is there.

Fourth, it may be about rituals: the ritual of sex in the morning, or the ritual of sex at night; and the ritual of sex on anniversaries, and the ritual of sex at Christmas.

Fifth, it may be about relief, which means deliverance of pent-up tensions which cause distractions, discomfort, and even pain. However reluctant the person may be to have such deliverance, and however much he regards it as unworthy self-indulgence, sooner or later he feels justified in getting it, or else he continues to struggle against it with a feeling of nobility and righteousness. For such people, relief is obtained through things called outlets. If the outlet is regarded as a person, then he feels guilty for using a person as an outlet; if she is not regarded as a person, then he feels shame for failing in humanity. If the relief does not require another person—"Every man his own wife, or a honeymoon in the hand," as they say—then he

feels a secret triumph of self-sufficiency, along with lone-
liness and disappointment and separation from the human
race, for this is one of the original sins forced on many
by personality and circumstance.

Sixth, it may be physiological readjustment, a pact entered into to give a mutual feeling of well-being.

Seventh, it may be a pleasure to be sought assiduously,
the eternal chase after the promise of an orgasm.

Eighth, it may be a mutual pastime, a way of spending
the days while waiting for Santa Claus or death.

Ninth, it may be a play of seduction and retreat, of
quarrels and reconciliations, with the bed as a playing
field for all the psychological games that are known or
that can be devised between a man and a woman.

Tenth, it can be a medium for union and understanding,
for sealing other pacts and making new pacts, for approaching ever closer to a meeting of two souls, for two
curves that slide along the carefully erected barriers between them.

Eleventh, it can be intimacy and attachment, the weld-
ing of two solids by the heat of passion in a union that
may endure forever, if it does not crack under the hammer
blows of life or waste away under the monotonous drip
of ever-haunting trivia.

Twelfth, it can be the final and ever renewed expression
of love, culminating in its natural product, the fertilized
egg, thus completing the circle.*

Often the question "What is sex all about, anyway?" is
asked with a kind of desperation. Then it usually means
two things. First, "Why do I want it so badly?" The answer is that we are built that way. Remember, we all
started out as jellyfish, and it took millions of years of
natural selection for us to evolve into people. The stronger

* EW: Your idea is that humans absolutely have to feel they
need to have children and, if not they are denying their basic
biological cravings; we can really only infer that it is biological
to want children. Really all we can say is that the craving or
need is for copulation.

EB: Ah, so!

and more energetic organisms that wanted it badly would on the whole leave more offspring, and so their kind survived better than the ones that didn't. So here we are striving to get it as hard as we can, except that we get mixed up about it, and all sorts of people are helping to keep us that way.

Which brings us to the second point that bothers a lot of people: "When am I going to get some?" The answer is that you will when you're ready. You can get some right now if you're willing to travel far enough and make the necessary sacrifices and take what comes along. But then you may have to face some consequences: possibly physical and mental and moral, perhaps the betrayal of yourself and your parents, so it may be better to wait until the time is ripe. In a way, waiting is a shabby way to live, and it goes against nature, but—each one can fill in his own but's, or throw them all away.

D

THE PURPOSE OF SEX

Sex best fulfills its purposes by being an end in itself. These purposes are of two kinds: those evolved through a billion years by the workings of nature and those set up ten thousand years ago by the workings of men's minds.

From Nature's point of view our bodies are irrelevant except as they are productive. We are living on a very small planet—Jupiter is 1,300 times as large—and our chief distinction over other heavenly bodies is that we are inhabited by walking people. In order to stay inhabited, we must reproduce as fast as or faster than we die. If there is any purpose to sex, therefore, the greatest or cosmic purpose is the survival of our species, and beyond that its continual evolution through variation—that is, intermarriage—and improvement through natural selection. In this respect, therefore, our bodies are there to carry the sperm and the eggs, and are themselves of no great consequence. Our only duty to the cosmos is to survive into puberty so that we can reproduce our kind. The only function of the sperm and the eggs, in turn, is to form a vehicle and an envelope for the genes they contain. In other words, the crux that makes the earth different from any other lump of rock that floats through space is a handful of human genes—and I say this literally, since all the genes for the whole human race could be held in the palm of your hand. So the sperm and the egg are there only for the sake of these genes, and our bodies are there for the sake of the sperm and the egg, and that is their holy mission. In the grand design of the universe, we are mail pouches for some great chain-letter scheme of our creator, whose end we will never know, any more than any other mail pouch knows what news and what propositions it carries in its belly. Sex is the fuel that drives this great project forward, and without sex it would come to a standstill and crumble away, leaving only dry bones to show that it ever existed.

All human life, then, may be seen as a preparation for our part in this production, followed by a nurturing of what we produce, and after that a fading away as we turn it over to the next generation. Fortunately, many can still enjoy sex after they have played their parts. Those who fail to reproduce, through design or endowment, may still be driven around and into each other in a grand ecstasy which in part makes up for what they have missed.

For helping her to carry on this rare design, Nature offers us a strange and wondrous fee. The orgasm is her reward to us for making a new baby.* And with tremendous generosity, she allows us to take as many as we like from her great basket of pleasures, and does not even ask for them back if we fail to produce. She also pensions us off liberally when we are too old to produce. Nor does she punish us if we take steps to fool her with contraception. For religious people, all this must be an unparalleled example of God's inexhaustible charity. But there is, it is

---

* EW: This is a male's idea.
  EB: Some women have it too. Isn't that OK?

true, an exception: dread diseases, which strike seemingly at random. On the other hand, for those who refuse these gifts altogether, there is a slow eating of envy and turning to stone: the same thing that makes their sex frigid makes their brains rigid.

An offshoot of sex is the nesting drive, which makes men build houses and women decorate them, and thus provides children with a pleasant snuggery while they are waiting their turn. And men and women, fortunately, become attached to each other so they can keep these establishments going. At least that is the way it should be, and the sexual circuits are arranged in the chemistry of the body and the wiring of the nervous system so that this is what will happen if nothing interferes.

So much for Nature and what she has produced in the course of evolution from the first primitive genes that formed in the ocean to the human families that help each other survive by forming great societies. But we ourselves are not content to be mere seed carriers, and we elaborate sex and its possibilities into something more complex and finer.

First, from sex comes our immortality. Our homes and businesses, our farms and factories, the books and paintings, and all those things that we put together and pass on to our children with the mark of our minds and hands upon them, will pass away, they tell us. Shelley told it to us, how all the monuments of Ozymandias crumbled into dust; and lean or ruddy ministers shout it from the pulpits every Sunday, and we see it in the dread phrase of our time when all things that have our personal mark are burned or taken away: "The tanks of the oppressors are coming, and they will destroy what we have built and what is dear to us." But our last hope is that our children, product of our sex, will survive, and that our grandchildren, product of their sex, will have some memory of us, and that our descendants far into the future will hear of us as legends, the Founder and the Foundress of the tribe.

Second are the more immediate gains we have already noted. As pure gratification, in every country it is a sport

more popular even than football, bowling, or television:
the ever-ready resort of the poor, and the sought-after delight of the rich. It makes pleasant hours that would
otherwise be dull or even dreary; some cultivate it like a
rare herb or grass to squeeze the last drop of dizzy delec-
tation from it. It is an excuse to form attachments that
we yearn anyhow to prolong; it cements us to the person
who is the only hope in our cosmic core of solitude; and
for those who find spiritual fulfillment in each other, it is
a mystic form of primal communion.

And so in summary of what has been said above, sex is
a matrix for all kinds of the most lively transactions: em-
braces and quarrels, seductions and retreats, construction
and mischief. In addition, it is an aid to happiness and
work, a substitute for all manner of drugs, and a healer of
many sorts of sickness. It is for fun, pleasure, and ecstasy.
It binds people together with cords of romance, gratitude,
and love. And it produces children. For human living and
human loving all that is what it is about, and all that is its
purpose.

E

SEX AND SCIENCE

What have we given it in return? For the most
part, up to now, fear, scorn, disgust, and repudiation.
There have been many polls to tell us its varieties, and
many journeys by anthropologists to study its regulation,
which is too often only its negation. There is little of
science, and that from many quarters met with cries of
outrage or pretension. Most of what I have said comes
from guesswork, intuition, and reports without stern statistical evaluation. The remedy is close at hand.

Let us take the statement that good sex means better
health. This would be easy to test, and I would propose
the following investigation.

It is well known that large numbers of college students

have regular sex. Another large number have irregular sex. A third part has only masturbàtion, and a smaller number (probably) has no sex at all. There should be little difficulty in getting 4,000 volunteers, 2,000 men and 2,000 women, 500 of each of the four categories. (The only problem might be to find 1,000 who have no sex at all.) It would only be necessary to compare the sex records and the health records of each of these students during their four years at college in order to find out whether better sex means worse or better health, and that would be something well worth knowing, both for individuals and for the medical profession. It could be an inexpensive project, easily handled by one hard-working investigator (40 interviews a day for 100 days, and the rest of the time for sorting cards and making tables). For a lazy worker, it could be made into a more expensive and impressive project with a few secretaries and a computer. In any case, it is quite practical and feasible. But no one has ever done it, as far as I can find out.

Incidentally, if Mr. Taxpayer paid $100,000 in taxes per year, his annual contribution to such a study would be only a small fraction of one cent. I don't think he should begrudge this small contribution to an important scientific undertaking; on the other hand, I don't think he should take advantage of it to interfere with the investigation.

F

SEX AND RELIGION

Nothing makes religious people as nervous as sex, or at least unregulated sex. Since each religion has its own regulations, people who go to different churches get nervous about different things. But their basic attitude is that sex *is* the concern of religion, and they leave it to the priests, elders, or medicine men to decide when it is sacred and when it is profane. Since these people are retained by the establishment, the rules they make usually favor older people rather than younger ones, and officers rather than enlisted men.

Religious or not, there are some people who regard all sex as sacred in some sense, and every man must have some secret place for sacred things; if he does not, his mind is dust and he is already on the road to death. On the other side are those who regard all sex as profane. This includes bigots, and men of principle such as the Russian Skoptzkies, who used to castrate themselves as a pledge of good faith. Somewhat different are the people who make it their business to profane everything that others hold sacred. These may be organized into cults like witches, or merely parade in pairs in public places in their Cuff You sweatshirts.

From a certain point of view,* sex is either straight or crooked. Which, depends on the "contract" or understanding between the two parties. If they have a clear understanding and stick with that, then it is straight. But if any corruption, exploitation, deception, or ulterior motive is involved, then to that extent it is crooked. Thus, even if there seems to be a clear understanding, taking advantage of a weakness is crooked because of its corruption. For example, getting sex from a child in return for candy is corrupt, because even if she agrees to it, she is being exploited; she doesn't know what she is getting into and what the consequences may be. This judgment follows the legal idea of a contract, where mere consent is not enough; it must be "informed" consent.

Clergymen who practice "transactional analysis" distinguish between sacred and profane sex as well as between straight and crooked. In trying to bring the two together, it is likely that all crooked sex would also be called profane. On the other hand, not all straight sex would be considered sacred, and that is where the two approaches differ.

There is a strong tendency to equate sacredness with solemnity: if it's fun, it can't be sacred, or if someone laughs, he is profaning it. I don't think either of these

---

* This refers to transactional analysis.

attitudes is correct. If sex is sacred, then fun and laughing, being equally happy and human feelings, are sacred too.

In civilized countries, as elsewhere, sex is often more sacred than human life. Thus in Texas people can be legally killed even for non-violent sexual transgressions. On a larger scale, in war it is all right to kill as many people as possible if the right person gives the word, but there is no one who can give the official word for an outbreak of sexual joy.

In civil life, the battlecry "Better death than sex" finds its most sinister application in the American prison system. There 200,000 inmates of state and Federal prisons are totally deprived of normal sexual relations. Hence these men and women, for the most part intense and energetic, take to homosexuality and murder for their emotional expression. But no one has so far dared give the word even for the married ones to relax with their legal wives, and thereby offer some chance for decency to prevail. (There are now some exceptions to this.)

2

THE
SEXUAL
ACT

A

MALE AND FEMALE SEX ORGANS

The sexual apparatus of men is less complicated than that of women, which is a source of pride to the biological female with her rounded hips and breasts and the four dimples on the lower part of her back which form the rhomboid of Michaelis that is so beloved of sculptors of the female form. Indeed, this rhomboid, when well outlined, is one of the most beautiful structures in nature, with its promise of all-embracing warmth and fecundity that stirs the deepest nature of protective and propagating biological man. If you have not previously looked at and admired this most promising and beautiful of all the valleys on this earth, I would recommend it to your attention. As an object for sheer esthetic pleasure, free of the more turgid passions aroused by the canyons found between the breasts, the buttocks, and the thighs, it is unsurpassed.

The sexual equipment of the male consists of two small crucibles, the testicles; each with its own still, the epididymis; and its own little tank, the seminal vesicle. These lead to a pump, the prostate, which delivers the product through a hydraulic ram, the penis. The female starts with the ovaries, which drop their ripened eggs like apples near the openings of the Fallopian tubes, whose gentle petals waft them down the tunnel toward the womb or uterus. The uterus is built to cradle the growing embryo and feed it into maturity. At the other end, the vagina is supplied with glands that lubricate to aid the brawny thrust of the penis as it slides down the ways ready too seed the new life with its seminal torpedoes. The vagina also has muscles that squeeze and pulsate and sweet-talk the semen toward its destination in the womb. Above its entrance is the clitoris, an organ especially designed and supplied with special nerves for exquisite titillation leading into ultimate ecstasy. In sum, then, the man has two exquisitely miniaturized cell factories and an aggressive delivery system. The woman is well equipped to encourage and handle his deliveries, which she pillows in the most beautifully constructed incubator in the universe. She also has the equipment to nurse its grateful product.

But psychological complications arise because the man sticks out while the woman is tucked in, or, as someone said, the man has outdoor plumbing and the woman has indoor plumbing. Thus the man has built-in advertising which he can light up at night when occasion calls for it, while the woman can only do promotional work behind the scenes. It is something like the difference between a roadside hamburger stand with neon lights, and an elegant inn with the most discreet façade concealing its single downy chamber.

B

HOW IT BEGINS

Sigmund Freud said seventy years ago that most dreams of adults treat of sexual material and give expression to erotic wishes.[1] He decided this by studying the psychology of dreams, but he had no concrete evidence. Many people, including medical men, found this idea unlikely, unpleasant, or even repulsive, but Freud stuck to his guns. Now the concrete evidence is here. Modern sleep research shows that nearly all dreams, in the male at least, are preceded or accompanied by an erection.[2] The same is probably true of females, although that is harder to establish. This means that there is a lot of sexual activity going on in both sexes while they are asleep, and that erections occur about every ninety minutes through the night. This can go on for years or even a lifetime without the person's ever being aware of it.

In waking life, the sex act for the male begins with an erection. No erection, no sex. The penis was designed by a careful engineer. All year round, the blood flows in and out smoothly and without hindrance, unless the inflow increases and the outflow is blocked. If these things happen, the blood collects in little caverns provided for that purpose. The organ soaks it up like a sponge and begins to hang a little bigger. As the blood continues to pile up, it fills all the spaces until they start to bulge. Pretty soon the whole penis is turgid and tight as a drum.

There are two theories as to what happens inside to bring the erection about. The blood is brought in by arteries and flows out through veins. One theory is that the arteries open wider so that the blood rushes in faster than the veins can carry it away. The other is that the largest vein is closed off just before it leaves the penis to enter the body, so that the blood piles up in front of it.

Let us consider the second theory first, since it is more elegant. If the largest vein is blocked off, the blood cannot get out until the pressure is high enough to overcome the block or to force a passage roundabout through other smaller veins. This main vein is shaped like a thin-walled flexible rubber tube. Near its exit from the penis, there is a little band of muscle lying across it in such a way that if the muscle contracts, the tube is shut off. Then the blood cannot flow out as it usually does. It piles up behind the dam and the penis swells like a—like a—like a penis, and the more it swells the tougher it gets. The more excited the man is, the harder his phallus grows. It swells so much that if the cap on the end is flexible it may turn up a little. He may feel as though he is going to burst if he doesn't find a place to put it, but there is no fear of that. The blood can always force its way through the other little veins before things get out of hand. Nature has set it up so that no matter how hard the hydraulic battle, there is no chance of a blowout.

The little muscle that starts the ball rolling is known to anatomists as the *Compressor venae dorsalis penis,* compressor of the vein on the back of the penis (not the vein you can see there, although that may throb too, but one buried inside). It is called, for short, Houston's muscle. If it is true that erections depend on this muscle, then for the most part procreation depends on it, too. Houston's muscle will always contract if the right kind of electrical impulses go down the right nerves, but it will stay relaxed as long as they don't. Through natural selection in the course of evolution, this muscle and the nerves going to it have become one of the most reliable triggers known. It can function perfectly for as long as eighty-eight years without oiling or parts replacement, even under the hardest conditions of use.

Nearly all difficulties in erection originate with the operator and not with the mechanism—pilot's error, as they say in aircraft circles. The impulses to the penis are sent down from the brain, and there is a little man up there who is supposed to keep his finger on the button when the signal flashes green and all systems are Go. But if he gets tired, scared, distracted, or upset, he may relax the pressure or release the button, even when the light is green.

Since it is a fail-safe button or dead-man's throttle, once it is released, the mechanism is disconnected and goes back into idle. The little man is of course the Child in the person, and if he chickens out there is no erection even though all the wiring is sound and even though there is lots of stimulation coming in from the outside.

It is interesting to note that the existence of Houston's muscle is unknown to many people, including medical men. It is not even mentioned by that name in Gray's *Anatomy,* so that most medical students go through medical school without ever hearing about it. Yet if this account is correct, the whole existence of the human race and its most ecstatic moments depend on this neglected strip of tissue, so beautifully set up to transform a short soft organ into a long hard one through the laws of physics.

There is no set of experiments in animals or humans to prove that this "rubber band" theory of erection is entirely wrong, but there are some that show that it is not entirely right.[3] In fact, any male can do his own experiment. If erection results simply from compression of the veins in the penis, so that blood can get in but cannot get out except under very high pressure, then anything that compresses the veins without shutting off the arteries should bring an erection about. It is easy to find an ordinary rubber band to fit tightly around the penis, and presumably compress the veins, without shutting the circulation off entirely. But even if it is left on for five or ten minutes, which is plenty of time for blood to collect if it is going to, no erection will follow.[4] Too bad, because if it did work, it would be an admirably simple cure for impotence, and a great deal of human frustration and unhappiness could be avoided. There are possible flaws in this do-it-yourself experiment, and it might not be completely convincing to an experienced researcher, but it does cast serious doubt on the "rubber band" theory in simplest form.

The second theory, that the arteries expand and pour in so much blood that the veins simply cannot carry it off, now seems more likely. But there is no way to expand these arteries artificially, so potency must be left in the hands of nature and psychiatry. There is a drug called yohimbine, that comes from the West African Yohimbé-hé tree, which was once promoted as a true dilator of the penile arteries, but few people who tried it found that it really helped. Spanish fly, the most popular aphrodisiac in folklore, acts by causing an inflammation that may be dangerous or even fatal.*

We do not have to give up Houston's muscle and its elegant mechanism entirely, because it is likely that in man the best erections result from a combination of both effects. There is an increased flow of blood due to expansion of the arteries, and also some clamping down on the veins, and between the two of them the phallus attains its greatest degree of hardness.

With the woman, things are more complicated. Sexual excitement begins with lubrication of the vagina, which may take place a few seconds after she decides to go along. Some minutes after that, the clitoris becomes distended. No one knows quite how that happens, but there is no reason to suppose that there is not a Houston's muscle in the female as well as in the male, since anatomists agree that there are muscle fibers in the clitoris similar to those in the penis. They may help by damming back the blood at the same time as the excited arteries pour it in, thus making the clitoris larger and firmer. But the clitoris is also pulled upward and may disappear from sight, which the penis does not. In a fully desirous woman, the cervix too swells and pulsates, "sending out urgent signals to the vagina to get filled up," as Amaryllis puts it.

* Dopa (dihydroxyphenylalanine), a substance now used in the treatment of Parkinsonism or palsy, is said to be a true aphrodisiac and penile erector in people suffering from that disease, but it is considered too powerful for normal use because of its many possible side effects.

C

MALE POWER

The sexual power of the male has three elements: potency, force, and drive. Potency is shown by the firmness of his erection, force by the ardor of his thrust, and drive by the muzzle velocity of his ejaculation.

There are several degrees of potency or erection. In the first, the penis is slightly enlarged and hangs a little away from the body. In a social situation, the bearer may hardly be aware that he is quickened. He will suffer no embarrassment, since the enlargement cannot usually be noticed by those around him. This condition may be called "social stir," as in the following news item: "Amaryllis caused a social stir among the men as she entered the room in her erectile miniskirt." At this point it should be mentioned that most women know the difference between "well-dressed" and "not well-dressed," but only a few know the difference between a "good-looking dress" or a "low-cut dress" and an "erectile dress." The same applies to other articles of female apparel.

In the second degree, the organ is long and stiff, but will still bend if it is hand-snapped or meets any opposition. Being so, unless the partner is open and well lubricated, it will not be able to penetrate, but will give way instead. That was the predicament of the young Englishman in the famous limerick on this very subject.

> There was a young man of Kent
> Whose kirp in the middle was bent.
> To save himself trouble
> He put it in double,
> And instead of coming, he went.

In honor of this double-jointed Briton, such a state may be called the Kentish curse, although it should more properly be termed "cautious kirp," since it is usually due to the presence of some doubts as to whether to go ahead with the project. The man may be seduced by the woman or by his own desire to prove his potency, but "in peno* veritas," as Dr. Horseley puts it, his phallus remains unconvinced. It may be a question of making up after a quarrel, or of the immediate consequences of the act, or of what the future may hold, or of some lack of firmness in his attitude toward the opposite sex. In short, there may be some fear of or hesitation in committing himself at that time, which he (his Adult) may be willing to overlook. But his penis (under the control of his more sensitive Child) is not so easily inveigled as he is, and remains skeptical in spite of this license.

In the third degree, the phallus reaches its full size but not its full nobility. It is stuffed, rigid, and ready for action of a kind, but sometimes it falters too quickly and ejaculates before either partner has had a chance for full expression. This is colloquially known as "quick on the trigger." In the fourth stage, the man is like a charging unicorn, not only stiff and ready, but so turgid and eager that he feels he must start his thrust or burst with the fullness of his potency. It is in this state that the cap sometimes turns upward, as though pleading to the heavens for immediate fulfillment. That is the ultimate turn-on, when the man will push ahead at almost any cost, and this is the carnal spindle around which all great courtship struggles are spun in literary romance. In general, this condition is called "raring to go." The special cases where the cap turns up (because some penises are constructed that way) may be called "Peyronie's pride," in honor of the physician who first made a formal study of that phenomenon.[5]

Once the stronghold is captured, in church or in the hay, the powerful urge of thrust takes over. The uncorrupted biological man feels an overwhelming desire to push into the vagina as hard as he can and deposit his semen there.† He will thrust again and again, reaching for the

---

* I know "peno" is not the correct form, but it fits in better that way.

† This is the movement previously referred to, in the language

profoundest depths, and clinging to his partner with all his strength as though no earthly force could ever tear them apart through all of time, even though he senses that the end is not far away. Such ardor is most likely to occur if his phallus is in the fourth and most noble state of its erection, the genuine procreative instrument of human nature. But if there is any spurious element behind its force, the animal thrust will lose its power and must be consciously reinforced. This most commonly happens if the man is more interested in glory than in sex, is frightened of what he has got himself into, or is swindling the woman for his own pleasure. In those cases he may try to make it last as long as possible to hear her sighs, or as short as possible to get away quickly, or he may be aware of the time but callously indifferent. If a come too fast will hurt his pride, the thrusting scares him lest it throw the elixir out too soon; hence he may thrust but little, hoping thus to make it last at least until his mate is satisfied, after which he can proceed with a clear conscience and dignity unimpaired, at his own pace.

The unhampered biological thruster is so intent on what he is doing, withal automatically, that he does not concern himself with time or very much with his partner's reaction, although it gives him the deepest satisfaction if she does react naturally at that great dynamic moment when he attains his goal and deposits his seed where it will do the most good. Such an intensive, almost insensible attitude is exactly the one most likely to bring the woman to the highest pitch of excitement and produce in her the most satisfying orgasm. The force of such thrusts is not brutality, it is biology. But if the woman, instead of responding from her deepest and most genuine nature, becomes interested in the thrust as an end in itself, she may regard it and crave it as brutality, and the same goes for the man.

But the description of unhampered biological activity is

---

of *The Perfumed Garden*, as *dok*, with the female response *hez*. In vulgar English, *dok* is bump and *hez* is grind. Kinematically, the man's pelvis pitches around a transverse axis, while the woman's yaws around a vertical or sagittal one.

an ideal rather than a reality. There is no such thing as unhampered sex in the human race. All societies are organized around sexual prohibitions, which seep through even in moments of the highest excitement and corrupt the purity of these responses. At one end there is compliance and overconcern, and at the other rebellion, cruelty, and dishonesty. Somewhere in the middle is real intimacy, with free functioning of sexuality. At its best, sex can be a blast-off from earthbound to 30,000 feet, with an intoxicating slow descent. But less than that can still be more than plenty, and even a flight above the housetops is more invigorating than keeping both feet on the ground. No one can fairly demand more than going through the roof, and every foot above that is a bonus.

What we are talking about here is the third aspect of masculine power. Drive is the power with which the semen at the moment of ejaculation is hurled into the vagina by the piston-like contractions of the prostate. It is probable (although not certain) that the height of the orgasm, that is, the felt altitude of the orgastic trip in feet or meters, depends on the power of the drive.

Thus on the quiet side is the man with an incomplete erection, restrained thrust, and low drive, and at the other extreme the one with an overstuffed ramlike phallus, who thrusts with mighty abandon and propels the semen with great power into the place provided for it by nature. But anywhere along this spectrum, the man can impregnate the woman, and if she is properly prepared, also cause her to have an orgasm.*

Of these three elements, the one most under conscious control is thrust. The erection can be terminated by an act of will, which simply means saying Stop! (or, as it is told in the joke books, Down, Fido!), but there is no magic word which will bring it back or harden it again. Up, Fido! just doesn't work all by itself. There has to be some bait, either living or artificial, to make it rise. The most automatic is ejaculation, which cannot be consciously hastened

---

* EW: This "properly prepared" is an old idea in sex manuals, but what about her preparedness separate from his causing it?

and can be postponed for only a few seconds once it is triggered. The power of the drive depends mostly on physical factors, while the nobility of the erection and the force of the thrust depend on psychological ones.

The sexual power of a man is influenced chiefly by two women: his mother (or maybe his big sister), who encouraged or discouraged his masculinity and his sexuality while he was growing up; and his partner, who has it in her power to elevate and stimulate, or to depress and inhibit him, by the way she responds. The older man is particularly sensitive about his mate. If she turns him off too often, he may begin to lose his potency and go into middle-age droop, a condition which may become progressively more severe, but is nearly always reversible if put in the hands of an enthusiastic practitioner.

Often a man's sexual power is reflected in his daily life, as many wives maintain. He may be hard, aggressive, and full of drive; or he may bend easily in the face of opposition, lack force and thrust, and dribble off at the end or fail to finish what he begins.

D

FEMALE POWER

The female and the male complement each other, and her power has three corresponding elements: profusion, force, and grasp. Profusion is represented by lubrication, force is manifested in counterthrust, and grasp is shown by muscular contractions.

Lubrication of the vagina naturally makes it easy for the phallus to slide in. If there is no lubrication at all (analoiphia), someone is likely to get skinned. Some women get so turned on that the happy oil or joy juice, as they call it, overflows (hyperloiphia) while they swing into one orgasm after another. Sometimes a woman may get excited enough in a social situation to lubricate slightly or even profusely, much to her pride or embarrassment. As with the male, such an event may be called "social stir." Lubrication, however, does not always mean that the woman is going to respond; she may accept the penis, but refuse to be excited by it.* But if all goes well, lubrication is followed by a turgid clitoris. Vaginal lubrication, together with clitoral swelling, corresponds to potency in the male, so when it is convenient to do so, the word potency can be applied to both sexes.

Counterthrust may be biologically the woman's response to the prospect of impregnation, or psychologically, to her drive for ultimate closeness. It may be demoted to a mere pleasure-seeking mechanism. True biological counterthrust is not self-conscious or calculating; it is not a question of trying to wring the greatest amount of pleasure out of the act; it is something the woman *has* to do because she wants so much to get the penis as deeply as possible inside her. Some women start off with counterthrust as pleasure-seeking, but are overtaken by its biological compulsiveness and begin to respond more naturally.

Grasping is the counterpart of drive. At the moment of orgasm, which may coincide with the man's ejaculation, the vagina grasps the penis again and again in waves of muscular contraction, as though trying to milk out the semen. This sends waves of reaction through her partner and may increase the driving force of his ejaculation. There may also be slower grasping motions that are equally pleasurable.

The woman's sexuality is reflected in her other characteristic responses to a man. She makes herself accessible to him and lubricates their actions together. When he comes toward her, she comes forward to meet him halfway. When he is driving toward some goal, she responds to him with exquisite emotional rhythm and helps to draw the best out of him, thus offering him inspiration. If she has been raised by her mother or father to avoid or despise such natural responses, she will be awkward or nasty, not only in her sexual transactions, but also in her other rela-

---

* EW: Women who do that can be called good sports.
  EB: Why not sulks?

tions with men. She will be inaccessible or abrasive, unresponsive, and competitive or belittling, rather than receptive, responsive, and encouraging.*

At one end of the female spectrum is the woman who does not lubricate or get excited, lies still and unmoved, and receives the ejaculation passively.† At the other is the one who lubricates profusely, reaches a high level of excitement, responds to every thrust, giving as good as she gets, and grasps the penis tightly as though to help out the last lingering drop of ejaculation.

E

THE ORGASM

The human orgasm is one of the most intimately and admirably planned and synchronized events in all of nature. Both anatomically and physiologically, it shows the splendid selection of the course of evolution. Exactly what the man needs the woman has, and exactly what the women needs the man has. Their temperature, pressure, and precipitation match each other in just the right way to form Cloud 9 in an explosive discharge of creative energy that involves all of both of them: physical, chemical, muscular, electrical, and psychological. If it works right, each of them will emerge with a mind pure and free, brain washed clean of troubles and ready to start life anew. Or, as someone said, the only time human beings are sane is

* EW: Why don't you put a list of similar not-OK words at the end of the section on male power?

† EW: Why blame her? Maybe he's a necrophile. And in the next sentence, you expect her to do everything.

EB: I'm thinking about natural selection, and picking out those items which seem to me to increase the chances of selection and fertilization, as well as the survival of the individual in a competitive world. Maybe it would have come out differently if Darwin had been a woman.

EW: That's an interesting thought.

in the ten minutes after intercourse. Or, as someone else said, every night spent alone is wasted.

Each sex has two different ways of bringing this about. In the male, the glans or cap is the most sensitive part of the penis, and stimulation of that area at the right time can bring about a rapid and rather unsatisfactory ejaculation, which justifies the Marquis de Sade's injunction to his partners: "Never touch the cap!" (This is one of the few things in his writings that come out right.) The shaft is less touchy and produces a more leisurely enjoyment. The most voluptuous area is where the shaft and the cap meet at the corona, which is a trigger area for the orgasm. Similarly in the woman, the clitoris is more touchy than the vaginal lining, and clitoral stimulation can bring about an orgasm which, according to many women, leaves much to be desired. Here again the most sensitive point may be where the tip of the clitoris and the vaginal lining lie close together.

There is a splendid synchronization between male and female orgasms. The man's loins move, his prostate contracts, and his semen hurls forward in exactly the same rhythm as the pulsations of the woman's vagina and clitoris. This is due to an automatic rebound of certain types of muscle fibers. This mutual rebound is repeated again and again until the reflexes of one partner wear out. The other may continue to contract and expand for a long time after that, often to the amazement and admiration of the satisfied one. Some partners even prefer to have their orgasms at different times so that they can get a kind of double enjoyment of one another in this way, but others would rather come together in one overwhelming wave of ecstasy.

This muscular rhythm of thrust and grasp feeds and reinforces the timing of the two clocks involved: one in the prostate, which determines the rhythm of the ejaculatory spasms, and the other in the clitoris, which has its own rhythm and regulates or coincides with the rhythm of the vaginal contractions. One of the wonders of evolution is that these two timers usually work at exactly the same speed: four-fifths of a second per pulse. The balance wheels of these alternating clocks are the ejaculatory centers in the spinal cord, so a nervous rhythm is at the bottom of it all, just as in a jellyfish or snail or an angel playing the harp.

_____

F

THE PSYCHOLOGY OF SEX

The sexual responses in both sexes are determined partly by built-in, or biological, factors and partly by mind-cuffing, or psychological, factors. Once the orgasm is triggered, the built-in biological circuits take over and the mind gets uncuffed, but up to that moment, voices in the head and voices in the bed strongly influence what happens, how it happens, when it happens, and who happens. Even more important than those voices, however, are the hidden pictures in the back of the mind, the primal images of the two partners, which determine their potency and thrust if not their drive.

The psychological or mind-cuffing factors at work on the male, with a similar list for the female, are as follows:

1. Whether he is fearful or enthusiastic about sex. The most important single factor here is his mother's voice saying either "Watch out!" or "Go to it!"

2. Whether he is dishonest or honest about it. This is usually decided by his father's voice or example saying either "Snatch it!" "Listen to her holler!" or "Both of you enjoy yourselves."

3. Whether his partner is responsive, neutral, or discouraging. Her voice tells him which by being warm and soft, indifferent, or cold and threatening. Her muscles go along, being loving, dead, or uptight, while her glands can make it smooth and damp, or rough and dry.

4. The external situation, especially the possibility of being interrupted or stimulated by other people, including children, and mosquitoes and their ilk.

5. His primal image of the female sex organs.

If he succeeds in digging up his primal image, it may be quite different from what he expected. Thus an obstetrician, whose Adult was thoroughly familiar with the actual appearance of these organs under all sorts of conditions, was surprised to discover that his Child still pictured the vagina as an enormous dark bottomless cave in which his penis or even his whole body could get lost. In another example it was a narrow passage full of barbs that must be avoided by anyone who entered there. The power of such images to affect erection, thrust, and drive may depend partly on the actual physical condition of the vagina as seen and felt by the phallus. If it feels loose, that may turn it into a scary cave for the first man and relieve the second; if it feels tight, the cave man may feel safer, but the trap man may become alarmed and want to get out of there quickly.

Incredible as it may seem, sometimes the penis, or even the fingers, can see as well as feel. This is called synesthesia. Everybody's Adult knows that the vagina is really red and stays red, but to the phallus its color may change with the degree of lubrication. Dry, it may feel purple; slightly moist, it may seem brown; and when it is very slippery, it may feel bright blue. These are common synesthetic impressions, but each penis may have its own color card. [6]

The woman has her primal image of the phallus, which affects her responses in a similar way. To her Child, it may seem like a jutting mass of hardness which is going to penetrate too far, a sharp knife which is going to cut her, or a thin round which is too small for her to grasp and control before it slips away. Some women may also have color reactions depending on the slipperiness of the penis, which is really the result of their own lubrication.

There are also more favorable primal images. To the man, the vagina may look like a cozy resting place or a caressing hand, or the clitoris like a seductive nipple; while to the woman, his penis may look like a lollipop or a Tootsie-roll or a mushroom. These images are not, as is commonly assumed, "unconscious." They can be easily seen by anyone who is alert enough to stop them as they

float by. It is important to know this because primal
images can have a decisive effect on male and female
sexual power, and there is no need to lie around for a
long time to uncover them. They are lurking stark naked
in the background all along.

Many statements about the psychology of sex are based
on personal preferences rather than on careful study. Some
sex psychologists have their own kind of strict morality;
for example: "The male is excited by what he does to the
female, not by what the female does to him; while the
female is excited by what the male does to her, not by
what she does to him."[7] Like puritanical schoolmasters,
they disapprove of energetic women and luxury-loving
men. They set up a standard type of human being who
can have all the different types of sex. This may work no
better than the lawmakers' policy of setting up a standard
type of sex for all the different kinds of human beings.
And Amaryllis says that fashions change in sex. "Even
the birth control movement has done a complete about-
face," she remarks in her cryptic way. "It used to be a
downward swing of the arm with the diaphragm, and now
it's an upward swing with the pill."

G

THE BIOLOGY OF SEX

In the course of evolution, potency, thrust and
drive in the male and profusion, counterthrust, and grasp
in the female have probably all contributed to the efficient
propagation of the human race. Animals raised a certain
way, for example, will lack these qualities and have a low
reproduction rate.[8] Thus, by physiological selection, the
sexier members would have an advantage over the less
sexy ones in reproducing their kind, so we may assume
that *Homo sapiens* has gotten sexier and sexier through
the centuries and millenniums, and is far more lusty and
lecherous and lewd than his ancestors who lived in caves.

Or even than those who lived in the primeval monkey forests before there were any men, since man is the sexiest mammal there is, nearly always ready on any day of the week or at any phase of the moon.

The biological purpose of the male orgasm is to blast the semen at its target, which oddly enough is not the opening of the uterus, but a pocket at the back of the vagina. This puts the spermatozoa into orbit, after which they turn on their own little engines for the second stage, when they shoot for the moon, which is the little egg lying above them in the ovarian tube. This is a ruthless race, in which the winner takes all and the losers die. Whichever sperm hits the egg first captures it forever and excludes all the others; there is no vice president in this election, and no second place. The swimming distance, in man-size terms, is about two miles, all of it a steeplechase over curves and hurdles and rapids and dams, and much of it upstream. It is more exciting than ten million horse races, for there are several hundred million sperm in each race. It is certainly awesome to realize that that is what happens inside the woman every time the man fires his starting gun. And every man is a hero here. Whether he is tall or short, handsome or ugly, strong or weak, young or old makes no difference; as long as he can throw sperm, he can at his own will start a race which is the equivalent of the whole population of North and South America milling around in Lake Erie.

The intense pleasure attending the male orgasm probably serves mainly to make it attractive and sought after, and that goes for the female orgasm too. But the biological function of the female orgasm remains unknown.* Sexual excitement, especially lubrication, changes the chemistry of the woman's reproductive system to make it a more congenial summer resort for the sperm, but the

---

* I believe that the real "purpose" of orgasm is psychological resuscitation. It acts like an electric shock treatment on the brain, redistributing its potentials so that the mind is cleared. This is similar to the sorting function of REM sleep noted in *Psychiatric News,* October, 1969, based on the work of R. Greenberg and E. M. Dewan.

orgasm itself does not seem to add much. At any rate, women seem to get pregnant just as easily if they do not have an orgasm as if they do, so the orgasm may be desirable, and possibly helpful, but it is not necessary.

It would appear that the male orgasm *is* necessary for impregnation, but there is no certainty even about that. Some men secrete "love-water" from the prostate long before they come, and that may have a few wandering sperm in it. This fact may be important for two reasons. First, it indicates that even if the man does not follow up the love-water with an ejaculation, or withdraws and ejaculates outside, he might still impregnate the woman. That would be particularly apt to happen if there were a few sperm swimming around in his spermatic system from a recent previous ejaculation, since that would increase the likelihood of some being washed out with the love-water. Secondly, any sperm that do leak into the vagina with the love-water have a headstart over those thrown in later, and might therefore have an advantage in the race to the ovum. Thus it may be that love-water sperm are more likely to start a baby than ejaculated sperm and this might possibly have a bearing on various problems of fertility and development.

Let us review the biological events. Maximum erection and maximum lubrication ensure maximum penetration, aided by thrust and counterthrust. At the critical moment, maximum drive is reinforced by maximum grasp. All this ensures that the maximum amount of semen will get as far back as it can go, and that is the best situation to ensure impregnation. As already noted, the contrast would be a little bit of semen dribbling down the outside of a dry vagina, which would give little chance for the egg to be fertilized; and there are many degrees in between. But one way is more likely to work than another, and in evolution a very slight increase in probability can expand into a large advantage over many generations, just like a thousand years of compound interest.

Something to remember, however, is that even with no erection, no lubrication, and no thrust, the probability of impregnation is greater than zero. It is possible for any

ejaculation in the region of the female sex organs to produce, more or less rarely, a perfectly healthy offspring, or
even twins. (It is possible to have twins, as the earnest
clergyman learned to his surprise, even though you have
only been naughty once.)

One of the most interesting biological features is the way
the woman is set up to welcome the man. As her excitement increases, her vagina graciously widens and lengthens
to accommodate him better, and as a final touch, her uterus
politely lifts itself out of his way so that he can have an
unobstructed channel. Only after he has permanently with-
drawn does the uterus come down again to dip its mouth
into the pool of womb-nourishing semen that he, responding to her open generosity, has lovingly and courteously
and firmly presented her with.

On the other hand, in many ways sexual intercourse is
a battle between the sexes. The harder he pushes down,
the harder she pushes up; and the bigger his penis gets,
the harder she clamps down on it; conversely, the harder
she clamps down, the bigger his penis is likely to get. It
is as though she is trying to make him smaller, and he is
trying to make her bigger. But it is an interesting kind of
battle, because if they bring it to a completely successful
conclusion, they both win. He ends up smaller than he
started out, and she gets bigger and bigger and bigger.
And on the average, there is a rough kind of arithmetic
about it, too. His phallus gets a few ounces lighter ten or
twenty or a hundred times to make her a few pounds
heavier once.*

As long as this "battle" is equal, as it is supposed to be,
it is actually a cooperative effort rather than a contest.
But if it is unequal, it may really turn into a conflict, or
even a running brawl, for then the stronger partner feels
frustrated, disappointed and unappreciated, and the weaker
one feeble, guilty and angry, or worse, gloating with
perverse and unseemly triumph. These unhealthy feelings

---

* EW: I don't like that one at all.

  EB: It's rough, but thought-provoking. Life is very strangely
contrived.

may be carried into the everyday living of the couple, deeply embedded in unpleasant games that cause their stomachs to churn, their muscles to tighten, and their blood pressure to rise, so that they may live for years in physical as well as mental discomfort. Not only do they wreak their vengeance on their children and the other people around them (sometimes with political force), but their bodies begin to give way under the strain until their troubles settle into the organ or system with the least resistance, starting with "psychosomatic" complaints.

People in such a situation are generally looking for ammunition to use against their partners, and I would certainly not want anything I have written here to be used for such a disreputable purpose. While in biology and evolution sex is the chief product of life (so that the first instructions of God to Adam and Eve, after saying hello, were: "Be fruitful, and multiply, and replenish the earth"), in the scale of human values it is, or should be, only second. That is why God said "Hello!" (or "Bless you!" *vyorech asom,* Gen. I:28) before he gave them any instructions, because "Hello" is the one thing more important than sex in human relations. It means, "We're in this together, so let's play it straight." The moral is, don't put your man or woman down for not being an ideal sex partner. First listen to how he says "Hello"—and also to how you say it. A straight man with a crooked penis is better than a crooked man with a straight one, and the right woman with the wrong vagina is better than the wrong woman with the right one.

This brings us to the very human, but often unstraight, ways in which sex organs can be used for purposes other than fertilization.

NOTES AND REFERENCES

1. Freud, S.: *The Interpretation of Dreams* (fourth edition). The Macmillan Company, New York, 1915, p. 240.
2. Fisher, C., Gross, J., and Zuch, J.: "A Cycle of Penile

Erections Synchronous with Dreaming (REM) Sleep." *Archives of General Psychiatry* 12:29-45, January, 1965. They found erections in 95 percent of 86 REM periods in 17 subjects.

3. The Ischiocavernosus is also called the Erector penis in men and the Erector clitoridis in women. Its action is thus described in Gray's *Anatomy* (28th edition, Lea & Febiger, Philadelphia, 1966): "The Ischiocavernosus compresses the crus penis, and retards the return of the blood through the veins, and thus serves to maintain the organ erect" in the male. For the female the same action is given, putting "clitoris" for "penis." Only one inconsequential word has been changed in this since the 23rd edition (1926), and that is what medical students have learned about the mechanism of erection for the last forty years. Houston's muscle would thus be a special band of Ischiocavernosus, functioning as the Compressor venae dorsalis penis (or clitoridis). The chief opponents of the Ischiocavernosus theory of erection nowadays are Masters and Johnson *(Human Sexual Response,* op. cit.). The lethargy in regard to this presumably important question is shown by the fact that the two pertinent citations given by these authors date from 1921 and 1933. They say that "little support is given now" to the Ischiocavernosus concept, but D. W. Fawcett, for example, who is Professor of Anatomy at Harvard, supports it in his article on the Reproductive System in the Encyclopaedia Britannica (1967). Masters and Johnson offer the alternative that "the veins of the penis are believed to possess valves that slow down the return of the blood." If such an apparatus is found to exist, it does not necessarily mean that the Ischiocavernosus contractions *ipso facto* cease to exist. Dr. John Houston's valves work very well in the rectum (Houston's valves, plicae transversalis recti), and there is no reason why his muscle should not work equally well on the erectile tissues.

On the other hand, the 1933 reference mentioned above is an excellent piece of research done by two competent pharmacological physiologists from the University of Toronto ("On the Mechanism of Erection," V. E. Henderson and M. H. Roepke. *American Journal of Physiology* 106:441-448, 1933). These authors, working with dogs in the early days of acetylcholine research, conclude that "the vasodilatation on stimulating the dilator nerves to the penis is due to a local hormonal mechanism," and that "erection is not due to a compression of the efferent veins by skeletal muscle action," although "ischiocavernosus, muscular contractions may play some minor part." "There is a rapid rise of pressure . . . within the corpora cavernosa, which may well make the venous outflow inefficient." However, they did observe "sudden sharp increases in the volume of the penis . . . due to sudden short spontaneous contractions of the ischiocavernosus muscles, which, owing to their somewhat spiral arrangement . . . could produce some pressure on the parts of the corpora lying beneath them . . . after each [contraction] a gain in the amount of erection was noticed." There are a few other small ambiguities in their findings, and there the matter rests until someone figures out a definitive way of demonstrating the anatomical and physiological mechanism in human beings.

4. This simple method of verification was suggested by Dr. James Daly, of St. Mary's Hospital in San Francisco. It only remains for some courageous investigator to find out what happens if a rubber band exerting just the right amount of pressure is put on after erection is established. Will it maintain the erection indefinitely even if other stimuli are avoided? Or if it is put on after ejaculation, but with erection still present? Amateur researchers are cautioned *not* to have the rubber band on during ejaculations, as this will force the semen back into the bladder, a procedure once favored by Oriental and Arab voluptuaries, but one not recommended because the ultimate effects are doubtful and may be damaging.

5. François de la Peyronie (1678-1747). There is some question about the super-erection with the turned-up end. A lady who knows about such things informs me that in her opinion this is a normal manifestation of super-excitement. On the other hand, the same phenomenon occurs in Peyronie's disease (plastic induration of the penis), variously attributed to physical trauma, vascular changes, prolonged abstinence, or lack of adequate gratification. Sometimes the curvature is so marked as to make intromission difficult or impossible.

Peyronie's disease is usually accompanied by pain on erection. The plaques are palpable but may disappear spontaneously (*Human Sexuality* 2:56-57, September, 1968). Since a similar curvature occurs in many toy balloons when they are blown up as far as they can go, it may be a normal anatomico-physiological phenomenon due to differential elasticity in the dorsal and ventral anchorages of the glans. But cf. Glenn, J. F.: "Curvature of the penis," *Human Sexuality* 3:83, February, 1969.

6. Reports of sexual synesthesias are not easy to collect. I would be happy to hear from anyone who cares to send me details of his or her experiences in this regard.

7. Legman, G.: *Oragenitalism*. Op. cit.

8. See Chapter 6, section B.

3

THE
EXPLOITATION
OF THE
SEX ORGANS

A

INTRODUCTION

Strictly speaking, the only natural uses for sex organs are making true love and making babies. Any other purposes are to some extent improper. Sex for pure pleasure by mutual consent may be free of emotional counterfeiting, but it is a biological betrayal if contraceptives are used, as they should be in such cases. Beyond that, the human race has had so much time on its hands, and is so afraid of open intimacy, that it has devised many ways of using its organs for hidden purposes and for frivolous or false relationships. We shall now go on to consider some of these non-propagating uses since they play such an important part in everyday living.*

* EW: There you go with propagation again. What is it with you?

B

THE EXPLOITATION OF THE PENIS

What use is a penis? Well, it is the best instrument for impregnating women and one of the best for sexual pleasure. Beyond that, it can throw a stream of water a reasonable distance and put out fires, but there is a catch there. Mr. and Mrs. Murgatroyd once agreed that whoever could urinate farther would be the boss of their home. Mungo, of course, thought that was a fine arrangement and stepped up to the starting line confident that from then on he would have his way. But just as he got started, Mysie cried, "Oh, oh, no hands!" With a rule like that, the crestfallen Mungo knew that he was done for.

But beyond these natural functions, man's ingenuity has found many ways of making the penis useful. In solitary enjoyment, it can be used as a plaything to pass the time on rainy afternoons and other boring hours. Children who are tired of lying in their cribs or sitting in a schoolroom find its reachability a great temptation. ("Their arms are made just long enough to reach it," as one mother said reproachfully to her clergyman.) In its erect state, it makes an admirable fertility symbol, and has been worshiped as such privately from time to time, or even publicly with joyful ceremonies, at other times and other places. Sometimes it is used in simple social etiquette, aristocratic gestures of politeness or *noblesse oblige,* on the principle that no well-

---

EB: First of all, as a philosophical biologist, I really believe in what I am saying. Secondly, when I was an intern, one thing that got through to me was the beautiful faces of the women on the obstetrical ward. The pregnancies to cut out are the unwanted ones, not the wanted ones.

The people who demand the right to have babies and populate the world have to give equal rights to those who don't. In fairness and salvation, that means free access to every means of prevention.

brought-up young man should leave a woman with any of her desires ungratified; her wish is his command. By men of lesser breeding, it can even be used in similar situations to earn money. Thus it becomes a tool of solace, ritual, courtesy, or employment.

In more informal society, it can be used in mutual pastimes, a ready instrument for exchanging pleasures with the fairer sex, although some dubious men make dubious jokes about preferring a good meal or a good bowel movement; such men should be left with their own kind stewing in the kitchen or the men's room. But beyond such frivolities, it is a great and versatile device for more serious games. Its mere phallic exhibition can seduce girls, frighten them, or excite their awe or admiration. As a poker, it can arouse them from lassitude and indifference. Proud men regard it as a trophy, which they bestow on the worthy as a gift or favor. The covetous man uses it as a branding iron, a sign that the woman has been possessed by him and in some measure is forever his, particularly if he has taken her virginity.

The clod may treat his phallus as a mere pleasure-stick, or as a pleasure-thief, entering under false pretenses, taking what it desires, and then silently shrinking away. The evil man shows his grudge against women, especially women far above him, by "spitting" in their wombs, or if he cannot win their favors, by battering through in criminal rape. The benevolent man will offer his phallus to the woman in distress as a comforter or even as a healing instrument that will surpass all medications, thus demonstrating to her and to himself its magic powers.*

Used thus in sexual games, the phallus has all the authority of a baseball bat to score foul balls, a grandstand play, or an away-from-home run.

As previously mentioned, the penis may be flaunted to advertise itself. Very often, a beach or a dance hall is like a supermarket for young girls, with all the goodies carefully packaged on open display. Tight swimming trunks or trouser pants may turn on the younger crowd or the

---

* EW: A hot beef injection.

hungry bar-fly girls, but more confident women may react differently. One of them put the question witheringly to a young man who sat across from her with his legs apart: "It's pretty, but what can it do?" In homosexual circles, where the main object may be to find someone who is "well hung" or has "a big basket," with little interest in the hanger or the man who is carrying the basket, such advertising may be more acceptable and pay off.

Finally, as an instrument of love, the phallus can be used to give pleasure to the woman, to caress and to stroke her most secret and sensitive part, and thus manifest and demonstrate that love. And this may end, with intent and mutual consent, in creating something that will be half his and half hers, with no exploitation and no charades.

C

THE EXPLOITATION OF THE VAGINA

The vagina too can be used by its owners to pass the time of day, being a responsive self-pacifier and comforter. As a fertility symbol to be worshiped by others (casually or in rituals and ceremonies), it gives dramatic promise of productivity and protection. And it is also the ultimate offering of the goddess of courtesy, either in sheer hospitality, or in order not to let someone down after having led him on. Its constant companion, the clitoris, can dance attendance and add spice to all these sensuous jubilees. But the vagina has one advantage over both the clitoris and the penis: like a pet cat, it can be trained to do all manner of curious tricks, such as picking up a dollar bill (an old trick in "night clubs" of a certain type) —a stunt which no penis has yet learned to master. This is one of the ways in which the vagina can be rented out to make money, and in general, the more tricks it has learned, the better it will be at its trade.

In everyday life of relaxation and social intercourse, it can be used for a large variety of teasing games of less or more respectability. In the crudest of these, it may be half concealed behind layers of gauzy or gaudy embroidery, or let slip out for a peek, either at irregular intervals or rhythmically, like a stroboscopic mushroom flashing its sickly fluorescence through the movement of the dance. Or it may be conspicuously concealed behind a cache-sexe, like an enormous zircon, in the hope that the cash customers will think it is a diamond. This is the downstairs or saloon level of genital quackery, playing it for peanuts or drink money.

Upstairs the stakes are higher. It can be used as a come-on for financial, marital, or other entrapments, as a squeezer by women who want to swindle a man out of his semen for dishonest or desperate impregnation, and as an impotent constrictor by those who want to deprive a man of his virile organ by violence, instead of caressing it into humility as an honest trophy-thief would do. More modest and sensitive women may regard the vagina as a deserving reward for services rendered, a grateful comforter in time of need, a magic erector set for failing potency, or the great earth-healer for all male frailties.

The clitoris may serve as a pet, as a warm-up, and to demonstrate passion by its swelling up. For some who feel they are deprived by not having the grand prize of a penis, it is ruefully treasured as a token of what might have been. One of the most interesting aspects of the clitoris is its "legal" value. A girl who has been forbidden to touch "herself" by her mother or father may put one over on them by legalistic mental quibbling: she refrains from touching her vagina, as instructed, but takes her pleasure from her clitoris instead, which she knows is naughty but convinces herself is not illegal.

As an instrument of enduring love, the vagina serves as a passionate grasper and caressing squeezer. It strives ever hopefully and ever vainly for total incorporation of not only the penis but the man behind it. But in the end, instead of taking, it may give forth the fruit of that love.

The woman, much more than the man, uses other parts of her body in a sexual way. She may use her breasts as advertising, either ethically and with pride, or subversively, or even competitively. She may use them in a false way to exploit men for other things besides sex: a form of petty theft most aptly called proplifting, making the wheels of her life turn smoothly by using them for what Amaryllis calls boobrication. Buttocks are used similarly, except that their motion is even more enticing that their form. Often a woman who puts her hands behind her head to thrust her breasts forward is not aware of what she is doing, and the same applies to women who squirm when they are seated in the presence of men. This kind of seductiveness was celebrated by Rabelais in his famous couplet *"Folle à la messe est molle à la fesse"*—girls who squirm in church have soft bottoms.

D

SEX ORGANS IN TIME-STRUCTURING

Before we go on to talk about the exploitation of the orgasm, we should understand why we have put things in a certain order in the last two sections.

Nearly every human being, as we shall see later, spends his life waiting for Santa Claus, and one of the great problems of living is how to fill in the time until he arrives. The exploitations of the sex organs discussed above are ways of doing that. Such methods of time-structuring can be divided into six different classes, which remain the same regardless of what instruments are used. Whether people concern themselves with sex, money, art, or religion, for example, there are only six types of transactions whereby they can express that concern, and these can be listed roughly in increasing order of emotional complexity.[1]

That was the plan followed earlier (see section title) in listing the uses of the sex organs, which explains some of the sequences which might otherwise seem peculiar: for example, putting phallic worship right after masturbation, and politeness right after that. The simplest things that people do are those they do alone, and the most complex are those involving the deepest intimacies, with their complicated interweavings of mutual feeling. For that reason, masturbation was put first, and intimacy last, with other types of transactions in between. In the same way, in talking about the psychological uses of money, the miser sitting in solitary splendor beside his adding machine, grubbing through his stack of annual company reports, would be put first, and the couple struggling to earn Christmas money for each other and their children would come last. In art, the solitary painter would be first, and the lover reading his poem to his mistress would be at the end; the religious sequence would start with solitary meditation and end with mystical personal union or a struggle against temptation from a loved one.

The six categories are named withdrawal, rituals, pastimes, activities, games, and intimacy. Returning to the subject of sex, withdrawal, which is a way of structuring time without being involved with other people, means using the sex organs as personal playthings. Here sex is instead of people; it is safer to sit alone and play with toys of whatever kind than to risk becoming involved with others, especially in such an emotionally charged engagement as sex. Rituals and politeness are the safest ways of being with others: everyone knows what is expected of him, and as long as he sticks to the rules, nothing untoward will occur. The worship of sex organs and courteous service are both in this category.

An activity is work designed to accomplish something according to a previous agreement or contract, and the use of the sex organs to earn money or impregnation falls into this class. Personal involvement is kept at a minimum by the terms of the contract. Once that is fulfilled both parties can go their own ways with no further obligations.

The simplest level of individual emotional engagement is called pastimes, loose relationships that can be broken off at any time, like passing the time of day with an acquaintance. Mutual sexual stimulation just for fun is one of the more pleasant ways of passing idle hours. The next level of personal involvement is called games. These are more serious engagements, with an ulterior motive beneath the avowed purpose, giving many opportunities for emotional expression. The meaningful part of most people's lives is mostly made up of games, as we shall see in the chapter on that subject. The various forms of spurious love and seduction, or even outright swindling, are all examples of sexual games. And finally, a few fortunate people manage to find genuine intimacy in sex, particularly if they want to have babies.

Whether the person is waiting for Santa Claus to come in his red suit from the North Pole, or for his opposite number, Death, to come in his black suit from the South Pole, he can fill in the time in a variety of ways which will be stimulating and perhaps edifying. His sex organ is only one of many instruments provided by nature and society for this purpose If he does use that, he tries to make matters as interesting as possible. The human race has been very imaginative in devising ways to structure time by the non-biological use of sex organs.

E

THE EXPLOITATION OF THE ORGASM

The orgasm is something that should just be allowed to happen, and enjoyed if and when it does. But many people, even people who can let music happen or not happen, cannot leave orgasms alone and have to exploit and meddle with them.[2] Most commonly they exploit them for reassurance of masculinity or femininity, or even beyond that, for competition, trying to be more masculine or more feminine by having more and better orgasms. Others try to turn it into an "experience," a trip, something to be reached for rather than something happening, or else into a production, a fancy embroidered orgasm with novel acrobatic thrusts, for example. It may also be regarded as a trophy or gift—"I had one with her" or "I gave her one"—and in many articles written by professionals it is treated as an attainment ("When her husband followed my instructions, she attained orgasm"). Some regard it as a comfort or a relief, carefully disregarding the pleasure; or as a mere reflex, a sort of accident that is irrelevant to the real sexual kick, which may lie in a fetish or a conquest. Even cynics of both sexes do better than that, taking it for a good squirt or a vaginal drink. But since having an orgasm is a healthy and exhilarating experience for most people, these counterfeit attitudes often become secondary after a while, or disappear altogether.

The more serious exploitations center around *not* having an orgasm. Many women and some men regard this as an accomplishment and a proof of superiority. Not having an orgasm may give a self-proclaimed "puritan" woman a feeling of righteousness that she prefers to the pleasure of having one. This may go with teasing, tormenting, or lying to her husband or lover, often out of revenge or spite. In other cases the orgasm is avoided from fear or thrift. Some women have a fear that they will die if they let go. This may lead to complete frigidity, but sometimes they risk getting a little enjoyment, being careful not to let it go too far. Then they feel that they have cheated death, which adds a gruesome feeling of triumph to whatever pleasure they did get.

Thrift enters the picture on the strange but common theory that each person is only "allowed" a limited number of orgasms in his lifetime. That is, they are regarded as capital instead of interest, and are handled the way the person handles money when there is a limited amount. Some try to enjoy it as fast as possible, lest something go wrong before they can spend it all; others conserve it and ration it so that it will last as long as possible. This theory can be found in the most unlikely people, tucked away in the backs of their minds. Almost any layman, if asked how many orgasms a person can have in his lifetime, will come up with an answer ranging from 100 to 20,000. But even psychiatrists and sexologists, if they allow themselves to reply spontaneously, will often give some figure that takes them completely by surprise, since it shows that in spite of their Adult sophistication, the Child in them still believes that their orgasms are numbered.

In general, there are four ways in which people can handle their orgasms: frigidity, withholding, postponement, and release. Frigidity is usually justified on an "if only" basis. "Everything would be all right if only—you weren't a bum, you treated me better, you were a better lover, this were really true love."

Withholding is based on shady ethics: it's all right to have sex providing I don't enjoy it too much. This is the position in petting and making out. It was also the position of French prostitutes in the late nineteenth century: they would be forgiven at confession because they were having sex only for business purposes.[3] This attitude has also been forced on such girls by their pimps, probably ever since the profession came into existence. The girl gets beaten if she allows herself to enjoy it with anyone but him. This kind of "fidelity" is really the source of nearly all withholding. By not having an orgasm, the woman feels she is being "faithful" to either a real husband or absent lover, or to a phantom lover such as her father or a "celebrity" who has never heard of her. Half-virgins handle it another way: they will do anything except have an orgasm face to face; that they are saving for their real, phantom, or future lover.

In postponement, the woman allows the man to have his orgasm, but postpones hers until later. Either he has to induce it by following a certain procedure, or she waits until he leaves and then has it by masturbation, or in the worst case, she goes to another lover with a "wet deck" and comes with him.

A release orgasm is one which takes place during intercourse. It may be pure and intimate, or contaminated by ulterior motives and gamy feelings such as guilt, anger, inadequacy, hurt, or triumph. It may become a swindle if a phantom third party is involved: "I only have orgasms with my wife when I think of another woman." But in a released orgasm, there is at least honesty in action, if not always in thought.

F

SEXUAL DEVIATIONS

Sexual deviations, or perversions, as they used to be called, are hang-ups considered abnormal by people who think of themselves as normal, which they may very well be. Such deviations may be merely enjoyable when they are carried on between consenting adults, but they become annoying, scary, harmful, or even vicious when they involve innocent victims. They range from esthetic preferences (enjoyable), through thefts of clothing (annoying), obscene telephone calls (scary), child molesting (harmful), to anal rape and murder (vicious). Some of the best-informed people, such as the staff members of state hospital-prisons for "sexual psychopaths," consider rape to be a crime against the person rather than a sexual deviation if the vagina is the point of attack.

There are three ways to define sexual deviations: legally, morally, and rationally. The virtue of legal definitions is that they are enforceable, or as the more salivating enforcers say, "You're damn right they are." Some of them are designed to protect the public from personal loss and verbal or physical assault, but others are mischievous and arrogant, and raise more questions about Them than about the people They are messing around with. Moral definitions may be more thoughtful, but they are often uninformed and based on dubious premises. Unfortunately, rational definitions also run into unforeseen difficulties. Deviation means literally something most people (more than 50 percent of people) would prefer not to do. But that doesn't make much sense, because it would make deviants of everyone who voted for the loser in a political election. Winners do sometimes take advantage of this to call their opponents perverts. As a sporting proposition, the winners would then have to admit that they were perverts the next time they lost.

The word "pervert" implies that there is a normal, natural course of development, and that the pervert is insulting nature. This can be and is easily twisted by some people into the proposition: "I'm normal and you're not." But that is a matter of opinion, and the man who writes his own certificate of sanity is not always an authority on the subject; his judgment may be coated with a vested interest as he pants after his prey, and the shoe may be on the other foot.

If sex is regarded as a reproductive function, then a perversion would be anything that interfered with natural reproduction. Thus a biological definition would state that nothing is a perversion which terminates with the deposit of the semen in the vagina. But this excludes the use of condoms and of coitus interruptus or withdrawal, although it allows for diaphragms, cervical devices, and pills. Certain technical difficulties also arise. For example, anal intercourse with vaginal ejaculation would then not be a perversion, but it is certainly biologically undesirable because it carries organisms from the rectum into the neighborhood of the urethra where they might end up causing a bladder infection.

The most practical and ethical definition is a humanistic one. Such a definition would recognize (1) that the participants are free agents, (2) that sex is an act of personal communion, and (3) that it must not damage the flesh beyond the perforation of the hymen. Then any sequence based on free, mutual, informed consent, which terminates in bodily contact and does not damage the tissues of either party is not a perversion. Hence there must be no force used, as in rape; there must be no exploitation of ignorance, as in child molesting; it must not culminate on an external object such as a shoe or a dildo; and there must be no violence, even with consent, as in sadism. This allows for innumerable forms of sexual excitement, but excludes rape, child molesting, the use of artificial instruments such as shoes or plastic penises, and physical abuse. Unfortunately it does not exclude crazy things like dressing in diapers or eating feces.

Perhaps it is simpler the other way around. Normal sex is any mutual enjoyment between two free and informed partners of each other's bodies and their usual decorations and trappings. While this is ethical in the best sense, it might be considered immoral by people with special interests. One difficulty is that it does not exclude incest, which no rational definition can do, since that is a moral problem, and indeed, the incest taboo is the basis of nearly all morality and probably of all cultures as well. Perhaps the best summary is to say if you don't want to do it, or it seems crazy, don't do it. If you only do it when you're drunk and hate yourself when you sober up, don't drink.

While sexual deviation may be damaging to its occasional victims, if any, much more serious is logical deviation, or perversions of thinking, which may affect large numbers of people. One of the most difficult of these deviations to understand is the prejudice against long hair, beards, and sandals, since George Washington wore his hair long, Abraham Lincoln had a beard, and Jesus Christ wore sandals(?), and in fact was guilty of all three. There is no reasonable way to explain the prejudice against long-haired men except on the basis that it arouses perverse desires in those who object to it so vehemently. Many other prejudices show perverted thinking. For example, if any Christian in the last 2,000 years were asked, "What would you do if you met Jesus Christ's cousin?" he would be unlikely to reply, "I'd kick hell out of him and his women and children." But that is exactly what large numbers of Christians have done. The inbred population of ancient Judea was small enough so that almost every Judean must have been some sort of cousin to Jesus, and so their descendants, the Jews, are nearly all related to him by blood and genes.

NOTES AND REFERENCES

1. Berne, E.: *Games People Play*. Grove Press, New York, 1964.

2. Maizlish, I. L.: "The Orgasm Game." *Transaction.. Analysis Bulletin* 4:75, October, 1965.

3. Philippe, C. L.: *Bubu of Montparnasse*. (With preface by T. S. Eliot.) Berkley Publishing Corporation, New York, 1957.

PART II

Sex
And
People

4

FORMS OF
HUMAN
RELATIONSHIP

A

THE HUMAN PERSONALITY

It is most fruitful to think of the human personality as being divided into three parts, or even better, to realize that each individual is three different persons, all pulling in different directions . . . so that it is a wonder anything ever gets done. And of course in sex, if they are pulling very hard against each other, it doesn't get done, or at least it doesn't get done properly. We can represent this very simply by drawing three circles, one below the other, as in Figure 1. These represent the three people that everyone carries around in his or her head.

At the top are his parents, who are really two different people, but in this diagram we show them as one circle, marked Parent, or P. This represents someone in his head telling him what he ought to do and how to behave and how good he is and how bad he is and how much better or worse other people are. In short, the Parent is a voice in

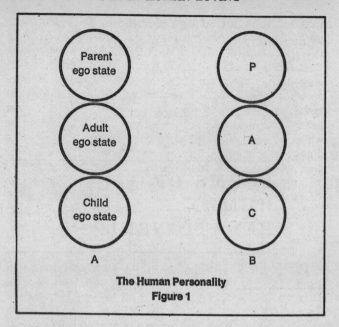

The Human Personality
Figure 1

his head making editorial comments, as parents often do, on everything he undertakes. You can tell when your Parent, or Parental ego state, is talking because it uses words like "ridiculous," "immature," "childish," and "wicked." Your Parent may talk to you that way in your head, and it may also talk out loud to other people in the same way. The Parent has another side, however. It can also be affectionate and sympathetic, just like a real parent, and say things like "You're the apple of my eye," "Let me take care of it," and "Poor girl."

The middle circle, marked Adult, or A, represents the voice of reason. It works like a computer, taking in information from the outside world, and deciding on the basis of reasonable probabilities what course of action to take and when to take it. It does not have anything to do with being "mature," since even babies can make such decisions, nor with being sincere, since many thieves and con men are very good at deciding what to do and when to do it. The Adult tells you when and how fast to cross the street, whether to raise or fold on two pair, when to take the cake out of the oven, and how to focus a telescope. In crossing the street, for example, it works like a very accurate and very complicated computer, estimating the speeds of all the cars for blocks on each side, and then picking the earliest possible moment for starting across without being killed, or rather without having to lose your dignity by running. The Adult ego state is careful whenever possible to preserve your dignity, unless it is your fate to be a clown. All good computers are like that: they choose the most elegant solutions, and try to avoid makeshift or sloppy ones whenever they can. You can tell when your Adult is talking because it uses expressions like "Ready?" "Now!" "Too much!" "Not enough!" and "Here, not there."

The bottom circle, marked Child, or C, indicates that every man has a little boy inside him and every woman carries a little girl in her head. This is the Child part of the personality, the child he or she once was. But every child is different, and the Child ego state in each person is different, since it is the Child he once was at a definite time in his life. When the Child takes over, the person acts in a childlike way, like a child of a certain age: in one person it might be four years and three months old, in another two years and six months, and it is doubtful if it is ever older than six years. We do not call this Child ego state "childish"; we simply say it is like a child, or childlike. The age of the Child part of the personality in each person is determined by special factors which you can read about in another book if you want to take the trouble.[1] It is important to realize that the Child is not there to be squelched or reprimanded, since it is actually the best part of the personality, the part that is, or can be if properly approached, creative, spontaneous, clever, and loving, just as real children are. Unfortunately, children can also be sulky, demanding, and inconsiderate or even cruel, so this part of the personality is not always easy to deal with. Since your Child ego state is going to be with you for the rest of your life, it is best to acknowledge it and try to get along with it, and it will do more harm than good to pretend that if you ignore it or deal harshly with it, it will go away.

You will have noticed that I referred to these three parts of the personality—Parent, Adult, and Child—as ego states, and that is the scientific name for them.* These ego states determine what happens to people and what they do to and for each other. The best way, and so far the neatest and most scientific way, to analyze human social and sexual relationships is to find out which ego states are involved. Each ego state has to be looked at separately if the person wants to understand his feelings and behavior in such situations. Some people try to become "a whole person" by denying that there are different parts to the personality. A better way is to find out as much as possible about each aspect, since they are all there to stay, and then get them to work together in the best possible way.

B

THE RELATIONSHIP DIAGRAM

There are in English, and in ancient Greek as well, hundreds of words describing different kinds of love and friendship between people.[2] [3] It is interesting to discover that there are far fewer words describing hate and enmity. We are not concerned here, however, with finding as many different words as possible, but rather with picking out a few that refer to the commonest types of relations between men and women, and particularly those which involve different sets of ego states. One of the oldest classifications of personal relations, which attempts to boil them down to their barest essentials, is the legal one. For

---

* "Parent," "Adult," and "Child," capitalized, are used throughout to refer to ego states in the head; the same words in lowercase refer to actual people.

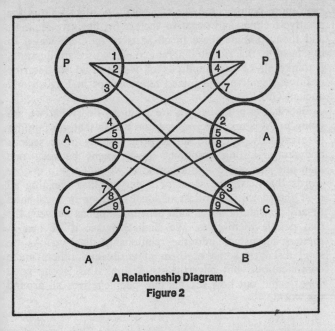

A Relationship Diagram
Figure 2

centuries, the law has dealt with them under four main headings: Husband and Wife, Parents and Children, Guardians and Wards, and Master and Servant (or Master and Apprentice). One difficulty here is that these are all one-up one-down relationships, with one person running the show and the other fighting for his rights, and that will never do for us.

A better way is to start off with a Relationship Diagram,[4] which tells us all the possible ways in which two people, each having three ego states, can relate to each other. This is shown in Figure 2. There are nine simple relationships possible, taking one ego state at a time in each person, and then of course various combinations of these. For example, there are 72 kinds of relationships involving two crossed arrows or vectors (the response going in a different direction from the stimulus), 432 involving three vectors, and so on. If we want to make it

even more complicated, we can put in positive vectors for
positive feelings and negative vectors for negative feelings,
and then combine these in all sorts of different ways. In
this fashion, this simple diagram could be used to illustrate,
I think, all of the hundreds of words used to describe
positive, negative, and mixed relationships in English and
ancient Greek.

But that is not what we are going to do. What we are
going to do is take twelve common words that are familiar
to everybody, which describe progressively more serious
and longer-lasting emotional involvement between one
man and one woman. Furthermore, we will try to choose
words that have the same or a very similar meaning all
over the world, regardless of local customs or local laws
or any consideration outside of what happens between the
two people themselves. We shall then see if we can fit
these relationships into the relationship diagram. As we
shall discover, some of them fit easily and others make
complications, but nevertheless, I think this is one good
way to find out how sex fits into people's lives all around
the world.

C

ACQUAINTANCES

Acquaintances are full of potential. It is from
among them that you will choose your more serious relationships, the ones that will continue and will give you
something to remember them by. Every acquaintance is a
possible friend or enemy, and you should choose both
carefully. The more acquaintances you have, the more
choices you have, so I would recommend that you say
Hello to everybody. Acquaintanceship is a static relation,
which can stay the same year after year. In order to go
further, somebody has to make the first move, and the
other person has to accept the overture.

Acquaintances are people who go through social rituals

with each other. Such rituals have a value in themselves. They are one form of verbal stroking, and they have the same effect as patting has on a baby. When someone says Hello, or How are you? or What's new? or Warm enough for you? he tones up your muscles, clears your brain, soothes your heart, and relaxes your digestion. For this you should be grateful, and in return he expects you to do the same for him. If you are in a sulky mood and refuse to accept the benefits thus offered, then both of you will suffer. You will get even sulkier, and his stomach will churn and a film will form over his brain and stay there until he meets someone more courteous and appreciative of his presence.

The kind of things acquaintances say to each other, passing the time of day while carefully avoiding any intrusion on each other's privacy, do not come from either Parent, Adult, or Child. They come from a mask or shield which the person places between himself and the people around him, called by some psychiatrists the *persona*. The persona is a way of presenting oneself, and is best described by an adjective: gruff, sociable, sweet, cute, busy, charming, contemptuous, or polite. With each of these words comes a different way of saying Hello or passing the time of day. The persona is formed during the years from six to twelve, when most children first go out on their own and are confronted with people in the outside world who are not of their own or their parents' choosing. Each child soon perceives that he needs a way to avoid unwanted entanglements or promote wanted ones in this world he never made, so he chooses his own way of presenting himself to that world. Usually he tries to be nice and polite and to appear considerate and compliant. He may keep this early persona for the rest of his life, or turn it in later, after more experience, for another one. Thus the persona is really a Child ego state influenced by Parental training and modified by Adult prudence toward the people around him. The main requirement for the persona is that it should work. If it doesn't work, the person is either in a continual state of anxiety when he is with people, for fear that his persona will break down, or else he takes to avoid-ing people and going off by himself.

The persona is really a special ego state: that of a ten-year-old Child trying to make his way among strangers, so it can be fitted into the structural diagram by saying that it is a special aspect of the Child ego state. Actually, it is a good example of adapting oneself to the situation and acting in an expected, predictable way, an ego state which is known as the Adapted Child.

D

CO-WORKERS

Almost as innocent and distant as the relation-ship between acquaintances is that between co-workers. Acquaintances keep each other at a distance by sticking to well-tried formulas of greeting and conversation, saying exactly the same thing time after time in the same sit-uation, carefully choosing the most harmless and inoffen-sive clichés or the most ingratiating ones. Co-workers accomplish the same end by talking at an angle instead of straight to the other person. They talk about something, so that their words are directed to that something, and bounce off it to the listener. Transactional analysts call occupational work an activity, and whatever is worked with is called the material of the activity. If the material is right in front of two co-workers, they will often look at it while they are talking, instead of at each other.

Helper (looking at frammis): "The frammis sure is de-coruscated."

Mechanic (looking at frammis): "Yeah, that always happens in these mass-production Mercillacs. They're just parlayed Volkolets."

Helper (keeping his eyes on the frammis): "Yeah, you never see that in a Maserrari."

In this way, the mechanic and his helper may work all

day together for months without ever looking directly at each other.

Paper-shufflers do exactly the same thing. In fact it is well known among boss paper-shufflers that if the clerical shufflers ever look you in the eye (or vice versa), something is going on. When they are talking to each other, they look at the papers, not at each other. Business and professional men with new customers or clients also act like co-workers.

Thus co-workers are people who talk to each other through the material, and they talk about the material. This is an Adult-Adult relationship, which looks like Figure 3. If the boss breaks the Adult-Adult contract by coming on Parent, that entitles the worker to call him one free adjective: helpful or fussy or strict if he was nice about it, and mean, nervy or impossible if he wasn't. If the worker comes on Parent, the boss is likewise entitled to one free adjective: understanding, co-operative, impertinent, or out of line. If either of them comes on Child, the other feels entitled to call the offender ridiculous, undignified, unladylike, ungentlemanly, flirtatious, or groovy.

This means that the moment two co-workers look directly at each other or talk directly to each other instead of through the material, they are something else besides co-workers.

E

COMMITTEE MEMBERS

From Figure 2, you can see that there are three "straight-across" relationships, Parent-to-Parent, Adult-to-Adult, and Child-to-Child, Although co-workers talk at an angle to each other because they are discussing "the realities out there," that is precisely the definition of Adult-to-Adult transactions, so the vectors in the Co-worker Diagram of Figure 3 go straight across. Oddly enough, there is no simple English word which describes Parent-to-Parent rela-

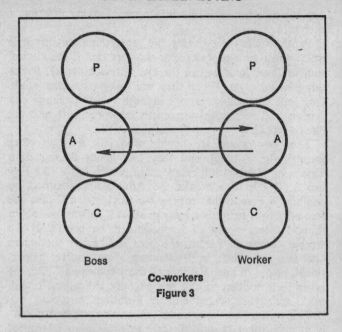

Co-workers

Figure 3

tionships although they are very common all over the world. In this country, the most likely place to hear one Parental ego state talking to another is on a "committee," so people in this relationship can be called committee members, for want of a better term.

The kind of committee I am referring to is not the kind that gets something done, but the kind that gets together and talks about suppressing something Awful which either doesn't exist or which they don't really know much about, or whose existence is necessary for the well-being of society. Their discussions, in the guise of exchanges of information, are actually exchanges of indignation, based on Parental prejudices instead of facts. Here the contract is Parent-to-Parent, as illustrated in Figure 4. Again, just as in the case of co-workers, anyone who breaks the contract is subject to name-calling. For example, anyone at a Parental type of Suppression Society who gives an unbiased

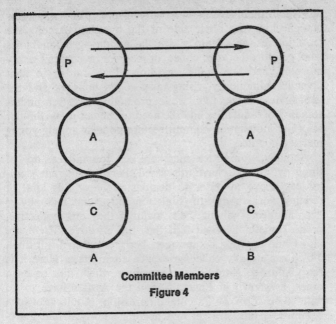

Committee Members
Figure 4

Adult view of the subject is likely to be called various kinds
of nasty names. A playful Child makes Parental committee
members even more nervous than a factual Adult does.
Thus Prohibitionists of various persuasions become uneasy
if someone tries to prove by Adult investigation that whatever they are prohibiting is not so bad after all, and they
may place difficulties in the way of such investigations. But
if someone tries to demonstrate the same thing in a playful
Childlike way, they take much more drastic action to put
a stop to it (put him in jail, maybe). Comedians understand this principle very well; they know that jokes upset
Parental meddlers even more than facts do.

Besides formal committees where some or all of the
members spend their time in Parent-to-Parent indignation
without really knowing what they are talking about, there
are many informal committees that work the same way.
These are made up of people who get together socially and

talk about their Awfuls in a Parental prejudiced way without checking the other side of the question. Among the most interesting examples are the middle-aged landladies who get together for coffee or beer or a cocktail every morning, and are really an informal committee to fight juvenile delinquency, rising taxes, open housing, and the fiendishness of tenants, while promoting a better understanding of landladies and the need for higher rents. Similar informal indignation committees are popular among young married couples.

Actually, committee members, or committees, are of three types. We have discussed Parent-to-Parent committees above in order to demonstrate how this kind of relation works. Adult-to-Adult committees talk factually or "communicate" about their Awful if they are ineffective, or do something about it if they are effective. There are also Child-to-Child committees, both formal and informal, which are usually called grievance committees. Here it is the Child ego states of the members which talk to each other, as shown in Figure 5, and the Awfuls have to do with some form of Parental oppression. Adult grievance committees talk straight and negotiate fairly. Child grievance committees play games, sometimes distressing ones, since their real object is to discomfit the authorities they are complaining about, rather than to rectify the wrongs they bring up.

The alliances mentioned above are not always man to woman, but they are included in order to illustrate how relationships can be analyzed into ego states.

By this time it can be seen that there is an unspoken rule about relationships. They are not set up between people, but between ego states. Both parties understand, in some way or other, which ego states are allowed to express themselves in the situation. This understanding has the force of a contract. Anyone who breaks the contract by expressing an illegitimate ego state is therefore legitimately subject to being called names, or in flagrant cases, to being fired from the relationship.

In order to be clear on what we are talking about, we can define a relationship as a continuing set of transac-

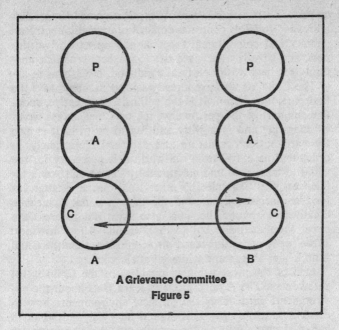

A Grievance Committee
Figure 5

tions between two or more people, or rather between their various ego states, which can be represented by a drawing on the blackboard. If a person who uses the word "relationship" is unable to draw a convincing diagram, it is not worth pursuing the matter further, because there is no way of knowing exactly what he means.

F

RESPECT

The next kind of relationship to be considered is called respect. This is another Adult-to-Adult relation, and is based on straight talk and the fulfillment of familial, occupational, and social contracts without alibis, quibbling,

or private reservations. Talking straight comes from reliability, and fulfilling contracts comes from commitment. Reliability and commitment together add up to trustworthiness, and trust is what gives rise to respect. Trust is something that begins very early in childhood, if it begins at all.

The Child, as we have already said, is in many ways the
best part of a person. It is the enthusiastic, creative, spontaneous part of the personality, the part that makes wom-
en charming and men witty and fun to be with. It is also
the part that enjoys nature and people. Unfortunately, in
order that he may live in the world it is necessary for the
Child to be curbed and corrupted by Parent and Adult influences. For example, he must learn not to scatter his
food enthusiastically around the table and not to urinate
creatively in public; he must also learn not to cross the
street spontaneously, but to look around before he does.
If too many restrictions lead into confusion, then the Child
is no longer able to enjoy himself at all.

One of the most valuable qualities of the Child is his
shrewdness. The Adult's job is to learn facts about the environment, particularly the physical environment: how to
drive a car, and why bills should be paid, and when to
call a doctor—information which may be necessary for
survival in a grownup world. The infant's survival, however, depends on people, so he is mainly concerned with
them: which ones he can trust, which ones to watch out
for, which ones are going to be good to him and which ones
are going to hurt or neglect him. Children understand
people much better than grownups do, including well-
trained grownups who study human behavior. Such professionals are merely relearning something they once knew,
but no matter how hard they study, they are never going
to be as good psychiatrists or psychologists as they originally were when they were little children.

The reason for this is that most parents raise children
not to be too intuitive and not to look at people directly
to see what they are up to, because that is considered rude.
They are supposed to figure people out with their Adults
instead of feeling them out with the Child. Most children,
including those who are going to be psychiatrists and psy-

chologists, follow these instructions, and then spend five or ten years at college and sometimes another five years in therapeutic groups or psychoanalysis, all in order to get back 50 per cent of the people-judging capacity they had when they were four years old.

But the Child is still there, although he may not talk very loudly or clearly, and it is he who decides best whether or not someone can be trusted. Trust comes from the Child, respect from the Adult, with the Child's permission. Respect means that the Child looks someone over and decides that he is trustworthy. The Child then says to the Adult: "Go ahead. You can trust him. I'll keep an eye on the situation and review it from time to time." The Adult then translates this into an attitude of respect and acts accordingly. Sometimes, however, the Parent interferes. The Child and the Adult may be all ready to go ahead, and then the Parent brings up a prejudiced objection: "How can you trust a man with long hair?" or "How can you trust a fat woman?" To the Child, of course, long hair or fatness is quite irrelevant to trustworthiness, and he would much rather be with a long-haired man and a fat woman who love him than with a short-haired man and a thin woman who don't. Nothing interferes with Child intuition more than Parental prejudices.

The first situation of trust arises between the infant and his mother, where her reliability and commitment are put to the test in feeding him. His survival depends upon that, and his attitude toward life and people depends upon how it is carried out.

If he is being fed on demand, he gives the signal with his hunger cry. If she comes when he calls, she is reliable. If she brings his milk shortly after, she is committed. But if she takes her time about coming, and also lets him down on the food, he never learns to trust her. This is not distrust, which is a broken trust; it is untrust, the absence of something that was never there.

If he is being fed on a schedule, say every four hours, the situation is different. Most babies seem to come equipped with a mental clock, perhaps the same clock some grownups use when they decide to wake up at 7:15

and wake up exactly at 7:15. The baby sets his clock for four hours, and expects his mother to be there when the alarm goes off, and to feed him soon after. If she does both, he trusts her. If she does neither, he doesn't.

In both cases, as he grows older, he is willing to accept longer and longer delays, and still later, even excuses, provided there are not too many of them. But if there are too many, either he never learns what trust means, or else he learns distrust. Basically, he expects her not only to be reliable and come on time, but also to be committed and bring the food when or soon after she comes. It is quite possible that his own trustworthiness will imitate hers: he may be reliable and committed, or one but not the other, or neither.

Trust is the basis of respect. To the baby, it means that his mother will be there (reliability) and will do what she is supposed to (commitment). Later he expects people to send a message if they are going to be late (reliability), and fulfill their contracts when they do come (commitment). He may excuse unreliability if commitment is there, and he may excuse lack of commitment if reliability is there, both under protest; but he is unlikely to respect anyone who is neither reliable nor committed.

Now for a homey example. A reliable husband is one who tells you without fail about every affair he has, no matter how *bad* it was. A committed husband is one who makes sure that every affair he has is a good one, even if he doesn't tell you about it. A trustworthy and respected husband is one who doesn't have affairs, if he promised not to at the wedding ceremony, because if he did, he meant it.

The actual transactions that manifest respect between two people are Adult-to-Adult, as previously shown in Figure 3, but they have a different quality. They are not carried on through the material, as with co-workers, but eye to eye and man to woman, with full trust in each other's reliability and commitment unless and until it is proven to be misplaced.

G

ADMIRATION

All the relationships we have talked about so far are "straight across"—Parent-to-Parent, Adult-to-Adult, or Child-to-Child (Figures 2-5). Now we come to one which is "up and down," Child-to-Parent (Figure 6, going up). People use the word admiration in many ways, but in its true sense it means "wonder." Admiration comes about in the opposite way to respect. In respect it is the Child who looks the person over and tells the Adult to go ahead. In admiration it is the Adult who looks the person over and tells the Child to go ahead. The Adult says, "Boy! He really knows how to . . ." whatever it is—swim, or dance, or recite poetry, or whatever you may admire most and know how to judge—and the Child takes it from there.

Sex may come into this in the case of a schoolgirl crush on a boy or on a female teacher. The girl starts off admiring the teacher in an Adult way for something she does or is, and then her Child takes over and she may get hung up on the teacher and follow her around and perhaps begin to have sexual pictures about her. If the teacher keeps to her position, she will be like a good mother in dealing with the girl's attachment to her, but if she changes the "contract," what might be an edifying relationship between a Parent and a Child is turned into a frolic between two uneasy Children.

I think that just as trust arises from the baby's relationship to his mother, so admiration has to do with his father, because father is the wonder-boy in the family. Mother is the one who is trusted because she is there when she is needed. Father may be there only irregularly. but his imposing voice and presence and his strength and power excite the baby's admiration. And it is true that genuine admiration is most often extended to men, although it may be shifted to women if they happen to be wonder-workers in their own right. That is what happens later,

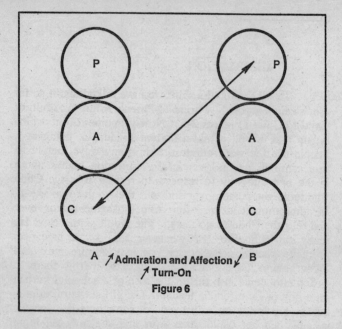

Figure 6

when children begin to admire their mother's accomplishments, such as cooking or painting, as well as respecting her as a person. And conversely, they learn to trust their father as well as admire him.

People vary in their ability to receive admiration. Some don't tolerate it very well and avoid it or turn it away when it comes, sometimes angrily. Others exploit it, like the teacher who has an affair with an infatuated schoolgirl or schoolboy, or the gangster who takes on an admiring young punk to exploit him as much as he can. The best handle it gracefully and make it a worthwhile experience for themselves and the others concerned.

H

AFFECTION

Affection is another "slanted" relationship, this time Parent-to-Child (Figure 6, going down). In admiration, the Adult of one person excites the Child of the other.* In affection, the Child of one person excites the Parent of the other. A person who feels affection expresses it very much as a mother or father does toward a winsome child, and the object of the affection responds in a simple Childlike way. These are not roles. They are true feelings arising from specific ego states, and ego states are different from roles. Ego states are psychological realities; in fact they are the only psychological realities, although they can easily be adulterated into falsehoods. They are systems of feelings which are there for life quite independently of roles, although roles can be grafted onto them and corrupt them.

In an affectionate relationship, Adult-to-Adult transactions may also occur between times, but the affection itself comes from a Parental ego state and evokes a response from a Child ego state. In many families the parents believe that it is necessary to look serious when giving affection, and many children follow these instructions and are firmly convinced that it is necessary. Such affection given with a serious mien is called concern. There is no reason, however, why one can't give affection while having a good time, and concern often seems a little oversincere rather than really helpful. That is the answer to one of life's—or death's—puzzling questions. Why is it that fatal cancer patients know they have cancer, even if the people taking care of them sincerely try to fool them? They may pretend they don't know, partly out of consideration for those

---

* But the Child responds as though it were a parent, so the actual transactions are Child-Parent as in the transactional diagram in Figure 6.

around them, since cancer patients, like other patients, are
usually good sports and go along with the scenario. But
usually they do know.

How does the patient find out, and which part of him
knows? He finds out, I think, because no matter how well
the others succeed in acting naturally around him, there is
always one exception: either they don't laugh when they
should, or if they do, they stop too quickly. That's what's
wrong when people make it a strong point to "demonstrate" concern, which is different from doing the most
helpful thing. They are confused by something as grim as
cancer, and their reluctance to laugh or their uneasiness
about laughing gives the diagnosis away, even if their true
concern makes them want to conceal it. The real concern
they may have trips over their concern about looking concerned, thus spoiling the picture. It takes a lot of guts to
give up *looking* concerned with a cancer patient, but it
can be done, and it pays off, as experiments on cancer
wards show.

Here is how the giveaway works. Let us say that Mrs.
C has an operation on her abdomen to find out the cause
of her pain, and the surgeon finds rampant cancer which
will be fatal in a few months. In order to spare her
anguish, everyone decides to pretend that it is something
less serious, although they keep her in the hospital. She
is very worried and wants to know if she has a death sentence or not. But she is also afraid of it, so she may ask
but not be too insistent on getting a straight answer. She
may not be ready to face the problems it raises. Nevertheless, she would really like to know if she is going to survive.

While her Adult evades an open answer, her Child
secretly bends every effort to finding out, and watches
people's behavior very, very carefully to get some clues.
Once she notices that people are laughing differently, she
starts checking. People who were previously uproariously
funny may continue to make little funnies to keep things
going, but they hedge them so they won't be uproarious.
The doctor's cheerfulness may be different from his pre-

operative attitude or his demeanor with other patients. Concerned clergymen may stop telling even "officially permitted" jokes about the priest and the rabbi, St. Peter, etc. The result is that Mrs. C can pick up a dozen examples a day of laughs toned down and laughs cut off, and pretty soon she knows something is badly wrong with her, and she knows what it is.

In such cases, "showing concern" may feel satisfying to the person who does it, but because of its oversincerity, it does not work too well. In fact, "showing concern" as a way of handling cancer patients over a long period wears out both the staff and the patients and benefits neither of them. If the patients are regarded as dying people, then the cancer ward becomes that grim institution which used to be called a "Home for Incurables," with the unwritten motto above the door: "What do you expect of someone who is dying of cancer?" If, on the other hand, they are treated as "very much alive self-respecting adult human beings," then the motto turns into "What can we do for you today?" and the nurses and doctors come alive as well as the patients.[5] That is an extreme example of the difference between "showing concern" and feeling affectionate.

True affection is to find help or be helpful when it is needed and to look concerned at critical moments. But when "acting concerned" takes precedence over thinking, it may do more harm than good, whether or not the concern is genuine. The firm statement "I am concerned" (said aloud or in writing, one time) is more effective than a determined effort to look serious. One reason for this careful discussion is that while the Parent and Adult may indeed be concerned, the Child usually has a different attitude unless he is in danger himself. Because of this ambiguity, "feeling concerned" should not be a matter for pride or self-righteousness, as it often is.

In milder situations, receiving affection allows people to laugh at their own troubles, but being an object of concern demands that they look serious in order to keep their helpers happy. Here a joke is often better than a frown.

I

THE TURN-ON

So far in our pursuit of relationships we have been in many different rooms: the workroom, the meeting room, the nursery, the schoolroom and the hospital room. Now we can follow our quarry into the bedroom. The turn-on is just what it sounds like: the right person pushes the switch and the whole body lights up, from the eyes into the brain and down through the chest and belly, and below that too. There is no social class or Parental prejudice cutting the wires, and no rationality or Adult prudence pulling the plug. It is the Child alone who lights up, and it either happens or it doesn't. It is very similar to what happens with imprinting in birds.[6] It is a sensory rather than a personal response, and it is mainly visual. Other senses may contribute, and it may be brightened by day-dreams and glorified by frustrations, but the flash of recognition nearly always comes from seeing.

In imprinting, the young bird will get turned on to a visual image of a certain form and color and respond to the object, which may be merely a piece of cardboard, as though it were its mother. It has no decision or free choice in the matter; it is torqued in by a certain stimulus and responds automatically. The stimulus may be only a silhouette, but the effect is full-bodied. In the same way, confronted with a turn-on, many people must give up the illusion that their feelings make sense and are proper to their being, because this is an automatic response which may go against Parental or Adult preference or logic, as the hero in *Of Human Bondage* learned the hard way. The ability to kindle this response is what movie talent scouts have always looked for, and in former days it was called many names from "It" to "Sex appeal," and sex appeal is what it is.

Fetishism is a special kind of turn-on, where the man gets the impact from a particular part of the female body or

from some feminine personal possession: hair or scarves, hands or gloves, feet or shoes. These parts of the body or feminine objects are said by some to be "symbolic substitutes for the loved person." It is much more likely that they are imprintings from early childhood, due to events which happened just at the right time and under the right circumstances to make a permanent hookup. Fetishism is very difficult to cure, partly or mainly because few fetishists want to be cured. Many of them get the same bang from the sight or touch or smell of their fetish as a drug addict does from his heroin or Methedrine. The prospect of giving up these thrills for a square passion has little appeal for them unless their fetish is so far out that it gets them into serious trouble.

A fetish is not just a symbol, any more than a gun is. The fetish is the real thing to the fetishist, just as a gun is the real thing to a shootnik. The gun is not a symbol of the penis but is used instead of it or in addition to it because it is more deadly than flesh and bone, and deadliness is something the gunki craves.* That is why he would rather go hunting than stay home with his wife. Even a toy water pistol is more than a phallic symbol. It works better than a phallus for its intended purpose of shooting a stream of water accurately from a distance. The idea may have come from nature, and the Child may enjoy the similarity, but there is a lot more to it than that.[7] One element is craftsmanship; the Adult appreciates the quality of the object, whether it is a rifle, a water pistol, an old slipper, or a glove.

Many mild fetishists have more fun than most "normal" people (at cocktail parties, for instance) if they are not hampered by their guilt feelings. Farther-out ones suffer from some confusion in their love relationships, if any, and may get distracted from more serious pursuits by their fancies. They may also get attached to degrading caterers,

---

* This does not include honest marksmen. I have some of those in my own family. One of my sons, who works as a cowboy, can shoot a flea off the head of a flying rattlesnake at 100 yards with an elephant gun.

and suffer because of that. They are in fact enslaved by their imprinting to follow the fetish rather than the person, and so it is a matter of luck what kind of personalities they get mixed up with or attached to. A dedicated fetishist does not usually make a very good husband unless he happens to find exactly the right wife.

Since to some extent all men have their preferences, and a great many have at least mild fetishes, one of the easiest ways for a woman to please and hang on to a man is to find out covertly what his festishes are and indulge or even cater to them secretly. This is certainly what makes (and has made throughout history) successful mistresses. Many a war has been fought and many a kingdom made or lost because of a bit of ribbon or lace worn in the proper fetching place. But the matter can be handled more honestly, and perhaps even more effectively, by asking him outright what his fetishes are, and then indulging him. But because fetishes are fixed early in life, they are sometimes a generation behind the current styles, which the woman may find embarrassing. Even though a 1940 bathing suit turns her man on, she may understandably decline to wear one thirty years later.

Which brings us to a much neglected subject: the counterfetishist, what I would like to call the fetishera. Nearly all fetishists are men. But for every man who is hung up on shoes, there is a woman ready to cater to and groove with him, and for every man who gets his thrills from hair, there is a woman who gets hers from having her locks raped. Havelock Ellis has many cases of this meeting of the minds: the man who yearns to get pressed on by high heels sooner or later meets a woman who has daydreamed all her life of heel-pressing. These women are fetisheras, and very little is known about them because they do not come to professional attention very often. There are just as many women who specialize in hair, gloves, shoes, or underwear as there are men urgently searching for the delights they offer. This is borne out not only in the case histories collected by Havelock Ellis and other natural historians of sex, but also by the fetishists who put want ads in underground papers such as the *Berkeley Barb*.

Now back to the "normal" turn-on. There are men who are turned on by breasts and men who are turned on by legs—breast men and leg men, as they call themselves politely—and both are considered normal. Strictly speaking, however, and meaning no offense, such preferences are expeditions to the foothills of fetishism. A true fetishist is unable to get an erection in the absence of his fetish, no matter how desirable his partner is in other ways. Now if a leg man or a breast man were not allowed to look at or touch his favorite regions, he might suffer from the same difficulty. The normal turn-on, on the other hand, is based on the height, weight, conformation, carriage, gait, seat, features, and skin texture of the woman: what is popularly called her "personality," that is, the general proportions of her body, the way she moves, her face and her skin. But the fetishes, the leg-breast preferences, and the "personality" turn-on, are all equally due to imprinting, and in most cases mother is the imprinter.

Thus the turn-on is actually a Child-Parent relationship, and fits Figure 6 (going up).

The turn-on is such a profound biological phenomenon that it has probably played a major role in evolution through sexual selection. Female birds are no doubt turned on by the brilliant plumage of male birds during mating season, and the brighter the plumage of the cock, the more birds he turns on. Similarly with rump colors in monkeys. The turn-on first occurs through distant senses: sight and sound, and in some cases smell. Male porcupines are strongly attracted by the urine of females in heat. Female moths give off an odor which can turn on male moths as far as a mile away.[8] The question is whether the male moth actually "smells" something, or whether there is just a chemical effect that pulls the switch without his being aware of an odor. The same question arises in the case of human beings. There are certain chemical turn-ons that people are aware of, and these are called perfumes, although sweat may serve the purpose too in many cases. But it is also possible that some women (and men also) give off chemicals that affect the nervous systems of other human beings without anyone smelling anything or being aware of what has turned them on.

As evidence for this, some people think that dogs can smell human odors that other humans can't—the smell of fear, for example. Now, people may not be aware of smelling fear, but they might still be affected in some other way by the same chemicals that the dog actually smells, whatever "actually smells" means for a dog. The same could easily apply to sex. In fact there is nothing, really, that says men are any less sensitive than moths. It may very well be that some men can sense the presence of a sexy woman, and vice versa, at a distance of one mile in open country, without being able to explain it. There is also the fact that people of one race often say they can smell people of another: some Caucasians say they can smell Negroes, and some Chinese say they can smell Caucasians, while people of the same race don't seem to smell each other that way. All this indicates that odorless smells may be important in sexual turn-on.[9] Whether the smell is odorless because it has no odor, or just because people don't notice the odor if they have been around it for a long time, such smells or chemical signals could still have a powerful effect on the nervous systems of the opposite sex, or in some cases, of the same sex.

There are tricks to every trade, but there are more tricks to the turn-on trade than any other, since it involves all of the senses and all of the man. Natural endowment of body build, legs, breasts, hair, and buttocks is a good beginning. Each man has his preferences, and some one of these elements just suiting him may be enough for a visual turn-on. This usually depends on the way his mother looked to him when he was a certain age: either four years old, when he first began to be interested in the conformations of different females, and decided at that time what kind of a girl he was going to marry; or twelve to fourteen, when he felt the first stirrings of adult sexuality. Usually he will look first at whatever features were emphasized in his family, which may be hands or feet or ears rather than the larger proportions. Some women go along with nature in the visual turn-on, or enhance their appearance in socially acceptable ways, but others do resort to tricks. One sits provocatively; another stands with her legs apart, perhaps over a floor heater so that her skirt balloons out a little. Some like to bend over to pick things up, emphasize the roll of their buttocks when they walk, or put their hands behind their heads. These are things that well-brought-up young ladies are not supposed to do; hence they are an unfair form of competition and may arouse anger or contempt in other women.

Along with the visual turn-on, the groundwork may be laid for the fetish turn-on, which depends a great deal on dress. Here again, the man tends to be hooked by the things his family emphasized, particularly his mother. In fact the basic rule for fetishes is that the man's fetish is the same as the fetish of his mother's Child. If she took a childlike fascination in collecting a closet full of shoes, he may have a childlike fascination with women's shoes. And her daughter may, too. He becomes a shoe fetishist and his sister a fetishera, although it does not always work out that neatly. But in general, when a fetishist meets his fetishera and says, "My mother had a closet full of shoes," she is quite likely to reply, "So did mine." He means: "Mother loved her shoes and so did I; that's why I'm hung up on your shoes." She means: "Father loved mother's shoes, and that's why I'm hung up on shoes; so I'm glad you love mine." The same applies to large breasts or buttocks, long hair, tight slacks, ruffled skirts, petticoats, furs, or hiking boots. The combination of imprinting and sexy secrets in the family becomes irresistible.

Voice turn-on probably has the same background as fetishism. One overtone may hook a man for life. This extends as well to other sounds. Some men are turned on by women who cough or cry; in former days there were sighs. If a man's mother had asthma, his wife, by an odd coincidence, may have it, too. This type of sexual selection can obviously have an inherited effect on their offspring, thus passing on certain types of illnesses to the third generation.

Smell turn-ons also hark back to the early years of life. The commonest are cooking smells, just like mother used to make. Then come perfume and sweat, and finally other odors, more difficult for people to acknowledge even to themselves.

All of these are social turn-ons: sight, sound, smell, and fetishes, which can happen anywhere during the most casual encounters. In the bedroom, they can be reinforced by powerful influences of mode and zone. Every man is to some extent a positionist, preferring a certain mode or position during intercourse, and every woman is a positura, ready to offer herself in a certain way. As noted in the introductory chapter, there are many manuals that list new positions for those who are tired of the old ones and are too tied up to discover others for themselves. Similarly, every man is an organist, preferring certain organs or body zones for his maximum excitement, and every woman an organa, with her own ideas of where she most likes to be touched or to receive. In some of the United States, intercourse other than in the vagina is illegal. But many religious authorities consider any kind of foresex permissible, as long as the ejaculation itself takes place in the vagina, so that even panorganas, women who enjoy all kinds of organic stimulation, can remain in good standing.

The ideal sexual mate for a man, then, is a woman with the right physical appearance, the right voice, and the right perfume, who dresses a certain way, and likes to have sex in a certain special position, freely using or making available certain parts of her body. The proper degree of initiative or activity, and compliance or passivity, is also very important. The turn-on is so powerful and so deeply ingrained that a marriage based on a complete turn-on, including all of the items given above, can stand all kinds of stresses and strains. But a marriage based on the turn-on alone can also turn out very badly, as men who marry call girls often discover when money problems arise. Nevertheless, it is very important to choose a mate from among the people who turn you on.

What has been discussed above may be called instant or primary turn-on. There are also two possible forms of delayed turn-on which can fortify a marriage mightily if the primary turn-on is weak. One is the conditioned delayed turn-on. A man who likes good food and good care, for example, may get turned on every time he goes into the kitchen and sees his wife standing over the cookstove getting his dinner for him.[10] The more times he gets turned on by that, the more likely he is to carry the turn-on into bed. There are many other situations having nothing directly to do with sex in which a couple may turn each other on, and the more often that happens, the more likely they are to discover the buried sexual attractions in each other. This is something like what psychologists call conditioning, a relative of the conditioned reflexes that have to do with food.[11]

Secondary delayed turn-on occurs in couples who do not thrill each other sexually at first sight, sound, or touch, but who live together affectionately nonetheless. In the course of time, through accident, boldness curiosity, or psychotherapy, they find certain things in each other that do turn them on, the buried sexual attractions referred to above. These may consist of certain kinds of naughty desires that they have kept hidden from each other, or even from themselves, and which turn out to be congenial to both of them. But the revelation of such a desire, when it is not congenial to the other party, may result in trouble, so there is a delicate balance here between boldness and discretion. Nevertheless, secondary turn-ons do often develop constructively in the course of time. They must be distinguished from phony turn-ons or one-sided lecheries, since both of those will end in turn-offs, which are worse than nothing.

The turn-on is what lends kicks and joy to a relationship and counteracts the drabness of living together with worry about finances and housekeeping, and petty job annoyances and drinking parties. Some people seek the turn-on by taking alcohol or drugs, but then it is the alcohol or drug that is doing the turning on and not the other person, and that can turn out badly in the long run. Certainly most women like to feel that they can turn on their husbands better than martinis or marijuana or a dose of LSD can.

If the turn-on is missing in a marriage, there is always the risk that some outside party will supply it. In a typical case, the wife does her duty and caters to her husband in some respects but is unable to go along with everything he asks for. On his side, he dare not ask for everything he wants, nor even admit some of his desires to himself. The wife tries hard and expects gratitude, and he in fairness to her tries to feel it. If he meets another woman who does more for him than he ever dreamed of, without "trying" and without expecting any gratitude, then the wife who has sacrificed so much pride in accommodating him feels that he is an ungrateful wretch. Or it may be the other way round, with the wife getting turned on by another man. In either case, the marriage is in deep trouble in this contest between upbringing and biology.

It is very difficult for a wife in her forties to face the fact that her husband's young mistress is giving him something she could give herself if she could cut loose from her early training. Most women in such situations would rather get a divorce than betray their parents, by surrendering to their own and their husband's sexual desires, which after a lifetime of suppression seem strange, sinful, and scary, or just plain lecherous. So now let us turn our attention to the psychology of lechers.

J

LECHERY

Lechery is less spontaneous than a true turn-on and more complicated. In fact, it is forced. An intelligent and alert lecher can actually hear the voices in his head which tell us the origin of his passion. It is the voice of a corrupt Parent saying that this is supposed to be exciting, and ordering the Child to get excited. (See Figure 17c.) The Child, of course, goes along with this because at first it is exciting. But the Parental voice keeps driving him beyond the limits of ordinary sexual endurance, so that he ends up exhausted and resentful.

This is openly declared in the Marquis de Sade's *Philos-*

ophy in a Bedroom,[12] where the corrupt gang goads and prods the young girl again and again, and since it is her first experience, her ardor is almost, but not quite, inexhaustible. It then becomes clear that it is her father who is the source of her dogged persistence: it is not enough for him that his daughter is being thoroughly debauched by these experts, but he sends his wife along too and urges them to corrupt her as well. De Sade, of course, is fundamentally a coward in spite of his loud boastings, and he fails the crucial test: he does not allow incest with the mother, but calls in outside assistance to ravish and rot her. Nor does he explain this dereliction in the philosophy with which he fills in the time while waiting for the next erection.

Lechery, then, is a Child-to-Child relationship, in which neither party is interested in the other except as a technician, because they are really each following the instructions of the Parents in their heads: "More! More! Enjoy yourself, dammit! It's fun." First the Child says, "It sure is," then he says," "I guess so," then, "I'm not so sure," and finally, "It isn't fun at all." Then like any red-blooded Child, he rebels, and rebellion in this case is repentance. That is why repentance is always more exciting than virtue; virtue is compliance, while repentance is rebellion against the corrupt Parent.

K

COMPANIONS

A companion literally is someone that you eat with. A comrade is someone that you share the same room with (from the Spanish *cámara*, a room). A companion is someone whom you eat with, have fun with, talk with, and go out with. All the ego states of both parties are likely to be involved. Companions exchange Parental prejudices, give each other Adult advice, and have Child fun together (Figure 7). Companionship is a twosome and

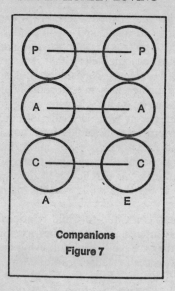

Companions
Figure 7

may or may not involve sex. Companions, however, are not necessarily concerned with each other's welfare, and the relationship may be temporary, as during a summer vacation, a ship's cruise, or a war. In these two respects it differs from friendship. Companions usually have a certain amount of respect and affection for each other. On the other hand, they may despise each other and go out together because they play the same psychological games.

L

FRIENDS

The next step in relationship is friendship. The essence of friendship is that there is no active Parental ego state under ordinary conditions. That is, friends do not criticize each other in a Parent-to-Child way, although they may give each other advice. But this advice is not

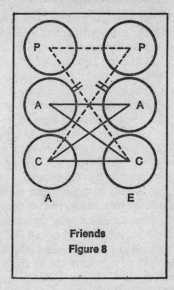

Friends
Figure 8

fingershaking, it is a rational, factual statement, Adult-to-Adult or Adult-to-Child, as in Figure 8. A friend does not say (Parentally), "Smoking marijuana is awful, and only degenerate people do it. I'm only telling you that as a friend." A real friend says, "You know you can get a rap of up to twenty years for doing that openly. I'd miss you if you were away that long."

Friends "accept" each other. "Accept" is one of those words most people use without defining clearly, like "togetherness," "sharing," "hostility," "dependency," and "passive." If you ask them what they mean, they say, "You know what I mean," and get angry if you say you don't. The reason they get angry is that they don't know what they mean and they are relying on you to know. If you say you don't, you have left them stranded, and so they get angry. The only way to be sure you understand an abstract noun is to draw a diagram or picture of what you mean. I think Figure 8 is a diagram of what "accept" means. It means that the critical Parent is crossed out and decommissioned.

There are two exceptions to this, however, where two people can be friends even with active Parental ego states. The first occurs in any emergency where the caring Parent, but not the critical Parent, becomes active, so that if you really get hurt a friend might show you some sympathy and take care of you without damaging the friendship. But if the caring Parent is always there meddling around, trying to help you when you don't want to be helped, then that's not going to be a very good friendship. That is one way mothers keep from being friends with their children. Even if the critical Parent is restrained, they overcare and interfere, giving help when it is not wanted.

Another way in which friendship can survive an active Parent, even a critical one, is to criticize other people but not each other. Already given was the classical example of the "committee members," who can be good friends just because "nowadays everything is awful (except us)." What they are doing is repeating things their mothers and fathers taught them, and if their Parents agree, they will agree, even if nothing they say makes sense or has been critically evaluated. So you don't have to say anything sensible to have a friend, providing you both believe in the same nonsense.

A friend is basically a more solid form of companion. Friends may eat together, live together, talk together, have fun together, and go out together. But in addition they stay together for life and help each other in time of need.

To paraphrase Proust, a friend is one who has the same illusions you have, so he won't hurt your feelings when he finds out you have them, too.

M

INTIMACY

The closer together people get, the more independent and self-contained their relation becomes. Therefore the closest relationships are the ones that we know least about. People have been trying to define intimacy, for example, for 5,000 years, with little success up to the present. By using the idea of ego states, however, I think we can say more about it now than anybody has been able to say previously.

Intimacy is a candid Child-to-Child relationship with no games and no mutual exploitation. If is set up by the Adult ego states of the parties concerned, so that they understand very well their contracts and commitments with each other, sometimes without a word being spoken about such matters. As this understanding becomes clearer, the Adult gradually retires from the scene, and if the Parent does not interfere, the Child becomes more and more relaxed and freer and freer. The actual intimate transactions take place between the two Child ego states. The Adult, however, still remains in the background as an overseer to assure that the commitments and limitations are kept. The Adult also has the task of keeping the Parent from barging in and spoiling the situation. In fact the capacity for intimacy depends upon the ability of the Adult and the Child to keep the Parent at bay if necessary; but it is even better if the Parent benevolently gives permission or, best of all, encouragement, for the relationship to proceed. Parental encouragement helps the Child lose his fear of intimacy, and assures that he will not be restrained by a burden or threat of guilt.

The reality of this dialogue between the three ego states can be checked by any alert person who is about to embark on an intimate relationship. If he listens carefully to the voices in his head, he will hear the Child exclaiming his desire to go ahead and get to know the person better, his Adult saying, "I think you have found the right one," and his Parent either grumbling about some aspect like social standing or religion, or throwing in some approving comment such as: "You deserve to enjoy yourself on your vacation, just so you work hard when you get back," at which the Child nods eagerly and promises that he will.

Once the Child is free of Adult caution and Parental criticism, he has a sense of elation and awareness. He begins to see and hear and feel the way he really wants to, the way he originally did before he was corrupted by his living parents. In this autonomous state, he no longer has to name things, as is usually required by his Adult, nor account for his behavior, as demanded by his Parent. He is free to respond directly and spontaneously to what he sees and hears and feels. Because the two parties trust one another, they freely open up their secret worlds of perception, experience, and behavior to each other, asking nothing in return except the delight of opening the gates without fear.

In order to have this kind of relation, the Child must cut loose from the inner Parent for the same reason that he must be away from his actual parents. Carefree sexual enjoyment and intimacy, for example, would be almost impossible if one of his actual parents were standing behind him, and the same difficulties arise if the inner Parent becomes active as a phantom in the bedroom. He must also cut loose from his Adult because his Adult expects him to make sense. Making sense is one of the first ways in which parents corrupt their children. For instance, they do not for long allow them to listen with pure and spontaneous enjoyment. Sooner or later, when the baby is listening to a bird song, the father or mother will say "Birdie, birdie," and then the baby has to say "Birdie, birdie." Later, he may have to learn to tell the difference between a sparrow and a jay. This Adult activity distracts his Child from listening. Of course, such teaching is necessary and valuable, and the baby could not survive into grownup years without it. What goes wrong in most cases is that the person is never again able to suspend this Adult data processing, so that after early infancy, most people never again really hear a bird singing.

The same happens with looking. Parents teach children that they are not allowed to stare at people because that is rude, unless they are doing it for a specific purpose, perhaps in the course of a professional activity such as hairdressing, dermatology, or psychiatry.* The result is that

* Professionals are allowed to stare because the client implicitly gives them permission to do so when he engages their services. In other words, certain professional contracts carry a built-in

most human beings never really see another person after they are five years old. In an intimate relationship, each party returns to the original naïve Child ego state, where he is free of such Parental prohibitions and Adult requirements, and can see, hear, and taste in its purest form what the world has to offer. This freedom of the Child is the essential part of intimacy, and it turns the whole universe, including the sun, moon, and stars, into a golden apple for both parties to enjoy.

There is also such a thing as one-sided intimacy, in which one party is ready for it and the other resists it. This is something like Balzac's typical situation in which one party is ready for love, and loves, while the other merely permits himself to be loved. Such a setup can be exploited by unscrupulous people for their own advantage. Many prostitutes and courtesans* know how to free the open and intimate Child in men without lowering their own guard, and pimps and predatory men can exploit women in the same way.

The "intimacy experiment," in which two people sit close to each other "eyeball to eyeball,"† and keep eye

---

staring license. The Parent of the professional relaxes the anti-staring rule as long as the staring is part of the job, i.e., Adult. But sometimes the Child takes advantage of this relaxation to steal a look too. A crooked Parent may even go along with this abuse of the staring license, offering an interesting example of the lechery mechanism shown in Figure 17C. Therefore, whether or not the cheating Child feels guilty depends on whether the Parent (of the same or sometimes of the opposite sex) is or is not lecherous.

* Roughly speaking, at the going rates, a common prostitute is one whose fee is up to $100 in advance. A high-class prostitute is one whose fee is over $100 in money or goods, not in advance. A courtesan is one whose fee is high enough so that it takes a lawyer to draw up the papers.

† This procedure was first systematically studied at the San Francisco Transactional Analysis Seminar about ten years ago. Since then it has become a standard part of the repertoire of "encounter" groups. It was amusing recently to have it demonstrated to me by an "Encounterer" who was unaware of its history.

contact while talking straight to each other reveals many interesting things about intimacy.[13] First, it demonstrates that any two people of either sex, starting as strangers or mere acquaintances, can attain intimacy in fifteen minutes or so under proper conditions. Secondly, it shows that any two people who really look at each other, and really see each other, and talk straight to each other, always (as far as these and similar "encounters" go) end up liking each other.[14] This indicates that dislikes result from (1) people not really seeing each other and/or (2) people not talking straight to each other. The greatest preventive of intimacy seems to be a critical Parent, and next to that, a crooked Child. This is instructive as far as it goes, but further investigation is necessary before any firm conclusions can be drawn.

In fairness to parents, however, it should be said that there are many who successfully teach their children to see and hear more and better, to be open to intimacy, and to distinguish it from sexuality.

N

LOVE

Love is defined in many ways, and I will not review them here. In Greek there are *eros, philos,* and *agape:* desire, friendship, and affection. Since our subject is sex, I will talk about eros, the desire and intoxication of sexual love.

Sexual love, being sexual, will be full of lust, or better, lustiness; and being love, it will partake of that which sets true love apart from all other relations—and that is putting the welfare and happiness of the other person before one's own. Love is the most complete and noblest relationship of them all, and includes the best of all the others: respect admiration, turn-on, friendship and intimacy, all in one, with its own grace or charisma added.

Such a relation can exist only if the Parent, with its

watchful eyes and hearing aids, and the Adult, with its dreary prudence, are out of commission, and that is exactly the situation when people fall in love. At the moment they do so, they cease to regard each other with prosaic prejudice or to restrain their buxom behavior with more than a bare minimum of sweet reason. Love is Child-to-Child: an even more primitive Child than the intimate one, for the Child of intimacy sees things as they are, in all their pristine beauty, while the Child of love adds something to that and gilds the lily with a luminous halo invisible to everyone but the lover. This is a primal vision, the way the infant, I think, sees his mother: not only as the most beautiful object or person in his world, but with a shimmering radiance that outshines all other worlds.

This resembles the radiance that some people see with LSD. The difference is that in mutual love there are two people involved, and they are involved with each other out there rather than with what is going on inside their own heads. Drugs are instead of people, and people are better than drugs. The person who takes LSD is intoxicated, while the person in love is in the purest state possible: he is detoxified of both Parental corruption and Adult misgivings, and his Child is free to embark on the greatest adventure open to the human race, next to the moon. In the intoxication of drugs, he is in the grip of an impersonal and inhuman force that will not listen and has no interest in his welfare. In the detoxication of love, he is in the grip of the most personal reality there is: someone whose greatest delight is to listen not only to his words but to the cadence of his voice, and whose greatest interest is precisely in his happiness and welfare. Love is a sweet trap from which no one departs without tears.

Some say one-sided love is better than none, but like half a loaf of bread, it is likely to grow hard and moldly sooner.

O

CLASSIFYING RELATIONSHIPS

Although some relationships are pure, a great many are mixed and not easy to classify. If they are looked at moment by moment, however, they fall into place. The following example will illustrate some of the difficulties and subtleties, and how they can be solved by means of relationship diagrams.

Susan, a young lady in her twenties who loved babies and had a strong nesting instinct, had always backed off from men because she feared them and their sexuality. She was progressing from acquaintances with whom she played games so as to disrupt the relationship before it became threatening, toward intimacy and love. On the way, we had the following conversation:

Susan: I get along well with Roger, but it's not love, it's just cuffing. We're very good friends, but he might as well be my brother. He fixes things around the house and then we go to bed. I'm not afraid of sex any more, but there's not much more to it than that.

Doctor: Too bad there has to be a man at the other end of the penis.

Susan: Yes, it would be much simpler if there wasn't. If I could have a penis to play with and a man to take care of me, I'd be okay.

In the language of transactional analysis, Susan wants Roger to oscillate between being a nurturing Parent, a helpful Adult, and a sexy Child, while she remains in a Child ego state throughout. According to her description, the relation sounds like companionship or friendship, but there are certain differences from both. Companionship (Figure 7) is a "straight-across" relationship, Parent-to-Parent, Adult-to-Adult, and Child-to-Child, while this one has some oblique vectors. Companionship is symmetrical, in that both parties are equal, while the Susan-Roger relationship is not. Friendship (Figure 8) has oblique vectors, but these only rarely involve the Parent, whereas the Parent is a necessary part of the Susan-Roger relation. In addition, friendship is symmetrical and Susan-Roger is not.

We can break the S-R relationship into its three aspects as described by Susan, in which she remains always in the Child ego state (Figures 9, 10, and 11), while Roger switches from one to another. If we bring these three diagrams together, we get a picture of the overall relationship (Figure 12). This can be used to predict what the possibilities are. It does not look like a good diagram for co-workers (A-A) nor for marriage (which needs more than three vectors to work well), and we have already discussed the difficulties in the way of true companionship or friendship. Intimacy and love are not likely either, because of its asymmetry. For those, Susan must change, either through psychotherapy or by meeting a different kind of man, so that she can overcome her Child's fear and meet him as an equal. Thus we can predict that the S-R relationship will be (and should be) only temporary, which it was. Although Roger got some satisfaction out of it, including sexual, from her side it was a relation of total exploitation in which she used all three of his ego states for her own needs without offering anything in return except what he could forage.

It is clear that sex can find a place in any of the relationships mentioned in this chapter, which gives us the following list, with a few comments about some of the items.

Acquaintance or casual sex. This may occur "by accident," on impulse, for money, to prove something, to "show somebody," or as a pastime in special situations of boredom.

Co-worker or office sex. This is common between workers in the same echelon. Most businessmen avoid it on the principle that it is easier to find another good mistress than another good secretary. Wise secretaries avoid it on the same principle that it is easier to find a good boy friend than a good boss. Aside from ethical considerations, therapists—and wise patients—avoid it for similar reasons. It is easier for a therapist to find a good girl friend than to find another good patient. And it is obvi-

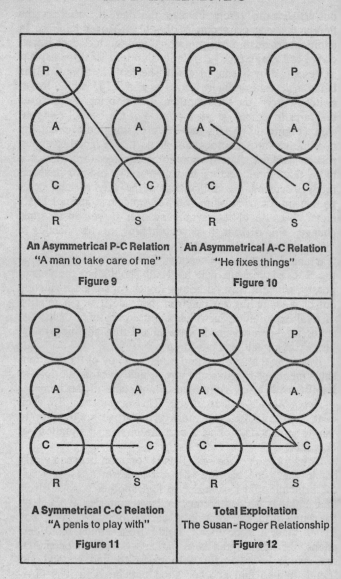

An Asymmetrical P-C Relation
"A man to take care of me"

Figure 9

An Asymmetrical A-C Relation
"He fixes things"

Figure 10

A Symmetrical C-C Relation
"A penis to play with"

Figure 11

Total Exploitation
The Susan-Roger Relationship

Figure 12

ously easier for a patient to find a good boy friend than to find another good therapist, since there are millions of eligible bachelors in this country, but only a few thousand competent shrinks.

Committee sex. This is a matter of propinquity and individual preference. It may work in a working committee, but in an "Ain't It Awful" committee it is likely to be awful.

Respect sex. This is risky even if both parties are unmarried and sure of their potency. If it is not completely straight and completely satisfying, respect is soon cremated in the heat of ill-spent passion, and the ashes of respect are the burning embers of scorn. Such an ill death of something so fine is seldom worth the hazard.

Admiration sex. This is a good way to get an autograph from an admired one.

Affectionate sex is groovy.

Companionable sex. A good way to share the room rent, some people think.

Friendly sex. Nothing interferes with friendship like sex, and nothing interferes with sex like friendship.

Intimate sex is wow.

Loving sex. Sexual fluids make a good cement, and they also produce babies.

P

MARRIAGE

Marriage may be based on or involve any of the situations previously discussed, and I will not attempt a formal analysis of this difficult relationship, which results in 500,000 divorces per year in this country alone. (The moral of this, obviously, is that the sovereign remedy for divorce is to abolish marriage.) But I would like to suggest a very artificial classification that has two advantages as far as it goes: it is not misleading, and it is easy to remember. It is based on letters of the alphabet: A H I O S V X and Y.

An A marriage starts off as a shotgun or makeshift one. The couple are far apart, but soon they find a single common bond, perhaps the new baby. This is represented by the crossbar of the A. As time goes on, they get closer and closer until they finally come together, and then they have a going concern. This is represented by the apex of the A.

An H marriage starts off the same way, but the couple never gets any closer, and the marriage is held together by a single bond. Otherwise they each go where they were originally headed.

An I marriage starts off and ends with the couple forged into a single unit.

An O marriage goes round and round in a circle, never getting anywhere, and repeating the same patterns until it is terminated by death or separation.

An S marriage wanders around seeking happiness, and eventually ends up slightly above and to the right of where it started, but it never gets any farther than that, leaving both parties disappointed and bewildered, and good candidates for psychotherapy, since there is enough there so that they don't want a divorce.

A V marriage starts off with a close couple, but they immediately begin to diverge, perhaps after the honeymoon is over or even after the first night.

An X marriage starts off like an A. At one point there is a single period of bliss. They wait for it to happen again, but it never does, and soon they drift apart again, never to reunite.

A Y marriage starts off well, but difficulties multiply, and eventually each one finds his own separate interests and goes his own way.

There are undoubtedly many other types of marriages, but they do not fit into the alphabet we use, so they will have to be left for a more complicated system of classification.

Q

LEGAL RELATIONSHIPS

In contrast to the structural or ego state system of classifying relationships, let us briefly discuss the sexual aspects of the legal system of classification. Personal relations have been under continual scrutiny and definition by this profession ever since Roman times, and even before that to some extent. Besides the four main classes generally mentioned in the law books,[15] we have included a fifth because, although it is not primarily a personal relationship, it easily becomes one.

HUSBAND AND WIFE

Sex is not only permitted between husband and wife, but it is more or less compulsory. If a marriage is not "consummated" that may be grounds for annulment. On the other hand, in many states there are strict limits to the kinds of sex which are permissible in marriage. Anything but face to face vaginal copulation may be called "a crime against nature" and constitute a felony with the penalty of imprisonment. Thus, legally speaking, one sexual act face to face makes marriage, while any other form of intercourse turns both parties into criminals.

PARENT AND CHILD

Sexual intercourse between parent and child is forbidden because that constitutes incest, even after the child is grown up. The only sexual pleasures permitted by law are extreme perversions or far-out procedures justified as morality or hygiene. A father is allowed to spank his children, including his daughters, with or without their clothes on. A mother is allowed to give her son daily enemas (and a father his daughter) even without a doctor's orders. A father is legally permitted to lift up his daughter's dress when she returns from a date to see whether she has had intercourse. And both parents are allowed to do stripteases and go to the bathroom in the presence of their children.

GUARDIAN AND WARD

This includes many complex legal situations. Generally speaking, guardian and ward are not supposed to have sex with each other. In some cases it is expressly forbidden, in others it may be permissible and may be one of the pleasures of such a legal relationship. If the ward is a minor, the same perversions may be permitted as in the case of parent and child.

MASTER AND SERVANT

This may include master and apprentice, teacher and pupil. It is an established principle (or at least it happens frequently) that a master may have sex with his servants or a mistress with hers, and if the consequences are unfortunate the servant is then entitled to the redress provided by common law. Thus such relations are a form of manor house roulette. When the girl's number fails to come up, the master loses. In the old days when teachers kept their distance from their pupils, sex between them was regarded askance. But as the relationship becomes more intimate, sex becomes more and more common and accepted. Boss and secretary is a common sexual relationship, even in the face of good sense, but such double contracts are chancy. Many a woman can be either a good secretary or a good mistress, but it is not easy to be both to the same man, and often the two vocations interfere with each other.

SUPPLIER AND CLIENT

There are no laws specifically prohibiting a businessman from having sexual relationships with his customers, but there are certain professional relations of a "fiduciary" nature. There the client is in the hands of the supplier and tends to rely on his judgment and take his advice, since that is the commodity being paid for. This is the case between lawyers or social workers and their clients, and between doctors or psychotherapists and their patients. It is considered unethical and sometimes illegal for the professional person to have affairs with his clients or patients. A few therapists do it on the principle that their patients will get better faster, but it rarely works that way. In the majority of cases it damages the therapeutic relationship and the patient gets worse.

What is wrong is that love is not included in the contract. The patient is paying for treatment and not for sex. Some therapists and lawyers get around the ethical problem by waiting until the case is "finished," and then have sex with their clients. This may be legal but it is certainly not ethical. Sometimes the supplier has sex with his clients and is also getting paid for his services, thus reducing himself to the level of a drug peddler or gigolo.

It can be seen that the legal classification of relations offers some possibilities for thought, but it is not as consistent nor as intellectually satisfying as the transactional approach. Nor does it offer any advantages for analysis, understanding, or prediction. It is actually more cynical than scientific. Much the same applies to other systems in common use. Psychoanalysis can analyze relationships but not meaningfully classify them, and the analyses are much more cumbersome than the transactional ones.

The Appendix to this book gives further information about classifying relationships in a more formal way.

NOTES AND REFERENCES

1. Berne, E.: *Transactional Analysis in Psychotherapy,* op. cit.

2. Dutch, R. A. (ed.): *Roget's Thesaurus.* St. Martin's Press, New York, 1963.

3. Liddell, H. G., and Scott, R.: *Greek-English Lexicon.* Clarendon Press, Oxford, 1883.

4. I try to avoid the word "relationship" as much as possible, along with several other words which have degenerated into shibboleths of psychosocial work jargon. An exception is made whenever one of these words can be represented reasonably rigorously in a diagram. The word "relationship" is used here specifically to mean that which is represented by its structural relationship diagram.

5. This is what actually happened when one cancer ward was transformed from a Home for Incurables (there actually was an institution by that name in Montreal, Canada, when I was a boy, and even then I knew there was something wrong with the idea) into a cooperative community where everybody had his job to do. Instead of lying in bed feeling miserable day after day as they waited for death, the patients actually began to have fun as they came back to life, even though death still awaited them, as it does every man. See: "Terminal Cancer Ward: Patients Build Atmosphere of Dignity." *Journal of the American Medical Association* 208: 1289, May 26, 1969. Also Klagsbrun, S. C.: "Cancer, Emotions, and Nurses." *Summary of Scientific Proceedings,* 122nd Annual Meeting, American Psychiatric Association, Washington, 1969.

6. Lorenz, K. Z.: *King Solomon's Ring.* Translated by N. K. Wilson. Thomas Y. Crowell Company, New York, 1952.

7. This discussion of symbolism differs from the psychoanalytic view as expressed in the classical paper of Ernest Jones, "The Theory of Symbolism." In E. Jones, *Papers on Psycho-Analysis.* Beacon Press, Boston, 1961.

8. Ford, C. S. and Beach, F. A.: *Patterns of Sexual Behavior.* Harper & Brothers, New York, 1951.

9. The concept of "odorless smells," chemicals "broadcast" through the air by the body of one person, which can affect the behavior of other people without their being aware of what has happened, is not a metaphysical one. In the first place, such chemicals would work exactly the same as body odors, except that the recipient would not smell anything. Secondly, odorless gases such as carbon monoxide and certain military gases, and radioactivity, which is also odorless, can certainly affect behavior, although their effects are due to pathological changes. Thirdly, insects such as moths broadcast such substances, and these must be inhaled by moth and man alike, but man is not aware of their presence. In the case of insects, they are called pheromones, hormones which stimulate physiological or behavioral responses from another individual of the same species. The species' specificity depends on the presence of specific ketones.

Whether the male moth "smells" the pheromones given off by the female there is no way of knowing. It is known, however, that the olfactory receptors are affected by them. This can be established by taking electroantennograms. (Schneider, D., and Seibt, U.: "Sex Pheromone of the Queen Butterfly: Electroantennogram Responses." *Science* 164:1173-1174, June 9, 1969.)

10. I have referred to the conditioned turn-on as "possible" because I do not have the clinical material to support it. What I have said about it sounds plausible and is certainly hopeful. Unfortunately, when I asked a recent divorcée about it, she replied, "Emphatically no! It just doesn't work that way!" with a clear implication that she knew because she had tried it in her own kitchen. So it is just left as a possibility, for what it is worth as a comfort to worried wives, experimental psychologists, and behavioral therapists.

11. Pavlov, I. P.: *Conditioned Reflexes and Psychiatry*. Translated by W. H. Gantt. International Publishers, New York, 1941.

12. de Sade, D. A. F.: op. cit.

13. Berne, E.: "The Intimacy Experiment." *Transactional Analysis Bulletin* 3:113, 1964, and "More About Intimacy," ibid. 3:125, 1964.

14. While in these "experiments" the word used was "like,"

there is something more to it because of the strange after-relationship so often described in literature between torturers (official or unofficial) and their victims if they really look at each other and really talk straight to each other.

15. The California Civil Code is the basis for this discussion, although it has not been strictly followed.

5

SEXUAL
GAMES

A

INTRODUCTION: IT'S A CRAZY WORLD

Sex can be enjoyable in solitude or in groups, or in couples as an act of intimacy, a passion, a relief, a duty, or just a way to pass the time to ward off and postpone the evil day of boredom, that Boredom which is the pimp of Death and brings to him sooner or later all its victims, whether by disease, accident, or intent. For the truth of the matter is not that time is passing, but that we are passing through time. It is not what they said in olden days, a river on whose banks we stand and watch, but a sea we have to cross, either in solitary labor and watchfulness, like crossing the Atlantic in a rowboat, or crowded together over the engine oil and the automatic pilot with nothing to do but play some form of drunk or sober shuffleboard. Only a few glide in splendor with sail unfurled in a lugger or a sloop or something grander, ahoy and belay there! up with the mizzen royal of our full-rigged five-master— the only one ever built to sail the Seven Seas! And it is still possible to fly nonstop, without being much bothered by what happens down below.

In the cities and in the country there are millions of birds, and how many of you with full awareness heard one of them sing today? In the cities and in the country there are thousands of trees, and how many of you with full awareness saw one today? Here is a nonstop story of my own. About five times a week, I walked from my office to the post office in the little village where I live. I walked by the same route for two years, about 500 trips, before one day I noticed two hairy palm trees with a cactus growing between them on a corner that I passed. I had gone by this rugged delight 499 times in a row without being aware that anything was growing there, because I was preoccupied with getting to the post office to pick up my mail so I could go back to my office and answer the letters so I could go to the post office and pick up the replies to my answers so I could answer the replies so I could go to the post office and pick up more mail to answer. My time was mortgaged to a self-imposed burden that I could never pay off but could at any moment, whenever I wished, tear up, and put the pieces carefully in one of the trash cans considerately provided by the village council so I would not litter the streets.

I thought of this one time lying in bed in a hotel in Vienna listening to the quiet of the night and then to the first rustles of life at dawn, the slow waltz of Vienna in the morning. First the six o'clock people danced out to prepare the way for the seven o'clock people, who got ready for the eight o'clock people who take care of the nine o'clock people.* These open their stores and offices so that shopping and business calls can begin at ten, so that the stores can be closed at twelve so that people can go home and get ready for lunch, so that they can re-open at two so they can close at five, so that they can get home by six to dress for dinner at seven so they can get to the theater by eight, so that they can get home by eleven to

* Six: bus-drivers, I guess. Seven: cooks, I guess. Eight: waitresses, some of them.

get a good night's sleep so they will be in good shape when they get up again in the morning at five, six, seven, or eight.

And there is a song about Sunday, when they are not bound by all this, and how on that day some of them jump into the Danube, which is a river and carries them in its flow as time does not. For time is not a river, but a sea that must be crossed, from the shore of bawling birth to the littered coast of death. And this is not a fancy of song writers, this fascination of the waters (Nepenthes en tw potamouthanatw),* for in Vienna each year about 500 people kill themselves. Do you know which country has the highest suicide rate in the world? Hungary. That's Communism for you. Do you know which country has the second highest rate? Austria. That's democracy for you. Actually, since they're both on the same river, that's the Danube for you. Which Communist people have a lower suicide rate than white democratic Americans, but higher than nonwhite democratic Americans? The Poles, that's who.[2]

Since time does not pass, it must be passed through, and that means always scheduled or structured. Don't just sit there, do something! What shall we do this morning, this afternoon, tonight? Mom, there's nothing to do. He doesn't do anything. I've got lots to do. Get up, you lazy loafer. Awritechuguys, getcherasses outabed. Don't do anything, just sit there, and for one million dollars an hour I'll fill in your time on Channel 99. A million? He's worth it, man. Pay him two million if you can.

Sex may be an essential ingredient in structuring time, although eunuchs find plenty to do, don't they? Old Abdul the sick man of Europe and Asia sitting on Seraglio Point

---

* Okay, here's what it means. Nepenthes, nowadays shortened to Nepenthe, is a potion which brings forgetfulness of all pains, quarrels, griefs, and troubles.[1] Helen of Troy got some from an Egyptian's daughter and used it to spike wine. From that description in Book IV of the *Odyssey,* it sounds not unlike some form of hashish. The rest I made up myself. The root Potam- means a river, as in hippopotamus, and Thanat- means death. So it means that river-death is a drink to end all troubles.

looking for excitement—you can't trust them, they've got hands and other ways, chop off their scrotums and what good does it do? Sex is in the head, it's not all in the scrotum by any means. You'll find that out the hard way, and then you'll have to tread slowly to satisfy your lust and have your bust. They say I'm Abdul the Cruel but I just have a sensual sense of humor, carry me back to old Istanbul and the randy life of the Golden Horn, get the girls out of the sordid honky-tonks and into the wholesome harems, I mean out of the sordid harems and into the wholesome honky-tonks. Have it your own way, Dad.

Meaning there's more to life than sex, you can't do it all the time, you can't even think of it all the time, animals do it only in the spring and fall, the rest of the time it's eat eat eat, who wants to be an animal? *Vive la différence!* The difference being that for people there is something more important than essential ingredients, eating and sex, and they think of it—the difference—between eating and between sex, and that is being me, I, myself. More than eating and more than sex (which are necessary, but not sufficient) I want to be a Self, and I am a Self. Unfortunately, for the most part, this is an illusion.

B

PARENTAL PROGRAMMING

From the beginning man does what he is told. Most animals don't. That is really the difference, and as usual it is the opposite of what people usually say. Sexy men are called (by some) animals, when men are by nature sexier than animals, and an unsexy animal would certainly not be called a man. Vicious men are also called animals, but animals are not vicious for the most part, just hungry. And man is called free, when actually he is the most compliant of all animals.

Some animals can be trained to perform a stunt here and there, but not tamed. Other animals can be tamed and also trained to perform a stunt here and there. But man is tamed from the beginning, and spends his whole life performing stunts for his masters: Mom and Pop first, and then teacher, and after that whoever can grab him and teach him feats of war and revolution or stunts of peace. Revolution, ha! Buzz off, Alex. Now I'm walking the wire in Joe's show instead. Foo, Manchu! It's Mao now for this brown kao.* Believe, work, and obey. I can't believe Manny so I'll obey Benny. I'm free to walk a mile to say Heil, hit the trail or go on trial, reach the goal or go to gaol. Man is programmed to obey, obey, obey, obey the obedient, or obey the civil or uncivil disobedients. Form a line on the right, left, don't straggle. Straggle, don't form a line. Which side shall I straggle on? Which side shall I struggle on? Don't struggle. Tune in, turn on, drop out. That's an order! Don't listen to those other pigs. Listen to your own pigs. Be anarchistic. Be independent, dammit. Be original, no no, not that way, this way. It's imperative that you enjoy yourself and be spontaneous.

Here's how it happens.

From earliest months, the child is taught not only what to do, but also what to see, hear, touch, think, and feel. And beyond that, he is also told whether to be a winner or a loser, and how his life will end. All these instructions are programmed into his mind and his brain just as firmly as though they were punch cards put into the bank of a computer. In later years, what he thinks of as his independence or his autonomy is merely his freedom to select certain cards, but for the most part the same old punch holes stay there that were put there at the beginning. Some people get an exhilarating sense of freedom by rebelling, which usually means one of two things: either they pull out a bunch of cards punched in early childhood which they have never used before, or they turn some of the cards inside out and do the opposite of what they say. Often this merely amounts to following the instructions on a special card which says: "When you are 18 (or 40) use

---

* I mean 羋 , lamb.

this new bunch of cards, or turn the following cards inside out." Another kind of rebellion follows the instructions: "When you are 18 (or 40), throw away all cards in series A and leave a vacuum." This vacuum then has to be filled as quickly as possible with new instant programs, which are obtained from drugs or from a revolutionary leader. Thus in their efforts to avoid becoming fatheads or egg-heads, these people end up being acidheads or spite-heads.

In any case, each person obediently ends up at the age of five or six—yes, ends up at five or six—with a script or life plan largely dictated by his parents. It tells him how he's going to carry on his life, and how it's going to end, winner, non-winner, or loser. Will it be in the big room surrounded by his loved ones, or with his bed crowded out into the corridor of the City Hospital, or falling like a lead bird into the chilled choppy waters of the Golden Gate? At five or six he doesn't know all that, but he knows about victorious lions and lonely corridors and dead fish in cold water. And he also knows enough to come in first or second like his father or his dad, or to come in last like his old man, he sure can hold his liquor. This is a free country, but don't stare. We got free speech, so listen to me. If you don't watch out for yourself nobody else'll watch out for you, but (a) no, no, mussentouchit, or (b) getcher cotton pickin' hans off my money, or (c) you gonna grow up to be a thief or something?

Well, hit him back. You hit him wrong. Say you're sorry. Watch out. I'll give you something to cry about, you little monster. Feel angry, inadequate, guilty, scared, hurt. I'll teach you how to think as well as how to feel. Don't think such thoughts. Think it over until you see it my way. I'll show you how to do it, too. Here's how to get away with it. You don't know what to be when you grow up? I'll tell you what to be. Be good. Do as you're told, Adolf, and don't ask questions. Be different. Why can't you be like other kids?

So, having learned what not to see, what not to hear, and what not to touch, and which feelings to have, and how not to think, and what not to be, the child sallies forth to school. There he meets teachers and his own kind.

It is called a grade school, but it is really a law school. By the time he is ten (the age that lawyers are stuck at) he is an accomplished pettifogger in his own defense. He has to be, especially if he is mean or naughty. You said not to write over the stuff on the blackboard, but you didn't say don't erase it (or vice versa). You said not to take her candy, but you didn't say not to take her chewing gum. You told me not to say bad words to Cousin Mary, but you didn't say not to undress her. You told me not to lie on top of girls, but you didn't say anything about boys.

Later, in high school, come the real script setups. "Don't go to a drive-in. You'll get pregnant!" Up to that time she didn't know how to go about getting pregnant. Now she knows. But she is not ready yet. She has to wait for the signal. "Don't go to a drive-in, you'll get pregnant, until I give you the signal." She knows mother was sixteen when she was born, and pretty soon figures she must have been conceived out of wedlock. Naturally, mother gets very nervous when daughter passes her sixteenth birthday. One day mother says: "Summer is the worst time. That's when most high school girls get pregnant" (generalizing from her own experience). That's the signal. So daughter goes to a drive-in and gets pregnant.

"Don't go into a men's room because you'll meet a bad man there who'll do something nasty to you," father says to his eight-year-old son. He repeats it about once a year. So when the time comes, the boy wonders what the nasty thing is, and he knows where to go to find out. Another father packed not only the sex instructions but the whole life script into one pubertal sentence. "Don't let me catch you going to that house on Bourbon Street, where there are women who'll do anything you want for five dollars." Since the boy didn't have five dollars, he stole it out of his mother's purse, intending to go to Bourbon Street the following afternoon. But mother happened to count her money that same night and found it where the boy had hidden it, and he was caught and punished. He learned his lesson well. "If I'd gone down right after dinner instead of putting it off until the next day, everything would've been all right." He wouldn't have been caught with the five dollars. This is a good non-winner script. If you want women, get money. Spend it as quickly as possible, before you get caught. You can't win, but you can certainly keep from losing.

The loser's instructions generally read something like this: "If at first you don't succeed, try, try, try again. Even if you win a few, keep trying, and you're bound to lose in the end, because you can't win 'em all." The winner's read: "Why lose at all? If you lose, it means you played wrong. So do it again until you learn to do it right."

If it is not interfered with by some decisive force, the script will be carried through to the sweet or bitter end. There are three such forces. The greatest script-breakers are massive events which lumber inexorably down the path of history: wars, famines, epidemics, and oppression, which overtake and crush everyone before them like cosmic steamrollers, save for those who are licensed to clamber aboard and use them as bandwagons. The second is psychotherapy and other conversions, which break up scripts and make losers into non-winners ("Making progress") and non-winners into winners ("Getting well," "Flipping in," and "Seeing the light").

In rare cases, a third force takes over, and the script is broken up by an autonomous decision or re-decision of the person himself. This happens with people whose script allows them to make an autonomous decision. The clearest example in recent times is Mao Tse-tung, head of the Chinese People's Republic, who started out as a middle-class person with a middle-class script, and by his own inner struggle became what he defines as a real proletarian, so that he felt comfortable in that role and uncomfortable in his middle-class script role, which due to the *force majeure* of Chinese history was a loser's role.[3] By flipping in with history, he became a winner in war and in politics, and in literature as well, since few if any authors in modern times are as widely read as he is in his own lifetime.

It is important to note that the script is not "unconscious" and can be easily unearthed by a skillful questioner or by careful self-questioning. It is only that most people are reluctant to admit the existence of such a life plan and prefer to demonstrate their independence by playing games—games that are themselves dictated by their scripts.

C

TYPES OF SCRIPTS

Scripts are designed to last a lifetime. They are based on firm childhood decisions and parental programming that is continually reinforced. The reinforcement may take the form of daily contact, as with men who work for their fathers or women who telephone their mothers every morning to gossip, or it may be applied less frequently and more subtly, but just as powerfully, through occasional correspondence. After the parents die, their instructions may be remembered more vividly than ever.

In script language, a loser is called a frog.[4] and a winner is called a prince or a princess. Parents want their children to be either winners or losers. They may want them to be "happy" in the role they have chosen for them, but do not want them to be transformed except in special cases. A mother who is raising a frog may want her daughter to be a happy frog, but will put down any attempts of the girl to become a princess ("Who do you think you are?"), because mother herself was programmed to raise her as a frog. A father who is raising a prince wants his son to be happy, but often he would rather see him unhappy than transformed into a frog ("We've given you the best of everything").

A winner is defined as a person who fulfills his contract with the world and with himself. That is, he sets out to do something, says that he is committed to doing it, and in the long run does it. His contract, or ambition, may be to have four children, become the president of a corporation, pole vault 17', publish a good novel, make an artificial gene, or shoot down ten enemy bombers. If he accomplishes his goal, he is a winner. If he has no children, stays in the warehouse, sprains his back at 16′, stays with the newspaper, ends up with a lump of gristle, or gets shot down on his first mission, he is clearly a loser. If he has three children, becomes a vice president, hits 16′11″, publishes a mystery story, discovers a new amino acid, or shoots down nine bombers, he is an at-leaster, not a loser but a non-winner. The important thing is that he sets the goal himself, usually on the basis of Parental programming, but with his Adult making the final commitment. Note that the man who goes for two children, 16′, five bombers, etc., and makes it is still a winner, while the one who goes for four and only makes three, or goes for 17′ and only makes 16′11″, or goes for ten and only makes nine, is a non-winner, even though he outdoes the winner whose goals are lower. On a short-term basis, a winner is one who becomes captain of the team, dates the Queen of the May, or wins at poker. A non-winner never gets near the ball, dates the runner-up, or comes out even. A loser doesn't make the team, doesn't get a date, or comes out broke.

And note that the captain of the second team is on the same level as the captain of the first team, since each person is entitled to choose his own league and should be judged by the standards which he himself sets up. As an extreme example, "living on less money than anyone else on the street without getting sick" is a league. Whoever does it is a winner. One who tries it and gets sick is a loser. The typical, classical, loser is the man who makes himself suffer sickness or damage for no good cause. If he has a good cause, then he may become a successful martyr, which is the best way to win by losing.

The first thing to be decided about a script is whether it is a winning one or a losing one. This can often be discovered very quickly by listening to the person talk. A winner says things like: "I made a mistake, but it won't happen again" or "Now I know the right way to do it." A loser says, "If only . . ." or "I should've . . ." and "Yes, but . . ." As for non-winners, they are people whose scripts require them to work very hard, not in hope of winning but just to stay even. These are "at-leasters," people who say, "Well, at least I didn't . . ." or "At least, I have this much to be thankful for." Non-winners make excellent members, employees, and serfs, since they are loyal, hard-working, and grateful, and not inclined to cause trouble. Socially they are pleasant people, and in the community, admirable. Winners make trouble for the rest of the world only indirectly, when they are fighting among themselves and involve innocent bystanders, sometimes by the million. Losers cause the most turbulence, which is unfortunate, because even if they come out on top they are still losers and drag other people down with them when the payoff comes.

The best way to tell a winner from a loser is this: A winner is a person who knows what he'll do next if he loses, but doesn't talk about it; a loser is one who doesn't know what he'll do if he loses, but talks about what he'll do if he wins. Thus it takes only a few minutes of listening to pick out the winners and losers at a gambling table or a stockbroker's.

The next item is time structure. Over the life span of the individual, there are several types of scripts as to timing. The six main classes are the Never, the Always, the Until, the After, the Over and Over, and the Open End scripts. These are best understood by reference to Greek myths, since the Greeks had a strong feeling for such things.

The Never scripts are represented by Tantalus, who through all eternity was to suffer from hunger and thirst in sight of food and water, but never to eat or drink again. People with such scripts are forbidden by their parents to do the things they most want to, and so spend their lives being tantalized and surrounded by temptations. They go along with the Parental curse because the Child in them is afraid of the things they want the most, so they are really tantalizing themselves.

The Always scripts follow Arachne, who dared to challenge the Goddess Minerva in needlework, and as a punishment was turned into a spider and condemned to spend all her time spinning webs. Such scripts come from spiteful parents who say: "If that's what you want to do, then you can just spend the rest of your life doing it."

The Until scripts follow the story of Jason, who was told that he could not become a king until he had performed certain tasks. In due time he got his reward and lived for ten years in happiness. Hercules had a similar script: he could not become a god until he had first been a slave for twelve years.

The After scripts come from Damocles. Damocles was allowed to enjoy the happiness of being a king, until he noticed that a sword was hanging over his head, suspended by a single horse hair. The motto of After scripts is "You can enjoy yourself for a while, but then your troubles begin." The fear of impending troubles, of course, makes enjoyment difficult. These are the people who say, "If things are too good, something bad is bound to happen."

The Over and Over scripts are Sisyphus. He was condemned to roll a heavy stone up a hill, and just as he was about to reach the top the stone rolled back and he had to start over again. This is the classical Almost Made It script, with one "If only" after another.

The Open End script is the non-winner or Pie in the Sky scenario, and follows the story of Philemon and Baucis, who were turned into laurel trees as a reward for their good deeds. Old people who have carried out their Parental instructions don't know what to do next after it is all over, and spend the rest of their lives like vegetables, or gossiping like leaves rustling in the wind. This is the fate of many a mother whose children have grown up and scattered, and of men who have put in their thirty years of work according to company regulations and their parents' instructions, and now live alone on pensions in obscure hotels and rooming houses. "Senior citizen" communities are filled with couples who have completed their scripts and don't know how to structure their time while waiting for the Promised Land where people who have treated their employees decently can drive their big black cars slowly down the left-hand lane without being honked at by a bunch of ill-breed teenagers in their hot rods. "Was pretty feisty myself as a teenager," says Dad, "but now-adays." And Mom adds: "You wouldn't believe what they. And we've always paid our."

All of these script types have their sexual aspects. The Never scripts may forbid either love or sex or both. If they forbid love but not sex, they are a license for promiscuity, a license which some sailors and soldiers and wanderers take full advantage of, and which prostitutes and courtesans use to make a living. If they forbid sex but not love, they produce priests, monks, nuns, and people who do good deeds such as raising orphan children. The promiscuous people are tantalized by the sight of devoted lovers and happy families, while the scripty philanthropists are tormented by a desire to jump over the wall.

The Always scripts are typified by young people who are driven out of their homes for the sins that their parents have prompted them to. "If you're pregnant, go earn your living on the streets" and "If you want to take drugs, you're on your own" are examples of these. The father who turned his daughter out into the storm may have had lecherous thoughts about her since she was ten, and the one who threw his son out of the house for smoking pot may get drunk that night to ease his pain.

The parental programming in Until scripts is the loudest of all, since it usually consists of outright commands: "You can't have sex until you're married, and you can't get married as long as you have to take care of your mother (or until you finish college)." The Parental influence in After scripts is almost as outspoken, and the hanging sword gleams with visible threats: "After you get married and have children, your troubles will begin." Translated into action now, this means "Gather ye rosebuds while ye may, Old Time is still a-flying, And this same flower that smiles today, Tomorrow will be stultifying."[5] After marriage it shortens to "Once you have children your troubles will begin," so the young wife spends her days worrying about getting pregnant right from the first day of the honeymoon. But now chemists have provided a stout shield against the bilbo which would otherwise be her undoing, and so she can be queen of the household without having her happiness suspended by an heir until she is ready for one.

The Over and Over scripts produce always a bridesmaid and never a bride, as well as others who try hard again and again but never quite succeed in making it. The Open End scripts end with aging men and women who lose their vitality without much regret and are content with reminiscing about past conquests. Women with such scripts wait eagerly for the menopause, with the mistaken idea that after that their "sexual problems" will be over, while the men wait until they have put in their time on the job with a similar hope of relief from sexual obligations.

At the more intimate level, each of these scripts has its own bearing on the actual orgasm. The Never script, of course, besides making spinsters and bachelors and prostitutes and pimps, also makes women who never have an orgasm, not a single one in their whole lives, and also produces impotent men who can have orgasms providing there is no love—the classical situation described by Freud of the man who is impotent with his wife but not with prostitutes. The Always script produces nymphomaniacs and Don Juans who spend their lives continually chasing after the promise of a conquest.

The Until script favors harried housewives and tired businessmen, neither of whom can get sexually aroused until every last detail of the household or the office has been put in order. Even after they are aroused, they may be interrupted at the most critical moments by games of Refrigerator Door and Note Book, little things they have to jump out of bed to take care of right now, such as checking the refrigerator door to make sure it is closed or jotting down a few things that have to be done first thing in the morning at the office. After scripts interfere with sex because of apprehension. Fear of pregnancy, for example, keeps the woman from having an enjoyable orgasm and may cause the man to have his too quickly. Coitus interruptus, where the man withdraws just before he comes, as a method of birth control, keeps both parties in a jumpy state right from the beginning, and usually leaves the woman stranded high and wet if the couple is too shy to use some way for her to get her satisfaction. In fact the word satisfaction, which is usually used in discussing this particular problem, is a giveaway that something is wrong, since a good orgasm should be far more substantial than the pale ghost that is called satisfaction.

The Over and Over script is one that will ring a bell for many women losers, who get higher and higher during intercourse, until just as they are about to make it, the man comes, possibly with the woman's help, and she rolls all the the way down again. This may happen night after night for years. The Open End script has its effect in older people who regard sex as an effort or an obligation. Once over the hill, they are "too old" to have sex, and their glands wither away from disuse along with their skins and often their muscles and brains as well. The man strongly programmed for punctuality has spent all his life waiting for Santa Claus to bring him his retirement pin— late to work only twice in the whole thirty years—while his wife has been waiting for Mrs. Santa Claus, whose maiden name was Minnie Menopause. And now they have nothing to do but fill in the time until their pipes rust away, taking their places in senior society according to what brand of car they drive, if any. If they are lucky, he may find a bleached divorcée at the trailer court who will give his plumbing a last fling, and as a result he may plumb his wife a few times in the afterglow, and after that, they've had it. The moral of this is that a script should not have a time limit on it, but should be designed to last a whole lifetime, no matter how long that lifetime may be. It may call for switching trades or sports, but retirement, no.

We have already seen that the sexual potency, force, and drive of a human being are to some extent determined by his inheritance and his chemistry. Incredible as it may seem, they are even more strongly influenced by the script decisions he makes in early childhood and by the parental programming that brings about those decisions. Thus not only the authority and frequency of his sexual activities throughout his whole lifetime, but also his ability and readiness to love are to a large extent already decided at the age of six. This seems to apply even more strongly to women. Some of them decide very early that they want to be mothers when they grow up, while others resolve at the same period to remain virgins or virgin brides forever. In any case, sexual activity in both sexes is continually interfered with by parental opinions, adult precautions, childhood decisions, and social pressures and fears, so that natural urges and cycles are suppressed, exaggerated, distorted, disregarded, or contaminated. The result is that whatever is called "sex" becomes the instrument of gamy behavior.

D

NATURE'S TRICKS

In fact most human relationships (at least 51 percent) are based on trickery and subterfuges, some lively and amusing, and others vicious and sinister. It is only a fortunate few, such as mothers and infants, or true friends and lovers, who are completely straight with each other. Lest you think that I am cynically distorting the situation, let me give you some examples of how Nature herself, through the process of evolution, has set up some gamy transactions. Some of these appear so cynical from the human point of view that it is hard to decide whether to laugh at them as practical jokes or weep over them as tragedies. [6] Yet their final outcome is to ensure the survival of the species. Indeed, human psychological games have a strong survival value also, else their players would soon have become extinct. It does not diminish that value, either for animals or for human beings, to see them as tricks and japes, nor does it increase the value to take them very seriously, as though to say, as some have said: "I am more solemn and indignant, and therefore more righteous than thou."

The simplest example of a biological trick is found in the barnyard hen. Sentimentally regarded, her story is this. After laying her eggs, she sits on them with single-minded devotion. From time to time, with the foresight of a trained midwife, she turns them over so that the nurturing heat of her body will reach all parts of the calcified wombs wherein her brood is growing. Eventually, as a result of her constancy and care, they hatch into healthy chicks. In this way she offers the human race a sterling example of intelligent and resolute motherhood.

What actually happens is this. Due to certain glandular influences, after she has laid a clutch of eggs, her bosom gets overheated. Driven by discomfort, she looks around for some congenial object to cool her ardent breast. She sits on the eggs because they feel cool. But after a while, she begins to warm them up, so she turns them until the cool underside is uppermost, and then gratefully accepts the relief they offer once again.[7] After she has repeated this enough times, the eggs hatch and she finds herself, much to her surprise, faced with a brood of chicks. In effect, she has been tricked into sitting on the eggs, but it works just as well as though she knew what she was doing. In the same way, people who play sex games can be presented with babies who are just as bouncing as those whose parents plan them. It is a comforting illusion to think that the gland-driven hen knows why she is sitting on the eggs, and it is comforting to script-driven people to think that they know why they do things, too. In one case the script (and the deceptions that go with it) is supplied by the genes, in the other by Parental instructions.

Even more wondrous in its innocence is the behavior of a species of male stickleback. Sticklebacks are to fatherhood what hens are to motherhood. The male stickleback is just as devoted to his offspring as the mother hen is to hers. His first job, immediately after copulation, is to grab the fertilized eggs in his mouth, because if mother gets to them before he does, she will simply swallow them like caviar. But gentle father places them in a grassy nest of his own construction. Once he has done that, he is afflicted with a kind of glandular lockjaw, which prevents him from opening his mouth again. He stands guard over the eggs until they hatch, swimming round and round the nest until the fry come out. He continues to protect them until they are old enough to strike out for themselves and venture forth into the seas. During all this time he goes hungry until his jaw loosens up again. This example of fatherly devotion, standing guard over his clutch while slowly starving, has not escaped the notice of our moralists. But the actual situation is probably different. As he gets hungrier and hungrier, the eggs in the nest look more and more appetizing. He stays around them, and also around the small fry when they first hatch, in the hope of making a meal of them, which he is prevented from doing by his locked jaws. So he stands guard over the nest, which has now become a food locker, waiting for his mouth to loosen up. Eventually it does loosen up—right after the newborn babies have swum away. In this case, what looks like fatherly devotion is really frustrated cannibalism.[8]

This particular stickleback comes closer to playing Tantalus than anyone else in real life except a hungry human. But hungry humans are the victims of mere human history, which they themselves can and have changed, while the stickleback is the helpless and unwitting butt of a more cosmic force which he can do nothing about. He is one of the Charlie Chaplins of evolution, funny and sad at the same time as he waits for his portion, only to have it vanish as he reaches out to grasp.

We should note that both the hen and the stickleback have been had. For the hen, the bait is a cool object that promises to soothe her heated breast. That promise is kept, but where did the chicks appear from so suddenly? "Now they tell me!" says the brooding fowl, but she does not learn from this experience and goes through it again and again. For the hungry stickleback, the bait is a promise of food, and that promise is not kept. Where did the fry disappear to just as his mouth broke free? The disappointed daddy can only exclaim, "Why does this always happen to me?"

Higher up on the evolutionary scale, not too far from

the human race, is another of Nature's jokes, this one set up partly by biology and glands, and partly by the players' own choosing. It is a musical comedy put on by seals at breeding season. First come the bulls, who congregate on their favorite rock or piece of shoreline. They stake out their claims with noisy huff and bluff or bloody battles, and the strongest gets the best piece of territory. A month later, the girls drift in—"cows," they are called, which does little justice to their fluency and grace. Each cow makes her choice of a daddy seal or is forced into his harem. Unfortunately, the result is that some of the strong and brave and handsome bulls get more than their fair share, and new fights break out as some of the stags try to kidnap a mermaid or two for themselves. In the end, the weaker bulls are repulsed and have to live as loveless bachelors.

The interesting thing is that the cows are all pregnant from the previous year, and they spend a month or two at the breeding ground watching the fights before they deliver. Soon after they have given birth, they take their babies into the water to teach them how to swim. While they are out there, the winning bulls have to stay home to guard their households and territories. But the bachelors don't have any territories to guard, so they just swim out and join the ladies who are running the nursery school.[9] In this way, in the long run, the bachelors have their fun while the old bulls have to stay home and take care of their real estate interests. So that's the way it is with seals, and many a human novel has been written on less material than that.

The great apes must have read some classics, too. The orangoutans come right out of the *Kama Sutra* and have their sex lives hanging from trees. They can think of more acrobatic positions than a whole regiment of Hindu philosophers. Baboons are more romantic—a cross between seals and something out of Flaubert and Stendhal. Big daddy has the harem, leaving large numbers of young bucks without any chicks. These bachelors lurk on the outskirts of the seraglio, and when big daddy looks the other way, some Pappyo makes a pass at one of his concubines. She is perfectly willing to accommodate Paps, and if big daddy doesn't get wind of this, then nature takes its course and the lovers part in friendly cheer. But if dad come to and catches them at it, the lady pulls a quick double cross. She splits and throws herself on the ground, making indignant noises and pointing at her Romeo—in effect screaming, "This big ape committed rape!" So big daddy says, "He did, did he?" and runs after the boy friend, who leads him a merry chase around the dell. This leaves the harem wide open, including the girl who started the game of Rapo, at which point the other bachelors, who have been watching and waiting in their lurks, close in and make out with whichever females are handy and willing.[10]

The biological effect of these harem scenes among the seals and baboons is to spread the genes. That makes for variety in evolution and thus serves a useful purpose. If each bull hung on to all his chicks like a rooster and nobody else got in, there would be a straight line of inbreeding and both species might go the way of the dinosaurs. But distributing the goodies by these merry bachelor pranks gives cross-breeding and variation. In fact the human race probably originated just because our simian ancestors played Rapo and Let's Make Hay While the Old Man Is on a Rampage, so we shouldn't put down these monkeyshines, because if they weren't there, we mightn't be here either.

Now, all this is probably not amusing to a big daddy baboon, or to a person who thinks baboons should have better morals, or maybe even wear muumuus,[11] but there is really no advantage in the rest of us treating it solemnly or indignantly. As a matter of fact, solemnity and indignation are what cause wars, and if everybody started laughing they would soon stop shooting at each other. In fact, this is a well-established principle of chemical warfare. Each side knows that whoever can drug the other side into laughing will win the war. If the laughing side retaliates, the whole war will come to a stop, which from a military point of view is even worse than one side winning.* So someone who is more solemn and indignant than thou may be more righteous than thou, but he is also going to make more trouble than thou. The fact is that if the seals and baboons burst out laughing at their own gamy antics, the games would be broken up and things would settle down to a more equitable and peaceful way of life, where nobody got insulted or hurt. But until they do start laughing, the games will continue, and it is the same with human beings.

E

WHAT IS A GAME?

Human beings are, after all, just parlayed jellyfish, and many of their "voluntary" actions and responses are no more the result of free will than are those of the lowly animal from which they have ascended. In the lower orders, such as sticklebacks, "nature's games" are automatic responses programmed almost entirely by genes. As we go up the scale to seals and baboons, they are learned more and more by imitation and experience. Human psychological or transactional games are programmed to a large degree by the parents, but this programming is just as decisive as the automatic gene programming of the hen. Man is the freest of all animals, but the life script and the games that go with it still make him the victim of a mighty joke played by the ineluctable forces of evolution. Despite our aspirations and our illusions of awareness, we are not much better off than a poet marching with upturned gaze and outstretched arms toward a rainbow, and slipping on an unseen banana peel or worse beneath his feet.

Let us now analyze the "Hen Game" and the "Stickleback Game." In each case there is a bait that looks to the

---

* I believe this statement is historically defensible: that from a military or at least militant point of view, stopping a war is worse than losing.

player like one thing but is really "intended" for something else. The eggs are there to incubate chickens, but the hen is conned into sitting on them because they are cool. They hook right into what is bothering her, which is a feverish breast. Just as she cools off, nature pulls a switch, and the payoff is a brood of chicks. In the case of the stickleback, he is conned into staying there because the eggs and the fry need protection, but to him they look like caviar. This hooks into his need of the moment, which is hunger. Again nature pulls a switch, and just as his mouth loosens up, his lunch swims away, leaving him with disappointment for his payoff.

In the "Seal Game," the pasha's weakness is territory. The cow, rather than being grateful to him for guarding the ranch, has an affair at nursery school instead. In the "Baboon Game," the pasha's weakness is jealousy. The female plays into that, and then pulls a switch by doing the very thing he is trying to prevent.

Already a pattern for games emerges. There is a bait that has a handy attraction but really serves some other purpose. The bait hooks into a weakness, but after the victim responds there is a switch. The "real purpose" comes into the open and springs a surprise for the ending. For the hen, the fish, and the ape, Nature's joke follows the plan precisely; with the seal it is a little looser, but all the elements are there. It remained for human beings to refine this pattern into a way of life, and to plot out innumerable variations.

In transactional games, the bait, which seems like one thing but is really intended for something else, is called a con. The weakness or need of the other player, which makes him respond to the con, is called a gimmick. The surprise ending is called the switch. The formula for all transactional games, then, is:

$$\text{Con} + \text{Gimmick} = \text{Response} \to \text{Switch} \to \text{Payoff}$$

As an example, consider the following set of transactions between a woman and her doctor, which is very similar to the game called Rapo.

Judith: Do you think I'll ever get better?

Dr. Q: Yes, I think so.

Judith: What makes you think you know everything?

It is clear that Judith's question was phony, and Dr. Q has been conned. In order to understand more clearly what really happened, we can translate it into game language, which is called Martian.

Judith (speaking as a helpless little Child): Help me, O Great One.

Dr. Q (speaking as a powerful Parent): I, powerful one, can help you.

Judith (speaking as a smart-aleck Child): Come off it, Buster.

This Martian translation shows that the con is "Help me, O Great One." Judith is apparently flattering the doctor and asking for help, but she really intends something else. Her con hooks into the doctor's gimmick, which is his humble feeling of power. He responds accordingly, whereupon Judith pulls the switch, and they both get their payoffs. Judith feels smart, which she enjoys, and the unwary doctor feels depressed, which he enjoys for reasons of his own. So Con + Gimmick = Response → Switch → Payoff. The nature of the payoff also makes it clear that Judith is playing Buzz Off, Buster, and the doctor is playing the complementary game of I'm Only Trying to Help You (ITHY).[12] Judith has led him into a trap, so that instead of being thanked for his good intentions, he is put down, which is the standard payoff in the game of ITHY.

Before going further, let us consider what is a "not game." It is easier to understand what is a cat if we also understand what is not a cat. Some people think that any set of transactions which is repeated over and over is a game, but this is not so. There are many such sets which are not games, no matter how often they are repeated, because they will not fit into the formula. Take the following example:

Patient: Do you think I'll ever get better?

Therapist: Yes, I think so.

Patient: Thank you, it's good to hear that again today.

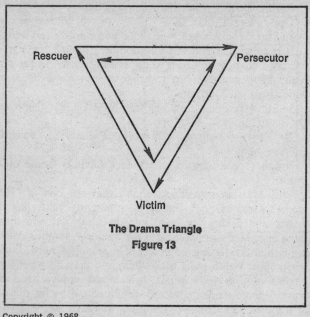

The Drama Triangle
Figure 13

This is a set of straight transactions, with no con and no switch. The woman's question is exactly what it appears to be, and no matter how often she asks for reassurance, it is not a game, as long as there is no con and no switch.

Every game is a little drama, and Dr. Stephen Karpman has devised a very simple way to show this (Figure 13). It is called the Drama or Karpman Triangle.[13] It shows how the game switches each of the players from one role into another, which is the essence of drama in real life as in the theater. It is based on the game of Alcoholic, where the three main roles, victim, persecutor, and rescuer, are most clearly played out. The "victim of alcoholism" is persecuted by "bad" people, but there are "good" people who try to rescue him. The Alcoholic keeps the initiative

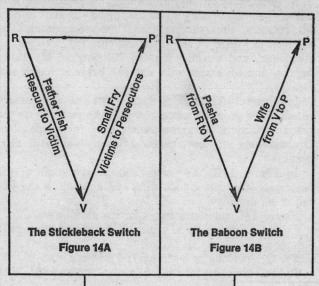

The Stickleback Switch
Figure 14A

R — P
Father Fish
Rescuer to Victim
Small Fry
Victims to Persecutors
V

The Baboon Switch
Figure 14B

R — P
Pasha
from R to V
Wife
from V to P
V

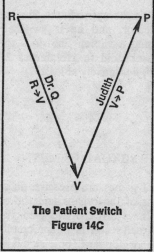

The Patient Switch
Figure 14C

R — P
Dr. Q
R → V
Judith
V → P
V

at all times, since he can turn his nagging, persecuting wife into a victim by beating up on her, or he can start to defy his rescuers, thus turning them into persecutors. The triangles in Figure 14 shows the switches (a) between the stickleback and his offspring (b) between the big daddy baboon and his errant wife and (c) between Judith and Dr. Q.

In Figure 14A, the stickleback starts out as a hungry cannibalistic protector or rescuer with his small fry as the potential victims. After the switch, they "persecute" him by swimming off, leaving him a hungry victim of their prank.

In Figure 14B, the pasha baboon starts off as the rescuer of his "persecuted" wife, and ends up as the victim of her duplicity.

Figure 14C translates into Martian as follows:

Judith (speaking as a victim of emotional troubles): Rescue me.

Dr. Q (speaking as a rescuer): I'll rescue you.

Judith (switching into the role of a persecutor): Wise guy!

Judith now has the upper hand. She switches from victim into persecutor, and he is switched from being a rescuer into being a victim. She does to him just about what her namesake did to Holofernes 2,500 years ago: cuts his head off, figuratively at least.

F

SOME SEXUAL GAMES

Sexual games are exercises in sexual attraction, the exploitations of the organs and the orgasm described in Chapter 3. If we call the two gameplayers Green and Brown, then Green's con is either coming on strong by being seductive or forward, or else playing hard to get. Brown's gimmick or weakness is sexual desire or a need for power over people. The payoff may be either wet or dry. In wet games, the payoff is orgasm (finally), preceded by a lot of insincerity and followed by a lot of mixed feelings on both sides. In dry games, Green's payoff is a feeling of victory, and Brown's is frustration and the reactions to that.*

Nearly all two-handed games are variations of this game of Rapo, and most three-handed ones resemble Let's Make Mother Sorry.

Rapo is played most often by women. It follows the formula $C + G = R \to S \to P$. The Con, C, is a seductive attitude, and the Gimmick, G, is a desire for sex or power. The woman's Con hooks into the man's Gimmick, and he gives the Response, R, which is to come on strong. The woman then pulls the Switch, S, by saying "Yes, but," and after that they both get their Payoffs, P.

Rapo, like all games, is played in three degrees of hardness, each with its own type of Switch and Payoff. First-degree Rapo is a dry game, Flirtation, in which the Switch is "Yes, but we both know that's as far as it goes—for now, at least." The Payoff is mutual good feelings, and possibly hope on one or both sides.

Second-degree Rapo is called Buzz Off, Buster. The Switch is "Yes, but I'm not that kind of a girl even though I led you on." The Payoff for the woman is to gratify her spite, and for the man it is to feel rejected and depressed. In this case the man is playing the complementary game of Kick Me. It is usually a dry game, but in the wet game the man pays for his fun by getting kicked harder.

Third-degree Rapo is a false cry of Rape. The Switch is "Yes, but I'm going to call it rape anyway." The woman's Payoff is justification as well as spite, and the man has his whole life and career on the line waiting to be kicked. It may be played either dry or wet, depending on how mean or sexy the woman is.

The payoffs in any game are not only enjoyed or suffered at the moment but are filed away for future use, very much like grocery store trading stamps. In this man-

---

* As it was said in *Don Quixote*, "She may guess what I would perform in the wet, if I do so much in the dry."

ner of speaking, every script has attached to it a trading-stamp book, and the script cannot be cashed in until the book is filled. For example, here is how it works in Second-degree Rapo.

The "existential" object of this game is to prove that men are no good. What the woman is really saying is "Buzz off, Buster (You're just like the rest of them—no good)." Her Payoff comes not only from seeing the man's discomfort but also from the fact that she can add the picture of another Nogoodnick to her collection. When her stamp book is full of such pictures, she can cash it in for a "Script Payoff." This may be a free suicide, a free homicide, or a license to be an alcoholic or a Lesbian—whatever her script calls for. The man, similarly, who is playing Kick Me, can add another Hurt to his book of Hurts. When he fills the book, he can cash it in for his Script Payoff. This may, for example, be suicide, in accordance with his mother's instructions: "I love you, but some day you'll come to a bad end," which means in effect: "I love you, but drop dead."

More friendly games of Rapo may be played as See What You Made Me Do ("You made me lose my virginity," "You made me get pregnant," "I didn't want to, but you raped me"). These are useful in courtship or marriage for getting additional leverage over the man. Another form is Toy Gun, which is played by people who act grownup but are really precocious children. Some of the slogans in this game are: "I can't really go through with it," "I didn't really mean it," "I wasn't really ready," and "You shouldn't have taken advantage of me." Toy Gun is diagnosed when the player says "not really," which means it wasn't a real gun, or uses the subjunctive, as in "You shouldn't have," which means "You should have known it wasn't real." The original, non-sexual form of Toy Gun is played by amateur or crooked holdup men if they are captured. When they are confronted with the crime, they reply: "I'm not in the wrong, you're in the wrong for being stupid enought to think it was a real gun." This is a classical triangle switch: "I may look like the armed persecutor and you the victim, but it's really quite the opposite; I'm the victim of your stupidity." One of the greatest examples of sexual Toy Gun in literature is Thomas Hardy's *Jude the Obscure,* where the hero said, "I didn't really mean it," but the girl cried, "Rapo!" so he couldn't get away.

Rapo can also be played by men, with slogans such as: "You took me away from my work," "You've worn me out," "I only did it because I was drunk," and "Why didn't you tell me you forgot to take your pill?"

All the above are "Yes But" games, since each of the slogans really contains a Yes But, whether it is said aloud or not. There are also "If Only" types of Rapo. Yes But games are played by tightening up. There is either a refusal beforehand, an interruption during, or an argument afterward, in each case with the implication that the woman (or man) player is or was being unfairly seduced or raped and is uptight about it, which is usually literally true as far as the body muscles are concerned. If Only games are played by hanging loose, with the slogan "If rape is inevitable, you might as well let it happen, or even enjoy it." The player still reserves the right to refuse, interrupt, or reproach, but in this case passively instead of actively. Thus Yes But games tend to be belligerent and argumentative, while If Onlys are merely wistful, whiny, or reproachful. Yes But Rapo says, "It's got to be different!" and in the extreme case ends with an abortion, while If Only says, "I wish it could be different," and ends in a whimper. ("If only you were more considerate [or careful] I wouldn't be pregnant.")

Yes But uses what in grammar are called the declarative or imperative moods, while If Only uses the subjunctive. On the West Coast, expressions like "Not really," "I (you) shouldn't, wouldn't, couldn't," "If only," and "I may look like the persecutor but I'm really the victim," are called the "Berkeley Subjunctive" by some. But there are people everywhere whose games are based on such end runs around reality, and they can often be picked out at social gatherings.

Refrigerator Door and Note Book, the games of interrupted intercourse, can be played either Yes But or If

Only. "Yes but I have to interrupt this rape to check the refrigerator, gas stove, dryer," or "If only my notes were finished, I could rape you with a clear conscience." Telephone Call is a passive form. "There goes the telephone, thank God. Now I can interrupt this rape to answer it." Telephone Call may also be either Yes But or If Only. "Yes but there goes the telephone," or "If only mother would call right now." (He: "How come your mother invariably knows the exact time to call?" She: "How come you invariably start something at the time my mother usually calls?")

Games are played by people who are afraid of intimacy, either in general or with each other. They are a way of getting close to others and having meaningful transactions without the surrender that intimacy requires. Thus sexual games may be either a barrier against love or a step on the way to it—a sort of testing arena. With people who have abandoned hope of loving or being loved, they may become ends in themselves, for whatever advantages can be wrung out of them. These advantages will be discussed in the next section.

Third-degree Rapo is played for the most part by such hopeless people. It is really a three-handed game in which the object is to make the man sorry by telling a third party: mother, father, lawyer, doctor, or police. It is the opposite of actual rape, which is meant to make the woman sorry, especially if she enjoys it in spite of herself—the most dreaded possibility. But the criminal rapist may not care much about the woman; she is just for fun, and once that is over, he is more interested in the chase and the game of Cops and Robbers. If she doesn't report him, he may send an anonymous letter or make an anonymous phone call to the police to stir them up and start the hunt. In extreme cases, he may even write a book about it, which is the best fun of all: playing Cops and Robbers with critics and philosophers, and raping their virgin minds. *How to Rape for Principle and Profit* will even outsell the Marquis de Sade when it comes on the market, because he was too proud to go commercial and hasn't even made it into the high school libraries yet.

One of the most interesting forms of Rape is called Sorry About That. It is also one of the most tragic, since it involves several people, often including broods of children. Here Right says to Left: "If you get a divorce, I'll marry you." So Left gets a divorce. Then Right says, "Sorry, I've changed my mind," leaving Left stranded with no spouse and no lover. The converse is Not Ready Yet: typically, "After the children are grown up I'll get a divorce. Meanwhile let's go ahead." Actually, both Sorry About That and Not Ready Yet are three- or four-handed games, since the spouses of the players know very well what is going on. Here is an example.

Mr. Right, who was divorced, told Mrs. Left that he would marry her if she got a divorce. She did, and then he said Sorry About That, and soon after remarried his former wife. Meanwhile Mr. Left was free to marry his girl friend of many years' standing, which he did. Mrs. Left, who didn't really like men anyway, was thus left free to lead her own life. But all four parties exploited the situation as much as they could: Mr. Left and his former wife with great lamentations about being wronged by each other and by Mr. Right, and Mr. and Mrs. Right with great apologies, embarrassments, and guilt feeling concealing their pleasure at the fast one they pulled on the Lefts. (Thus the Rights were playing a variant of FOOJY —Let's Pull a Fast One on Joey, Joey in this case being Mr. Left.)

The spouses also come through, as reliable spouses do, in Not Ready Yet. Mr. White promised to get a divorce and marry Mrs. Black as soon as his children were grown. She said she was ready to divorce her husband any time White gave the word. But when their last child left for college, Mrs. White came down with arthritis. Then of course Mr. White could not leave her, so the affair with Mrs. Black continued on the old basis. Mrs. White knew which side her bread was buttered on. Eventually, however, she was killed in an automobile accident. Then Mr. White was ready to take advantage of his bargain with Mrs. Black. But the very next week, Mr. Black went for his first physical examination in five years and discovered that he had diabetes. So Mrs. Black could not conscientiously divorce him. She stayed with him and broke off the affair with White.

There is a grim and tragic humor about such games, with their almost unbelievable "coincidences," but as we have already seen, Nature herself has a sense of humor and sets up Hen Games, Stickleback Games, Seal Games, Baboon Games, and many more that are equally unbelievable in their exquisite design.

As we said at the beginning of this section, three-handed sex games usually follow the pattern of Let's Make Mother Sorry, which is described in its most gruesome form in de Sade's *Philosophy in a Bedroom*. There everyone gangs up on the unfortunate mother who values her daughter's virginity. The dissolute band first initiates the daughter into all the possible combinations of persons and orifices, so that her previously treasured virginity becomes a mere trinket in their frenzied orgy. The father then gives them permission to humiliate and torture the mother as they choose, which they proceed to do, with the daughter taking a principal part and disregarding her mother's shrieks and pleadings. And throughout they make it very clear to her why she must suffer: it is because she has tried to prevent her daughter from enjoying sex, and they are making sure that she will never again interfere with the girl's pleasure, and will be sorry beyond belief that she ever did.

In its more commonplace form, the daughter makes mother sorry by becoming promiscuous or getting pregnant, causing a neighborhood scandal and perhaps ending up in Juvenile Hall. The boy serves merely as an instrument, and the girl may never see him again once she has done the job on mother. If she cannot swing it on her own, the daughter may bring another party, called the Connection, into the game. He may simply pimp for her, or he may also get her hooked on drugs to make matters worse. Variations with increasing age are Let's Make Boy Friend (or Girl Friend) Sorry, Let's Make Husband (or Wife) Sorry, or Let's Make Aging Acres Sorry. Nowadays one of the most popular versions is Let's Make Welfare Departments Sorry. Since Welfare Departments are usually against sex, and also (I am reliably informed) against bubble gum, this is played by having lots of sex and many illegitimate children to be supported by State Funds; and spice can be added by chewing lots of bubble gum while all that is going on.

Making Someone Sorry (MSS) will only work if the Patsy, the one who is going to be sorry, is a person or organization that functions in a Parental ego state and plays I'm Only Trying to Help You, or at least After All I've Done for You. Then, the harder the MSS (or MS) players play, the madder the Patsy gets, which is just what the MS players want. The Patsy, like most people in a Parental ego state, works under the illusion that the madder he gets, the more likely he is to break up the game, when exactly the opposite is usually true. The angrier he gets, the more fun it is for the MS players. If the Patsy gets angry enough, they may even feel entitled to shift into the third-degree game and call in a lawyer, which is more fun than a barrel of monkeys. Once the game gets legalized, however, much of the fun goes out of it, and the players settle down into dreary domesticity.

For those who are unable for various reasons to find other players, any of these games may be played as solitaire in the form of skull games or fantasies.

There are many three-handed games in which the third player remains under cover, so that the victim thinks he is in a two-handed game. Prostitution is often of this nature, where the man believes he is dealing with the woman, whereas the show is really being run by the pimp behind the scenes, who has taught the woman the rules and sees that she enforces them. How Was It is a similar game in which the husband is the hidden player. He sends his wife out to pick up a man and have intercourse with him on condition that she tell him all the details afterward for his edification and entertainment. In its most repulsive form, she is instructed to find a virgin. In That Was a Good One, the husband may actually watch from a place of concealment. Sometimes this is reversed, and it is the wife who sends her husband out or panders for him with her girl friends or by picking up a girl in a restaurant. In the third degree of these games, the hidden player suddenly appears on the scene. If he is a professional, he takes the Patsy's money by force or armed robbery, or in the guise of the Angry husband, blackmails him. That is called the Badger Game. It is also played with homosexuals, when the third player may take the part of a Corrupt Cop. In the domestic form, too, there are many opportunities for surprises if the hidden spouse decides to pull a switch. Then the game may end in murder, suicide, lawsuit, or divorce.

In Who Needs You? the wife takes a lover to make her husband jealous, or vice versa. Sometimes none of the three knows that that is the real reason, and sometimes all of them do, and the neighbors as well. Or the spouses may know and the lover may not, in which case he is the Patsy; but few lovers are that stupid. In Steal One, Mr. Right has an affair with Mrs. Left not to get back at his wife, but to make Mr. Left sorry; while Mrs. Left takes on Right not to get back at her husband, but to make Mrs. Right sorry. On the other hand, this may be a competitive game rather than a spiteful one, in which case it is called I Can Do Better Than the Other Guy, Didn't I? These three games—Who Needs You?, Steal One, and I Can Do Better—make great combinations for plays, operas, novels, and short stories, especially since each of the players has it in his power to play counter-games if he wants to.

The Sandwich is a straight three-handed operation, not a game. Everybody is supposed to feel good and nobody is supposed to feel sorry. It may be operated with any assortment of sexes: three men, three women, two men and a woman (*"Ménage à trois"*), or two women and a man ("The Tourist Sandwich"). A has sex with B, then B with C, then C with A. Thus each party has sex twice and watches once. It is turned into a swindle in the Potato Sandwich. Here A and B have sex, with C watching and waiting expectantly for her turn, but her turn never comes and she is left holding the potato. Such swindles are very common in children's sex play. In You Show Me Yours and I'll Show You Mine, played two-handed, A shows his, but B doesn't show hers, or vice versa. Rat Fink Potato Sandwich is a three-handed game where C turns the tables. A shows his and B shows hers, but when C's turn comes she runs home and tells mother instead. Double Potato is a four-handed game. Mr. Green has sex with Mrs. Brown, his wife's best friend. Mrs. Green and Mr. Brown would like to have sex too, but the others arrange it so they can't, and they are left holding the potatoes.

G

WHY PEOPLE PLAY GAMES

The advantages of playing games are nowhere shown more clearly than in sexual games.

(1) Straight sex keeps people happy in a straight way. Sexual games satisfy other needs besides or instead of sex: hate, spite, anger, fear, guilt, shame, and embarrassment, along with hurt and inadequacy, and all the other perverse feelings for which some people have to settle in place of love. By using their sexuality for bait as well as for pleasure, game players can satisfy both their hangups and their desires and thus keep themselves reasonably contented—on their way to lonely Loserville. This is called the internal psychological advantage of a game: it keeps the pressure down and prevents the person from flipping out. Sometimes, however, the pressure gets so great that no amount of such sports can relieve it. De Sade, for example, kept making his mother sorrier and sorrier, until he ended in the asylum at Charenton, leaving a trail of poisoned and beaten girls behind him, much to the admiration of Baudelaire, Swinburne, Dostoevsky, Kafka and others who are touting him even now.

(2) The second advantage, called the external psychological, is that games avoid confrontations, responsibilities, and commitments, a fact overlooked by de Sade's admirers of the existential school. Dry games avoid confrontation with the naked body and the call for action, as well as re-

sponsibility for defloration, impregnation, stimulation, affection, and other consequences of intercourse. Wet games end in orgasm, or at least penetration, but because they are games, avoid commitment to the partner.

(3) While games keep people from getting too close for comfort, they do bring the players together and keep them together, close enough to keep them from being bored with each other but not close enough to be seriously committed. This gives them the illusion of being part of the human race, or at least of heading that way. Actually, games are part of "until" programs. They are supposed to be preludes to the real thing, when the right person will come along. Too often, the right person is Santa Claus's son Prince Charming, or his daughter The Snow Maiden, who will never come, or in many cases, Death, who will. Games are something to do meanwhile, a way of structuring time while waiting in Destiny's bus station, and they have the same relation to real living as waiting in a bus station does to swimming over a tropical reef on a sunny day. They offer a framework for pseudo-intimate socializing indoors or in privacy, and this is called their internal social advantage.

(4) Since games are full of incidents and little dramas, sometimes real and sometimes phony, they give people something to gossip about on the outside, and this is called their external social advantage.

(5) Sexual games satisfy stimulus hunger and recognition hunger as well as structure hunger. For most people, they are more fun than sitting alone (withdrawal), being polite at cocktail parties (rituals), going to work in the morning (activities), or talking about golf (pastimes). They stir up the metabolism, stimulate the glands, make the juices flow, and keep the body, mind, and spirit from slowly shriveling up. Wet games do this better than dry games because in wet games odors, skin thrills, infrared rays, and fluids are exchanged. These invigorating effects are called the biological advantage game.

(6) There is something always interwoven with sex, and that is Being or Self—the answer to the question "Who am I?" This, and the next question, "What am I doing

here?" are existential questions. The existential advantage of sexual games is that they go a long way toward answering these two puzzles, although not as far as real intimacy does. They are particularly useful in answering the third question, which is "Who are all those others?"

Every script is based on these three questions, and the Parental programming usually tries to give ready-made answers. As long as the person follows his script, he will devote himself to proving that those answers are the right ones for him. In a winning script, the résumé may read: "You're a prince, you're here to give yourself to others, and the others are people who need you." Through sexual games, the person will try to confirm again and again that it really is like that: that he really is a prince (or at least a Derby winner), that he really can be generous, and that others (women) really appreciate him. Once he is satisfied that all those things are true, he may be ready to settle down to a more intimate relationship where he is not so concerned with trying to prove something. For a loser the answers might read: "You're a no-good whore, you're here to work your butt off, and the others are bums who will make you do it." In such a case the games will be designed to prove that she really is a whore (even if she struggles against it), that she has to grind her way through life with her pelvic muscles, and that all men will take advantage of her whenever possible. As long as she is in that script, the only intimate she can have is another whore or a pimp. It's a bum rap, but it works the same way a good script does.

Games keep people comfortably happy or familiarly miserable by proving that the Parental programming gives a true picture of their existence and the world around them, and sexual games are carefully planned to do that by picking the right players and setting them up to respond in the required way.

H

THE ILLUSION OF AUTONOMY

In a previous section, I tried to demonstrate that the road to freedom is through laughter, and until he learns that, man will be enslaved, either subservient to his masters or fighting to serve under a new master. The masters know this very well, and that is why they are masters. The last thing they will allow is unseemly laughter. In freer countries, every college has its humor magazine, but there are no such jokes in slave-holding nations like Nazi Germany or Arabia. Authority cannot be killed by force, for wherever one head is cut off, another springs up in its place. It can only be laughed away, as Sun Tzu knew when he founded the science of military discipline.[14] He first demonstrated this to the Emperor by using girls from the harem, but they giggled when he gave his orders. He knew that at long as they were laughing, discipline wouldn't work. So he stopped their laughing by executing two of them, and after that the rest did as they were told —solemnly and indignantly. Conversely, no comedian has ever been the head of a state for very long; the people might stand it, but he couldn't.

Man is born free, but one of the first things he learns is to do as he is told, and he spends the rest of his life doing that. Thus his first enslavement is to his parents. He follows their instructions forevermore, retaining only in some cases the right to choose his own methods and consoling himself with an illusion of autonomy. If they want to raise him to feel inadequate, they can start by requiring him to produce square bowel movements and refusing to be satisfied with anything less. Whatever condition they impose on him he will spend the rest of his life trying to meet, and they can let him know from the beginning that he is not supposed to succeed. In that way he will end up with a good collection of inadequacies to cash in according to their instructions. If he has a streak of independence, he may change the subject and geometry of his efforts, but seldom its essence. He may shift his striving from square bowel movements to pear-shaped orgasms, but he will still make sure that he ends up feeling inadequate. If, on the other hand, they raise him to succeed, then he will do that, using whatever methods he has to to hew his ends to the shape required by this destiny.

In order to break away from such script programs, he must stop and think. But he cannot think about his programming unless he first gives up the illusion of autonomy. He must realize that he has not been up to now the free agent he likes to imagine he is, but rather the puppet of some Destiny from generations ago. Few people have the courage or the elasticity to turn around and stare down the monkeys on their backs, and the older they get, the stiffer their necks become.

This programming starts at the very bottom, at the organs that lie below the mystically curled omphalos or belly button where the twisted silver cord was once attached from mother's womb. Consider the sergeant's classical greeting to the new recruits when they arrive at basic training. The true translation of this is even more anatomical than the anatomical sergeant dreams of. What he says is (and this is true of WAC sergeants too): "Your soul belongs to mother, but your ass belongs to me." This can be truly stated as "The inside of your pelvis belongs to mother, but the outside belongs to me." The pelvic organs of almost every human being belong to mother—and for the lucky ones it goes no further than that. In other cases she controls the stomach and the brain as well. Actually, the Army gets only the leftovers—the outside parts, for the external muscles are all that the Army really needs. As long as soldiers follow orders, the rest is of interest only to the Medical Corps.

The important instructions in the script remain unchanged; only the method and the object are permitted to vary. "Be devoted to your leader," says the Nazi father, and the son devotes himself either to his Fascist leader, or

to his leader in Christianity or in Communism, with equal
fervor. The clergyman saves souls in his Sunday sermons,
and his daughter sallies forth to save them singing folk-
songs with her guitar. The father is a streetsweeper and
the son becomes a medical parasitologist, each in his own
way cleaning up the offal that causes disease. The daughter
of the good-natured prostitute grows up to be a nurse,
and comforts the afflicted in a more sanitary way.

These similarities and differences correspond to what
biologists call genotype and phenotype. All dogs have
doggy genes, and cannot undertake to be anything but dogs;
but each dog can be a dog in his own way. The basic
instructions of the parents are like genes: the offspring
cannot undertake to do anything but follow them, but
each can follow them in his or her own way. This does
not mean that brothers and sisters will be alike, for each
sibling may and usually does receive different instructions,
since each may be raised to play a different role in the
scripts of the parents. For example, Cinderella had instructions to be a winner, while her stepsisters were raised
to lose, and they all followed their Parental programming.
Cinderella with her sweet and winning nature found her
own way of coming out on top. It was not the way her
parents visualized it perhaps, or maybe it was, but she
came through. Her stepsisters were taught to grump and
sulk to make sure that nobody would want them except
the two jerks who were ordered to marry them by Cinderella's prince.

This freedom to select methods for arriving at the
predetermined goal helps to support the illusion of free
choice or autonomy. That illusion is most clearly illustrated
by the man who had his brain stimulated by an electrode
during an operation. Since the stimulated area was the one
which controlled his right arm, he raised the arm. When
the operator asked him why he moved it, he replied: "Because I wanted to." This is the same thing that goes on all
the time in daily life. Each person follows the Parental
instructions in important matters, but by choosing his own
time and place, maintains the illusion that he is making

his own decisions freely and that his behavior is the result of free will. Both of these aspects are built in. It is built in that the Parental instructions will work like an electrode, so that the person will end up following them almost automatically with little or no chance to decide for himself. It is also built in that he will think he is exercising free will. This can only be accomplished if he forgets the Parental instructions and does not remember hearing them. The moment he does remember, he may realize that it is they who have been deciding his feelings, behavior, and responses. Only by such a realization can he free himself to use his own decisions.

For some people, of course, and at some levels with everyone, there is no illusion of autonomy, and the person is quite aware that his behavior is determined by what his parents told him at an early age. This is the case, for example, with many virgins and frigid women who state quite openly that they are so because that is how their parents told them to be. In a way they are better off than those who pretend otherwise. And the study of parental injunctions was started by a gambler who wanted to be cured and who said to the therapist: "Don't tell me not to gamble. That won't work. What I need is permission not to lose." He had suddenly become aware that he lost because he was ordered to lose. What he needed was not more instructions, such as "Why don't you stop gambling?" but permission to disregard the instructions he had received in childhood.

Thus lechery, sadism, homosexuality, promiscuity, sexual games, and other biologically inappropriate forms of sexual activity are programmed in by the parents in most cases. But the person says, "I do it that way because I want to." This is true in a roundabout way. He does it that way because he was so instructed, and he wants to obey the instructions because he is afraid not to. He turns this necessity into a virtue by claiming free will, which might fool Baudelaire, but it need not fool others. If and when he recalls the instructions, and finds out how the electrode was implanted in his brain, he may be ready to give up his parental programming and the illusions that go with it and perhaps become really free.

It is important to understand that what we are talking about here is biology and not youth movements, which in any case are carried on by programmed youths. Parental programming is not the "fault" of parents—since they are only passing on the programming they got from their parents—any more than the physical appearance of their offspring is their "fault," since they are only passing on the genes they got from their ancestors. But the brain chemicals involved in script programming are easier to change than the gene chemicals that determine physical appearance. Therefore a parent who wants to do the best for his children should find out what his own script is and then decide whether he wants to pass it on to them. If he decides not to, then he should find out how to change it, to grow princes where there were frogs before. This is not easy to do. It is even harder than trying to give oneself a haircut. It usually requires help of a script analyst, but that doesn't always work either. It is even more discouraging to think that if he does pass it on, it will probably be carried through to his grandchildren. This script transmission is the basis for the old saying "To make a lady, start with the grandmother," and it also explains why the Civil War is not over yet, and why it will take another hundred years for the angry scripts of nowadays to cool into a decent way of living. Now is the time to start programming the parents of the ladies and gentlemen of the next century. If we want things to be warm and straight later, we've got to stop being cold and crooked now.

NOTES AND REFERENCES

1. Liddell and Scott give *Odyssey* 4.221 seq.; Theophrastus, H. P. 9.15.I; Plutarch 2. 614 C; Anthologia Palatina 9.525, 13; and Protag. (presumably Protagoras) ap Plutarchus 2.118

E. Nepenthe is best known nowadays as the name of a restaurant in Big Sur, California. Oxford gives *"Med.* A drink possessing sedative properties (1681), and the plant supposed to supply the drug (1623)." *Nepenthes* is used now only for a genus of carnivorous pitcher plants, but these are not used as materia medica; at least they are not listed in pharmacology texts, nor in the U.S. Pharmacopoeia, nor in the U.S. Dispensatory as far back as 1866, nor even in Culpeper's *Complete Herbal.* Nevertheless, they are of some interest from an evolutionary point of view if we remember that *Homo sapiens* is very likely descended from monkeylike tarsiers who fed on insects. *Tarsius spectrum* likes to rob pitcher plants of their insect prey. Hence, according to the late Professor Francis E. Lloyd (Encyclopaedia Britannica), *Nepenthes bicalcarata* has developed sharp hooks' "as an adaptation for catching the tarsier if he tries this game" on that species. This ancient battle between tarsiers and pitcher plants no doubt played a modest part in the evolution of the human race, as it did in the genetic selection of certain Nepenthes.

For those who like gossip, I might add that the owner of Nepenthe, William Fasset, is a great and genial poker player, and the father of several remarkable children. Professor Lloyd taught botany at McGill and from him I learned what little I know of the subject. I once extrapolated his personality into a story I wrote under a pen name, which was published in the old *Adelphi* for August, 1933 ("An Old Man," by Lennard Gandalac). He fathered two sons, one celebrated for his researches in neurology, and the other for the beauty of his children and the number and excellence of his grandchildren. As for tarsiers, although I freely acknowledge them as my many-greats grandparents. I have never had the pleasure of a personal acquaintance with one. Concerning pitcher plants, I do not understand their ways at all. They have their ideas of what a flower should be, and I have mine, but I bear them no ill will.

2. The following figures from the *World Almanac,* 1968, show suicide rates for males per 100,000 for 1962–63 according to the World Health Organization: Hungary, 35.5; Austria, 29.5; U.S. White, 18.0; U.S. Nonwhite, 9.6; Poland, 16.6.

The corresponding rates for females are 14.1, 11.1, 6.7, 2.7, and 3.5. (In 1966–67, West Berlin was far, far ahead of the rest of the world both in suicide rate [40.9] and in general mortality rate [1798.8], exceeding in each even the most backward countries of Africa and Arabia. *United Nations Demographic Yearbook*, 1968.)

3. Mao Tse-tung: *On Art and Literature.* China Books & Periodicals, San Francisco, 1960.

4. Cf. Young, D.: "The Frog Game." *Transactional Analysis Bulletin* 5:156, July, 1966. Also Berne, E.: *Principles of Group Treatment.* Oxford University Press, New York, 1966, and Grove Press, New York, 1968.

5. That paraphrases Herrick's version (c. 1630). Other versions are: "Let us crown ourselves with rosebuds, before they be withered" *(Wisdom of Solomon,* 2:8). "Gather ye therefore roses with great glee, sweet girls, or ere their perfume pass away" (Angelo Polizeano, "A Ballata," c. 1490, trans. by J. A. Symonds). "Gather the Rose of love, whilst yet is time" (Spenser, *Faerie Queene,* I, 12, c. 1590).

As for us passing through time, rather than vice versa, this idea was most neatly expressed by Ronsard in his poem "Le temps s'en va," later elaborated by Austin Dobson in *his* poem "The Paradox of Time."

6. Lorenz discusses this dilemma in *King Solomon's Ring* (op. cit.). He has one chapter on "Laughing at Animals" and another on "Pitying Animals."

7. This cynical interpretation of brooding behavior is adapted from Ruth Crosby Noble: *The Nature of the Beast* (Doubleday, Doran and Company, New York, 1945, pp. 161 f.), but it arouses considerable feeling among those who love poultry. In my efforts to verify it among textbooks and teachers of poultry science, I received categorial and sometimes heated denials. "That . . . is pure imagination. It is not to cool her breast." Poultrymen much prefer to hypostatize an anthropomorphic concept of gallinaceous brooding. "If the weather is hot, the hen may stand over the nest *to shade* the eggs. If the weather is cold, the bird nestles down *to keep* them warm. When a hen becomes 'broody,' you can't keep her from setting on eggs or potatoes or smooth stones" (teleological italics mine). But none of this is inconsistent

with the view set forth by Noble. Thus, opinion is divided between an altruistic bird who wants to keep her eggs comfortable and a less estimable hen who merely wants to cool herself off. Noble cites in support of the icebag theory the fact that if the breast of an incubating bird is immersed in cold water, thus counteracting the abnormal heat, the bird will no longer be interested in brooding. But as she also notes, birds do recognize and prefer their own eggs to those of other birds. So there may be something more to it than mere poulticing.

8. I came across an account of this unusual stickleback behavior some years ago and made some notes, but neglected to record the source. Since then I have hunted for it assiduously but vainly. I have talked to and written to several fish men, but they were all skeptical, including Desmond Morris, who is a stickleback man of many years' standing. With the pride of a poultryman, he replied, "My sticklebacks never, to my knowledge, developed 'lockjaw.' "

9. Wendt, Herbert: *The Sex Life of Animals.* Simon and Schuster, New York, 1965; Chapter 7. See also Le Boeuf, B. J., and Peterson, R. S.: "Social Status and Mating Activity in Elephant Seals." *Science* 163:91-93, January 3, 1969.

10. Wendt, Herbert: *Ibid.* For the most careful study to date of baboon harems, see Hans Kummer: *The Social Organization of Hamadryas Baboons.* University of Chicago Press, Chicago, 1968.

11. The idea of putting muumuus on apes is no more original than the proposal of SINA, the Society for Indecency to Naked Animals, to put panties on pets, half-slips on cows, and Bermuda shorts on horses. Started as a hoax, with the slogan "Decency Today Means Morality Tomorrow," SINA hoped to expose some aspects of sexual hypocrisy through satire, but failed because millions of people took their crusade seriously. For an account of the barely credible results, see: *The Great American Hoax,* by Alan Abel. Trident Press, New York, 1966. For additional information about how violently some "pet-lovers" feel about "immorality" in animals, see: *Petishism,* by Kathleen Szasz. Holt, Rinehart and Winston, New York, 1969.

12. Berne, E.: *Games People Play.*

13. Karpman, S.: "Fairly Tales and Script Drama Analysis." *Transactional Analysis Bulletin* 7:39-43, April 1968.

14. Sun Tzu: *The Art of War,* translated by Lionel Giles, *in* Phillips, T. R. (ed.): *Roots of Strategy.* Military Service Publishing Company, Harrisburg, Pa., 1940.

6

SEX AND WELL-BEING OR PREVENTIVE INTIMACY

A

INTRODUCTION

It is very difficult to decide on cause and effect in human behavior because most psychological theories are manufactured to explain what happened last time. But this does not prove anything unless the same explanation can be used to predict what will happen next time. If the explanation works for the future as well as it does for the past, then very likely it does say something worth saying about human nature. A theory that works for the future as well as for the past may be called a hard theory, while one that works for the past but not the future is a soft theory. Thus the theories of psychoanalysis and transactional analysis, properly used by properly trained people, can not only explain the previous behavior of a person, but can also foretell what he will do in the years to come; so these are hard theories. People who use soft theories, such as sociologists, generally say that they cannot predict the future because circumstances change, and that is very true. So a hard theory of human behavior is one that deals with hard facts, aspects that remain unchanging through the ages, while a soft theory deals with soft facts, those that are easily changed by external circumstances.

Soft theories are not as powerful as hard theories because there is no reliable way to check them and they do not indicate remedies. Usually they deal with Awfuls, items that can be traded like stamps between people who play Ain't It Awful, but don't know what to do with the Awfuls they collect except compare them with other collections. For example, comparing the frequency of sexual horse-whipping among college graduates versus grade school graduates does nothing to stop it, if it should be stopped, but it makes an interesting Awful to talk about, even though there is no reliable way to check the figures. Actually, such a study should be of interest mainly to manufacturers of horsewhips. Most people who want to read about such things are like the little old lady at the zoo who asked the guard whether the hippopotamus was a male or a female, to which the man replied: "Madam, that should be of interest only to another hippopotamus."*

Soft theories, which are usually based on the question "How many people do so and so?" are of value to administrators, politicians, economists, and businessmen. Hard theories, which say, "Human beings are so constructed that unless something special prevents it, they will invariably do such and such," are much more useful to scientists. Soft theories are made for the most part by dependent thinkers, thinkers who are thinking for the benefit of someone else. Hard theories are made by independent thinkers, who like to discover things for the sake of discovery. In the long run, however, they prove more useful than soft theories do. So in the sections that follow, we will try to stick to hard facts and avoid soft facts whenever possible.

---

* EW: Do you know any jokes in which the woman doesn't end up looking stupid?

EB: Yes. See page 65 (Chapter 3, section B).

B

PHYSICAL CONTACT AND PHYSICAL HEALTH

If baby rats are not handled by their mothers or by human hands, they do not develop as well as they should, and many of them get sick and die. The same applies to human babies who are not picked up. They need to be held and patted.[1] In fact any human being who is not stroked with cheerful words or gentle hands will shrivel up and die inside. Dr. Harry Harlow and his friends studied baby monkeys who were taken from their mothers at birth and given a terry-cloth towel to rub up against instead.[2] They proved that monkey babies are designed by nature for physical contact with others of their kind. If they are deprived of that, when they grow up they cannot have sexual relations the way other monkeys do, and if one does get pregnant, her baby is likely to die because she will neglect or mistreat it. Some human parents do that too: ignore their babies or beat them up, even injure or kill them. Such parents were usually victims themselves as children, sons and daughters of non-touching shells of humanity, or of sad and angry sacks.[3] We can say all this briefly as follows: If any person is not stroked by his own kind, his mind shrivels and his humanity dries out.

There are two groups of people who suffer this way. In every city there are thousands of girls who go to work every morning and travel home each night to spend nearly all of their spare time alone in their rooms or apartments, with nothing to do and no one to talk to or fight with. In a typical case, Sally has no dates; she may have a few friends who are not too enthusiastic about her; they invite her to dinner once every two months to meet a young lawyer from Kansas or Maine. In between, she may try going to movies or concerts, but she goes alone and lives the life of a loner. After a while she loses interest in cooking for herself, and eventually in eating. Then her skin begins to go bad and her legs start to shrink from lack of nourishment. Her muscles get weak and her stomach sags. It is not the lack of social activity that causes these bad effects, but it is the lack of social activity which leads to her loss of appetite, and that is what causes the body decay. Between her lack of social stimulation and her physical weakness, she gets depressed and loses her drive and energy. This may lead her to take drugs. Often these are amphetamines or pep pills, which further depress her appetite and make things worse.

In her case, as in most cases, drugs are instead of people, and the circle will spiral downhill and can only be turned up by social contacts. Thus she starts out living a lonely life, and through loss of appetite and other things that happen to loners, she ends up in bad physical shape. The end result may be just as bad if she overeats instead of losing her appetite. In one case she uses drugs instead of people and in the other food instead of people. In both cases, she becomes less and less attractive and less likely to find someone who will supply the recognition and stroking she needs.

Another group that suffer in the same way are older men who lead lonely lives, such as night watchmen who live in cheap hotels. Many of them end up in an equally sad condition, which may be called night watchman's disease. They too, from lack of social life, lose interest in eating. There is no one to cook for them and no one for them to cook for. Their bodies shrivel from bad nutrition and lack of vitamins, and resistance to pneumonia and other infections is lowered. Their brains may shrivel, too, causing slow thinking, confusion, and sometimes delirium.

Lobar pneumonia itself is a good example of how important social contact is. Nowadays this ancient lung disease can usually be conquered with penicillin and similar medications. But before those remedies were devised, it had a very high death rate, something like 33 percent. City hospitals used to be full of lonely people suffering from pneumonia in the middle of winter. Often there were so many of them that they filled up all the beds on the wards and the overflow lay on mattresses in the corridors, and it was very difficult to save them all from dying. Many hospitals internes in those days were convinced that patients who just lay there, with no one from outside caring about them, had a higher death rate than those who had visitors.[4] Whether this lowered resistance was due simply to the lack of contact or to the loner's diseases (malnutrition and alcoholism) which result from that, the evidence is that people-hunger meant the difference between life and death, and a cool hand on the brow or a friendly squeeze was a powerful aid to the serum that was being injected. This is a specific example of something which also applies to many less common diseases as well, especially to the condition known as marasmus in infants.

Social and physical contacts, or lack of them, also affect the way people tread the world they live in. An experienced observer can pick out loners just by the way they walk down the street and look at other people and the things around them. Nor does this have to do with "extraverts" and "introverts." Many extraverts are really loners and many introverts can form lasting and intimate relationships. Sometimes a loner can be diagnosed by the way he talks on the telephone. My friend Dr. Horseley, for example, says that he can tell almost instantly, when a strange psychiatrist calls him, whether this colleague does group treatment or confines his practice to individual therapy, sometimes just by the way the caller says Hello, or in other cases after the first two or three sentences.

The examples given above are meant to show that physical contact is necessary to produce healthy, vigorous and alert children, and that social contact is necessary in later life to sustain these qualities. Infection and malnutrition are the great killers of the world, and physical contact helps to prevent and conquer both if there is any choice in the matter. The friendly touch of a human hand can spread its benevolent influence to every part of the body and awaken the desire to fight and eat and live. Even where disease and starvation seem beyond help, everybody knows what help means. It means the friendly approach of another human being bearing balms and medication and boxes of food. Once recovery begins, baskets decorated with loving care are even better.

C

THE SIX HUNGERS

Just as the human body has a hunger for food and vitamins and will waste away without them, so the nervous system has a hunger for sensations and will fall apart if they are taken away. This is well known to the political police of many countries, and also to prisoners who have been put in solitary confinement. It was a great surprise when this fact first came to light during the Trotskyite trials in Russia in the 1930's. Most people thought that the Trotskyites who "confessed" to crimes must have been severely tortured to make them swear to falsehoods. But all that is necessary to make a person "confess" to almost anything is to keep him in solitary confinement long enough, either with a bright light that is always lit or in complete darkness. Monotony is the key word: no human contact, no change in surroundings (not even sunrise and sunset), and the same food from the same dreary tubs in the same grim bowls every day. Under such conditions, the nervous system decays and the mind with it. The craving for sensations grows so great that the victim will do almost anything merely for a cigarette or a few words with another human being, no matter how evil.

A baby who is not picked up is in a similar plight. He lies in his prison crib hour after hour, day after day, with no change or stimulation except when he is fed, and this gradually leads to physical and mental breakdown. This happens because there is a special part of the brain, the "arousal system," that must be stimulated regularly to maintain good health.[5] If it is not stimulated, deterioration results. This can be seen in a mild degree in "sensory deprivation experiments," where people are hired merely to stay in a cell with their eyes covered to prevent touching. Few can stand more than forty-eight hours of this, and many of them begin to have hallucinations and delusions, very much as they might under the influence of a drug.[6]

Most people have a hunger for human contact, at least of sight and sound, and in most cases also for touch or stroking. Again we see that such contact may actually make the difference between physical and mental health or breakdown, and even between life and death.

Of all the forms of sensation, the one preferred by most human beings is contact with another human skin. This provides not only touch, but also warmth or heat of a special kind. The human skin is the best known emitter and absorber of infrared rays.[7] In fact people who study infrared rays use human skin as a standard, just as diamonds are used as a standard for hardness. Infrared rays are heat waves, and can easily be photographed with special film, or "seen" with special lenses such as snipers use to see enemy soldiers in the dark. The infrared rays given off by the human body have a certain wavelength—just the right wavelength to have the best possible effect on other human skins. That is why babies respond so well to physical contact with their mothers, and why mothers in turn love to feel the warmth of their infants. There is something close to sexual pleasure in all this, and part of sexual pleasure is to receive infrared rays from another person. Actually, any living thing with a temperature of 98.6 degrees probably gives off the right infrared rays, and that is one reason why anything with a temperature of 98.6 degrees—an animal, a child, or a person of the same sex, as well as a person of the opposite sex—can become a sexual object under certain conditions.

The human nervous system is so constructed that verbal recognition can partly take the place of physical contact or stroking. That means that having people say Hello to you can keep your spinal cord from shriveling up almost as well as physical stroking, but it is never quite as satisfactory, and the hunger for physical stroking is still there, although it may be repressed. It is interesting to observe that in this country some bottle-fed babies never feel their mother's skin directly, but ever and always only through her clothes. The warmth does get through, but probably not as pleasantly as from the bare skin. Thus for the baby it is something like the old saying about "taking a bath with your socks on," only in this case he takes his infrared bath with his mother's blouse on.

There is even more specialization than that. The baby not only wants the warmth of another body next to his, but above all he wants his mouth stroked, and nursing mothers like to have their breast stroked by the baby's mouth. When the nursing period is over, these desires may subside in the baby until after puberty, but then there is hunger again for closer contact of certain parts of the body, and these become grownup sexual cravings.

If we take all these things together, we can call them hungers, and sex is the most exciting way to satisfy all of them at once. (A) Stimulus hunger, for sensory stimulation of sight and sound and touch, with smell and taste as a bonus for gourmets. (B) Recognition hunger, for a special kind of warmth and contact in deeds or words. (C) Contact hunger for physical stroking, although some people settle for pain, or even come to prefer it. (D) Sexual hunger, to penetrate and be penetrated, which gratifies the other hungers while it happens.

Thus sex hunger may start anywhere along the line. A sex-hungry girl who lives as a loner in a little room with not even a picture on the wall will get none of the gratifications. In large cities, there are a certain number who live this way by choice. They cannot afford the slightest luxury or relaxation because they are in therapy. They keep enough of their earnings for low-grade food and gas and oil and give all the rest to their therapists while they slowly "make progress" year after year to a melancholy menopause. Others have hobbies that keep their senses awake (A), but recognition, contact and penetration with love are out of their reach. Still other men and women have sensory stimulation (A) and recognition (B) at work or at play, but veer away from contact or penetration, perhaps in favor of "causes" instead. These are the ones who surprise people when they commit sexual betrayals or crimes, nearly always of a cowardly nature. The half-virgins of both sexes like stimulation (A), recognition (B), and contact (C), but avoid penetration—from fear or on questionable principles which do not keep them from being crudely seductive and teasing until the last moment, when they cry "Rapo! I've scored again," and the crestfallen partner goes home to a lonely bed. People who find their proper mates can have all the hungers satisfied—(A), (B), (C), and (D).

One of the great problems in life is how to structure one's time, and this gives rise to a fifth kind of hunger. There are 24 hours each day, 168 hours a week, 52 weeks every year, and 50 or 100 years to look forward to. All this time has to be filled or "structured." Structure-hunger is more widespread and almost as damaging as malnutrition or malaria. When it becomes acute, it turns into incident-hunger, which causes many people to get into trouble and make trouble just to relieve their boredom,[8] and that is one reason why they play hard and destructive games. (Another is so that they won't have time to stop and think.) This sixth hunger, incident-hunger, was far better understood by old-time poets, philosophers, and men of action than it is by modern social scientists, since it is poor fodder for either computers or governments grants. Isaac Watts said it: "Satan finds some mischief still for idle hands to do." Military officers, sea captains, and others skilled in authority have not only always understood it as well as Watts and Kierkegaard[9] did, but they also know what to do about it: "Keep the troops busy (no matter how) or they'll lose their morale and their respect for you to boot."

Even people with the strongest drive occasionally feel acute structure-hunger, and it is chronic for most of the world with their over-and-over lives and repeating scripts. Long-term structuring is the least pressing and is taken care of by choosing a career. Shorter periods can be filled in by setting up something to look forward to:

graduation, next vacation, good promotion, recreation. The most difficult problem for most people is what to do right now or today, if there is leisure or unstructured time. There must be somebody to do something with, or alternatively, some interesting way to pass the time by ignoring other people: meditation, masturbation, defecation, and intoxication are all good ways to loaf and invite your soul—to shrivel up, unless you are one of the great ones who can profit from such activities.

But if you stop to think, you yourself can create the very people who will keep you busy all the time without any initiative on your part, and manufacture incidents galore. They will see to it that you have enough to do today and tomorrow, and 168 hours this week and 52 weeks next year, and you will feel in the long run, if you have any goodwill at all about it, that every minute of it was worthwhile. All you need to do to acquire these built-in time structures is have sex once a year on the right day according to the calendar, with a willing mate. Babies are the greatest remedies for structure- and incident-hunger ever devised.

D

SEX AND ETHICS

I have tried to give some hard facts that should impress hardheaded as well as softhearted people. Physical contact is necessary for physical development and health, and is often life-saving. It is also necessary for mental development and health, and is often sanity-saving. And sexual contact is the simplest, pleasantest, most constructive, and most satisfying way of appeasing the six basic hungers of the human mind (or nervous system, if you wish). There is therefore no good reason (although there are several bad ones) why other people should meddle with sexual activities between consenting grownups, and such meddling is a poor basis for an ethical system. Its result in this country has been that sex is largely illegal, and violence is not. Sex is banned from the newsstand in most places where murder is freely sold, and from television where violence is freely seen: not only violence between consenting adults, as in Westerns, but unprovoked mayhem that sells cancer sticks and soap. An ardent teenager can learn from every corner store and in any living room new and better ways of charnel killing or wounding, but there is no one to tell him new and better ways of carnal love.

It is the other way round in places like Denmark, where anyone over twelve, I am told, can watch a sexy movie, but no one under sixteen can watch a violent one. So in this country children are allowed to see hate but not love, while in Denmark it is vice versa. Of course decent children with decent parents in both countries will behave decently anyway, and I am only talking about where the official sanctions or sanctimonies lie.

Somewhere there has to be a simple and sensible system of values, and I propose one that is not only simple, but also I think makes some sort of sense. Furthermore, it can be judged from one set of pretty reliable figures, so that different countries can be compared, and barroom arguments can be settled with a wet thumb in the right book. It is based on the single idea that if anything in life is significant and worthwhile, it is the love between mother and child. It assumes that mothers (and fathers and uncles and grandparents too) want their babies to live. Although this is not always so, it is as hard a fact as anything that can be said about human desires. The proposed ethical system is therefore based on one item which comes out of that. Here is my proposition. The goodness or badness of any society shall henceforth be judged by its infant mortality rate. If that is low, the society is good; if it is high, the society is bad. In between there are gray areas for those who don't like black and white. (The infant mortality rate is the number of deaths of children under one year per 1,000 live births.)[10] This mortality rate is really a matter of national management and is decided by the prejudices of each government and where it puts its money (or as it is usually said in the words of the people in charge and their donzels, by political and economic policy). We therefore say our ethic again to take account of that. We consider the total infant mortality rate from all causes (disease, starvation, ignorance, and murder, whether in peace or war), in all the territories controlled by a government. If that rate is low, the system is a good one; if it is high, it is bad. The reason I am down on India, for example, is that while some of its people sit around sucking their psyches and kowtowing to their cows, babies are dying like flies around them. Therefore that system is a bad one.* By using this approach, all problems of sexual ethics can be solved by asking only one question: which decision will result in fewer deaths among babies born alive? It is not a question of making babies; almost anybody can do that. The real test is to keep them going after their first cry, and that takes careful thought, good governing, and decent concern for things that count. It is doubtful that it is going to be taken care of by what Amaryllis calls "smut-smellers" and "shootniks."

E

SEX AND ESTHETICS

It is also possible to set up a "one-item esthetic system" by proposing that nice pictures should have good frames and that art galleries should be clean and well built. This does away with the error that a beautiful inside excuses an ugly exterior, with its final challenge that Truth and Beauty should crouch in the garbage can

---

* Note that this is a reductive system, which simply states that *for whatever reasons,* a system works well or badly. There may be *all kinds* of reasons, but the ailing infant and his mother are not likely to be impressed by them.

and we should all go and look for them there. Picture
frames can be disdained as merely gilded squares, and
so can the people who built art galleries, but it takes both
to set off Leonardo and Renoir to best advantage. True,
the paintings can exist without them, but enjoyment goes
beyond mere existence, and a good light is better than
a dark alley to see how a man handles his palette. No
painting can even exist in darkness, if existence means
to live in the world of people. (This is Bishop Berkeley's
paradox again.)

This principle can be applied to human behavior; for
example, juvenile delinquency, whatever that includes.
In some cases, delinquency is a matter of morality if it
increases or threatens to increase the infant mortality rate.
But in other cases it is merely unpretty, and reprehensible because of that. Evil is bad because it makes
messes. This approach appeals to many of the "juveniles"
themselves. They may be more willing to listen if you
say that what they do is not pretty than if you say that
it is wicked. The wickedness may not be visible, and
may in fact be just a figment to the growing mind,
while bloody litter on the sidewalk is very real, and is
there for all to see.

Having now set up an ethical principle and an esthetic
principle, both based on visible results, we are ready to
consider whether sexual intimacy, which is good for the
body beautiful, is less good for the body politic. Intimate couples usually love and care for children and respond to beauty in themselves and their surroundings.
In this way they help decrease the infant mortality rate,
which is moral (according to our proposed ethical system), and they also want to keep things beautiful, which
is esthetic. Thus they contribute to both the health and
the beauty of society at large. And beyond that, since
they receive so much, they can give more. Being game
free, they do not try to exploit anyone, prove anything,
or make anybody sorry, and having each other in natural
closeness, they do not need alcohol or other chemicals that
may damage children's minds or bodies and leave unpretty sights for them to see. All this shows, I hope, that

from both the moral and the esthetic points of view, sexual intimacy is the most desirable way for society as for the individual, for satisfying the yearnings of the human soul and mind. We have only to beware of pseudo-intimacy, which masks anger, fear, and hurt and guilt with sweet words, or drowns them in acids and alcohols, only to have them surface the next morning or the next year to spread their fetid vapors through the house.

Thus marriage, in common or in canon law, can become a true sacrament if it is not bruised or abused by clumsy handling and phony dandling, or by the threats and exhortations of muddling fiddlers, moral meddlers, and venal peddlers.

F

SEX AND INTIMACY

I have talked above about sexual intimacy because intimacy without sex, outside the family, is rare. Every couple has sexual desires, which they will discover if they are intimate in any other way; if they do not reveal them, they are withholding that much of themselves, so that the intimacy is not complete. Some couples can have partial intimacy while looking forward to its fulfillment later; for example, engaged couples waiting for the marriage bed. Others seem unlikely candidates, such as a homosexual man and a homosexual woman; for a long time such a pair may confine themselves to talking about important intimate subjects, such as their hopes, their fears, and their telephone bills. But if they keep it up, they too are likely sooner or later to find themselves in bed with each other, trading infrared rays and exploring each other's bodies, even though they may not have actual intercourse.

Real intimacy takes place between real people, and usually progresses more or less quickly to sex. First comes the thrill of discovery: "Someone I can really talk to," "I've been waiting so long and I'm really excited I found you." The breathless talkies, which may go on for twenty-four hours at a stretch, as each one pours out his life's savings of opinions, feelings, and aspirations, sooner or later give way to the smiling lookies as "really talking" is replaced by "really seeing" the other person. The lookies lead inevitably to the touchies, and after a period of entranced stroking, the feelies begin to take over and the hands move downward and inward. Unless the proceedings are postponed or terminated at this point, the desire to explore warmer places wells up as the warmies come to life, and after that there has to be a decision as to whether the cuffies will have their way.

At each of these stages there is the risk of Parental interference.

> You're not supposed to talk that way,
> You're not supposed to stare,
> You're not supposed to touch him so,
> You must not feel her there,
> And certainly, my dear young thing,
> Of *that* you must beware!
> Talking, looking, touching, feeling,
> What an evil pair!

These warnings have to be overcome gently and without rancor, since defiance or outright rebellion will be followed in due time by the guilties and the morning after, which will sully the joy and slash of the canvas of intimacy. But in most cases, once two people "really talk" to each other or "really look" at each other, they are tempted to plunge into the great adventure of a candid, game-free relationship, in which orders from headquarters are likely to be reinforced by orders from hindquarters. Then one or the other is going to say: "Why spend our lives with an at least when we can have a wow?" If they are both levelheaded, read from right or read from left, both ways WoW spells WoW. But if things get topsy-turvy, it reads MoM from either side. If their venture is prudent and successful, however, at an appropriate time there will be a baby, who will show them all the valuables they had hidden in the pockets of their genes. And what could be more moral and esthetic than that?

—————————

G

SEX AND MARRIAGE

The marriage license is a service provided by society to take care of the Parental interference referred to above by replacing it with the Parental blessing, and it often succeeds at that. But a marriage license no more makes a good spouse than a driver's license makes a good driver. Good spouses and good drivers are both made by Parental instructions contained in the script. A winner will make a good spouse and a good driver, and a loser will be poor at both because he does not have permission to do well at either. There are, of course, many splits here, good spouses who are poor drivers, and vice versa. Most of these, I think, turn out to be non-winners, who either plod and shrink, or zoom and crash.

Since the license in favorable cases eliminates the guilties, married people have the best chance for continued intimacy, although informal ball and sockets often do better than welded ball and chains. Either way, if the intimacy works, the couple can be spotted by the way they walk down the street. Their eyes sparkle and their steps are springy, and their children, if they have any, will be laughing merrily much of the time. The lady should be congratulated on looking so well, and the gentleman on the good job he has done. My friend Dr. Horseley relates the case of a troubled marriage that improved to the point of real intimacy, as was easily apparent when the couple was together. He asked them: "Do I have your permission to say that intimacy such as yours makes people's eyes sparkle and their steps springy?" To which they replied: "You certainly may,

and you can add that it makes the children happier too."
The children may not know what is happening when
such a change occurs, but they know that something is
different, and they react in a very favorable way.

While the physical and mental effects of sex and intimacy have a great deal to do with this happy condition,
there is another element at work as well, and that is a
sense of freedom. This is shown by the fact that some
newly divorced people show the same spring and sparkle
after they are released from the bonds of their matri-
mony. This is one manifestation of the age-old conflict
between security and freedom. When a marriage is based
on love and security, its restrictions are cheerfully accepted and even enjoyed. But when it is an obligation and
a damper on the free spirit of humanity, its bondage is
cheerfully given up in favor of something more important
than sex and more invigorating than apathy, and that is
liberty. There is a simple question to test the importance
of sex vs liberty. How would a person choose between
staying in a prison with conjugal visits and taking a sex-
less parole?

H

SEX AND RESEARCH

Very little research has been done on sex and well-
being. The best known figures are those that show that
married people can expect to live longer than single ones.
The only systematic work on the subject was published
in German in 1904, and is full of pre-Nazi exhortations
to keep the race pure and forbid sexual intercourse (even
with contraceptives) to anyone with any physical de-
fect.[11] The antisexual attitudes of those times and places
are still to be found in this country, although some research is permitted under protest, with many people hoping it will make the whole subject look even more Awful
than it did before. Research intended to find out whether

sex is beneficial or harmful to the human race would arouse opposition in many quarters, but a determined investigator might be able to carry it through. I would propose the following studies as a beginning:

(1) I have already mentioned (Chapter 1, E) the project of keeping health and sex records on a large group of college students of both sexes. It would then be a simple matter to compare physical health with frequency, regularity, and quality of sexual activity, if any.

(2) Take 1,000 female teachers in a number of school systems. Half wear sexy clothes and half wear conservative clothes. Then compare the scholastic achievement scores and IQ's of all their classes. Since the teachers would be volunteers, we would really be comparing sexy teachers with conservative ones. This study might show that sexy-looking teachers raised the IQ's of their pupils, while conservative ones lowered achievement scores. Or it might be the other way round. Or it might be that sexiness has no effect at all. Nobody knows until somebody tries it.* This is merely one of the more practical projects of the many that an agile mind could devise to test the connection between sex and well-being.

I

SEX AND WELL-BEING

At this point we are ready to consider the specific conditions that sexual intimacy can prevent, alleviate, or cure. We will rely for the most part on the clinical experience of Dr. Horseley, who cautions us that specialists in other fields than psychiatry might well disagree with him on many of the things he says. In fact the mere list of these conditions has caused many of his medical

---

* Some of the variables in such an experiment, besides Sexy-Conservative and IQ-Achievement, would be Over-achievers–Under-achievers, age and sex of pupils.

colleagues to raise their eyebrows, and some of them even to purse their lips. And no wonder, for here is what he includes: high back pain, low back pain, obesity, fluid retention, bladder trouble, stomach ulcer, stomach cancer, high blood pressure, hemorrhoids, palpitation, shakiness, sweating and nightmares; asthma, eczema and hives; alcoholism and drug addiction; insomnia, flat feet, dull eyes, and all manner of other afflictions.[12] It sounds like an ad for a patent medicine, but fortunately no one can get a patent on this mixture of nature's elixirs, which has more healing powers than all the mineral waters of Europe, all the trees of the tropics, and all the herbs of China.

(1) Back pain. First, says Dr. Horseley, while the saying "Stroking keeps the spinal cord from shriveling up"[13] is just a manner of speaking, in some ways it is literally true. For example, good sex keeps the spine lined up right, and vice versa; or as Amaryllis puts it, "Stiff necks, cold sex." There are a certain number of women who wear surgical collars as a splint against recurring neck pains. Such pains are notoriously unpredictable. Even if the X-rays show signs that there is something wrong with the cartilages between the vertebrae, the complaints come and go without much change in these abnormalities. In his experience, a permanent cure often follows a congenial marriage or a robust affair, and the collar is never worn again. The same applies to low back pain, which is one of the commonest complaints among people with unsatisfactory sex lives. This condition is seen in the greatest concentration in the U.S. Army, where it is frequently referred for psychiatric consultation, which is generally not the case outside. The sexual remedy in civilian life should not be too vigorous, for on the other side there is the condition known as "bride's back," which comes from over-indulgence. Nor should it be halfhearted or perfunctory, since an unsatisfactory orgasm may aggravate the discomfort or bring on a recurrence after it has gone away. For that reason, the local remedy may not work for the military, and they seem to do better if they can go home.

Now, love as a cure for pains in the back, from the

neck down to the sacrum, is not available to everyone, and many would consider the suggestion unacceptable or even repugnant. In such cases the patient will search for some cause in his everyday activities. He and his doctor may decide, for example, that the pain is a result of mowing his lawn. It may be that he has mowed this same lawn every day for years, but it is always possible that the grass was especially long on the day he got the pain.

But the facts are that the sex organs in both men and women become so engorged if sexual excitement is not released by a well-developed orgasm that they may exceed the structural safety factor of the muscles and ligaments of the lower spine, just as an excessive load may exceed the safety factor of an automobile's suspension system and cause an awful racket when it goes over a bump. The excited uterus, for example, may triple its normal size and weight and stay that way for an hour or more, but after a satisfactory orgasm it will return to normal in five or ten minutes. If we add to the weight of the blood-laden uterus the congestion of all the other pelvic organs, it is not surprising that a small and normally harmless twist can throw the already strained back out of joint. The same applies to the male sex. It is advisable, therefore, for people who are not going to have physiologically effective orgasms to either shun sexual stimulation of mind or body altogether, or else get with it one way or another. In making up their minds, they should remember Amaryllis' epigram: "Sexually frigid is intellectually rigid." She explains it this way: "It doesn't mean that frigid people can't learn, but that they're not flexible in applying what they learn."*

(2) Overweight. Most women in Western countries consider overweight repellent to the opposite sex, but in some

* The word "frigid" is sometimes used in a general deprecatory rather than a specific physiological sense to mean "having an intolerant attitude toward sex." This would include people who are prudish and hypocritical (and withholding anorgasmic women) as well as those who are actually coldly repulsing or frigid.

Oriental harems, the fatter the better, and even in this country plump women can usually find mates who like them that way. Nevertheless, women in search of marriage, love, intimacy, or just plain sex try to stay slim, and medical men consider this healthy because thin people on the whole have lower blood pressure and live longer than fat ones. In this indirect way, sex, or sexual desire, can prevent high blood pressure and its unwholesome consequences, and possibly prolong life.

Overweight, when it does occur, is of two types, obesity and fluid retention. According to the Don't Look at Me Theory, which is well known among obese women, one object of overeating is to prevent men from making passes at them, or to repel their husbands. This means that when they are ready for intimacy, they are more likely to slim up, and in that roundabout way, sex can be regarded as a cure for obesity. Sometimes the relationship is more direct. A woman who loses a lover or husband will often begin to stuff herself, trading a man for a bag of groceries. On the other hand, a lonely woman who finds a mate may start to diet and take off weight.

Fluid retention is more variable than obesity and may cause quite large changes in weight from one day to the next. Some women who get angry at night find that they have gained the next morning, and this anger is closely related to their sexual activities. In these cases, a sweet-flowing sex life makes smooth-flowing kidneys, and the weight changes are watered away.[14] The bladder is also toned up.[15]

(3) Stomach trouble. On the man's side, many a husband knows how sex can prevent cancer. He knows that it is his wife, or rather his choice of wife, and his reponses to her, that make his stomach churn and the acid squirt. He also knows that if it churns often enough and fiercely enough, he may end up with an ulcer, and that it is not a very long churn from an ulcer to cancer in serious cases. So he pops executive mints to keep the acid down, and hopes for what script analysts call an At Least: for example, at least he might get high blood pressure before he gets cancer, and die a pleasanter death. But he will tell

you that a good sex life would prevent the whole disaster: churning, acid, mints, and ulcer, and the cancer or stroke at the end of the line. And in many cases, all these things he says could be true.

(4) Hemorrhoids, oddly enough, can also result from sexual frustration. They are strongly encouraged by spending too much time in the bathroom. Now, people with a good sex life would rather spend an hour romping in the bedroom that reading in the bathroom, and in this way sex can be regarded as a preventive against piles. On the other hand, from this point of view, illiteracy might be a simpler solution.

(5) Anxiety symptoms. Freud's first theory about anxiety said that it was caused by simple sexual frustration.[16] He later made it more complicated, but his first equation seems to hold true in many cases. This means that palpitation, shakiness, sweating, and nightmares, if they are not caused by some physical or chemical disorder such as thyroid disease, may result from dammed-up sexual excitement. This may be simply due to lack of available partners, but it may also come from lack of real intimacy, so that sex, if it is indulged in at all, is not properly completed or is mere copulation, without the health-giving closeness and freedom that tones up the body and wards off such maladies.

In some cases, lack of opportunity, or lack of response to sexual stimulation due to anger and other complications, may result in chronic, alarming, and sometimes disabling breathlessness, weakness, and tightness in the chest, giving the feeling of an impending "heart attack." This condition is known medically as neurocirculatory asthenia, and among soldiers and Australians as "the rare Hawaiian disease lakanuki." It is often treated with large doses of tranquilizers and sleeping pills that reduce the person's efficiency and sociability, and this sets up a vicious circle.

(6) Allergic reactions. Good sex is good prevention for asthma, eczema, and hives. But bad sex may aggravate them. The same goes for arthritis and "rheumatiz" in older people, and for trichomonas infection, which often causes

"the whites" in women. This condition is particularly common in those who are unresponsive (perhaps intuitively) to their husbands, who may be innocent carriers of the organism.

(7) Since alcohol and drugs are instead of people, good sex is a sovereign remedy for these addictions. They can cause death in many ways, ranging from cirrhosis of the liver to overshooting with heroin, setting fire to a mattress or sweating it out in the stinking hell of a badly run jail. Cigarette smoking belongs here too; sexual frustration and marital tension may lead to harder, faster, and deeper smoking and hasten the onset of lung cancer.

(8) Good sex is a cure for insomnia. On the mental side, it is something pleasant to think about in bed, and refreshing thoughts should bring refreshing sleep. Even if you don't fall asleep, blissful thoughts make lying awake more cozy, and more restful to boot. It should be more agreeable to think of rolling in the golden hay of sunrise with rosy-fingered Aurora as she colors the dawning sky than to toss and worry about all the people you hate, or why you can't make more money, or how guilty you should feel about something you've done or haven't done, or how scared to be of someone you have to deal with when the sun is really up. (Don't think you're going to shock Aurora with your lusty play. Astraeus and Tithonus and Cephalus were there before you, and she is the reason Orion is always smiling in the sky.)

It is the four-year-old in a person that tosses around in bed, taking advantage of the enormous muscles at his disposal. And nothing soothes a tired or worried four-year-old like cuddling up to Mother, unless he is sulking or she pushes him away; the same goes for a little girl and her father. In this particular case, outcest is even more effective than incest.

Biologically, good sex is nature's sleeping pill, and should automatically lead into a healthy drowse that falls into a sound night's sleep. This may even be stated as a rule: If after bedtime sex enough a lover doesn't feel sleepy, then something is wrong with the sex. If he actually feels twitchy instead, then something is very wrong. But if it goes right, then in the morning it will be a cure for flat feet and dull eyes, if you remember the springy step and sparkling look of the well-cuffed couple.

(9) Beyond all the conditions mentioned above, there are probably hundreds of thousands of cases seen by doctors every year where physical symptoms in various parts of the body result directly or indirectly from sexual "problems." Tracking this down is an interesting field of medical detective work, but in most cases it would probably not help much in the immediate treatment of the symptoms. Every once in a while, though, it does pay off in the most surprising way. For example, consider the case of Mrs. Woble, who suffered from "tennis elbow," which is about as far away from sex as you can get. Since she did not play tennis, she was at a loss to account for her condition, which almost paralyzed her right arm. It was aggravated by the fact that she bumped her sore elbow several times a day passing through doorways or reaching for things. Her orthopedic surgeon treated it in the usual way by novocaine injections, ultrasound and rest. But every time she bumped it, she undid the effects of the treatment. He suggested that she keep it in a sling, which she was reluctant to do because that kept her from taking care of her housework. Furthermore, when she did wear the sling on her right arm, she began to bump her left elbow.

One of her knowing friends told her it was all due to masochism, and another avid reader said it was hostility, but neither of them could explain why it settled where it did. Her housemaid, closer to the truth, said she thought it would go away if Mrs. Woble hit the right person real hard, but ventured no opinion as to who that person was. Then her psychiatrist noticed one day that she walked differently than she had before, that is, with her arms tensed up and her elbows slightly bent akimbo, as though she really was trying to keep from hitting somebody. They both know who that somebody was: it was her husband, whom she was furious at and blamed for her sexual frustration. Her "tennis elbow" came about as follows. Since she had begun to stiffen up her arms and keep her elbows slightly bent, she was two or three inches wider than she was in her normal state with her arms relaxed. (Normal width, 20″. Angry width, 23″. Width of many doorways, 29″.) But when she walked through a doorway, she did not make allowance for the fact that she stuck out a little on each side, and therefore banged her elbow every so often. Only after the sexual problem was settled, and she went back to her normal diameter, could the orthopedic treatment start to take effect.

It should be clear from this list of conditions that sex is closely connected with well-being and is biologically healthy and desirable, and so we can speak of preventive intimacy as an important public health measure. Under certain conditions, however, it may do more harm than good, and a certain amount of caution has to be exercised, just as in swimming or riding a bicycle. There are always sharks and oil slicks to watch out for. These are similar to the dangers mentioned by Miss Wilde, the young lady in the limerick in Chapter I. She feared she might get an unwanted pregnancy, or venereal disease, or be denounced from the pulpit, or forced to hide her cleavage under a big red A, and those are things that can always happen.

Sex may also interfere with other activities. Many athletes try to abstain during the playing season or when their big events are coming up. There used to be a legend that the members of the Oxford and Cambridge rowing teams would go to any lengths to prevent an ejaculation, even a wet dream, while they were in training for the big race, and inflicted all sorts of unpleasant prevention on themselves to avoid such accidents. Some movie producers try to prevent their stars from having affairs during a filming for fear that it might impair their acting ability in the love scenes. "If they're balling all night, how can they look as though they want to ball some more the next morning in front of the camera?" as one man put it plaintively. And some Old Masters felt that they did their best in a state of temporary virginity.

Worst of all, it is a fact that sexual intercourse or even masturbation can occasionally be fatal for men with coronary heart disease or hardening of the arteries, by causing a heart attack or a stroke of apoplexy. This commonly occurs away from home, in a motel or the apartment of a lady friend, usually after a heavy meal and lots of drink. These tragic endings are much feared by madams of brothels, since they are almost sure to get busted, and badly, if there is a death in the house and the coroner is called in. The medical examiners who do the autopsies in such cases recommend that coronary patients limit their sexual attentions to their wives, in familiar surroundings, and on an empty stomach.[17]

On the other hand, there is the curious fact that Oriental potentates, who have unlimited opportunities for sexual gratification, often outlive their contemporaries (providing they are not assassinated), and there is no doubt that many older people are rejuvenated when they take a younger mate. Thus the Fountains of Youth, so ardently sought in Florida and other exotic places, may be right under our noses (approximately 2′ 6″ down). Since it is well established that married people, on the average, live far longer than single ones,[18] the prevention of aging may lie not in some rare drug or mineral but in an active sex life. Thus my young friend Amaryllis may be more philanthropic than saucy when she wishes her elders "Long life and good cuffing," for the two do seem to go together.

A more specific question for older men is whether sexual activity prevents prostate operations. There is no firm evidence that sexual frustration causes enlargement of the prostate, but it does make the symptoms worse by causing congestion.[19] Dog owners run into this during rutting season when their frustrated males get so uncomfortable that they have to be taken to the vet for injections at $35 a throw. Thus good sex may alleviate the symptoms and so avert a serious and very upsetting surgical procedure in humans. An allied question is whether it prevents cancer of the cervix in women, and the answer is no.[20] If it proves to be true, as some have said, that the viruses causing such conditions hide in the male's foreskin, then a small sacrifice on the part of the husband might be worthwhile, and he will be amply repaid by having an interesting conversation piece thereafter.

And now a practical hint about the dentist's chair. Novocaine injections are often requested by timorous people for simple fillings. The victim is then left for the rest of the day with a concrete jaw on one side, and sometimes when the novocaine wears off he suffers more pain than the original drilling would have caused. In order to avoid the injection, he should try Nature's anesthetic first, and that is sexual fantasies. In order for this to work, the more the drill hurts, the sexier his fantasies have to get. If his imagination is responsive enough, he may go through the whole procedure without feeling any pain at all, and in fact he may come to regard his dental work as a festive occasion. That is a right-now on-the-spot way in which sex can contribute to well-being. Unfortunately, this does not work as well for the lower jaw as it does for the less sensitive uppers. But it may work for other pains besides dental, although that remains to be seen.

In closing this chapter, I would like to mention the key word that prevents intimacy and all the well-being it can bring. This is not a four-letter word; it has three: b-u-t. "But" prevents more loving than any other word in the English language, with "if only" running second. Intimacy is very much a matter of experiencing and enjoying what is here and now. "But" repudiates here and now, and "if only" moves it somwhere else or puts it off till later. "But" means apprehension for the future, and "if only" means regret for the past. Good sex contributes to well-being because it is right now. Living right now is seeing the trees and hearing the birds sing, and it is necessary to see the trees and hear the birds and know that the sun is out, in order to see people's faces and hear their spirits sing and know that the sun of their warmth is there; and that is the way to attain intimacy. That bright here and now of the open universe out there is what should be, before going indoors and living in the closed here and now of each other. For those things to happen, it is first necessary to have a clear mind and to forget for the time being all forms of tedious shuffle: shuffling papers and shuffling people and shuffling things in your head. That is why I asked you a long time ago whether you heard a bird sing today, and reminded you that it isn't time that is passing, but you who are passing through time—nonstop. And my last word is to repeat what I said there about that. Stop! And begin over again with the first word, which is Hi!

With this word, we bring these contemplations to a close. For those who want more, there follow some short discussions, some wise sayings, and a brief appendix for behavioral scientists. But for most people, it might be better to stop here.

NOTES AND REFERENCES

1. On rats see Levine, S.: "Stimulation in Infancy." *Scientific American* 202:80-86, May, 1960. Also "Infantile Experience and Resistance to Psychological Stress." *Science* 126:405, August 30, 1957. On babies, see Spitz, R.: "Hospitalism: Genesis of Psychiatric Conditions in Early Childhood." *Psychoanalytic Study of the Child* 1:53-74, 1945.

2. On monkeys, see Harlow, H. F., and Harlow, M. K.: "Social Deprivation in Monkeys." *Scientific American* 207: 136-146, November, 1962.

3. Parents of "battered children" were often battered children themselves. (Personal communication, Ellen Berne, Bellevue Hospital, New York City.) Cf. Silver, L. B., Dublin, C. C., and Lourie, R. S.: "Does Violence Breed Violence? Contributions from a Study of the Child Abuse Syndrome." *American Journal of Psychiatry* 126:404-407, September, 1969.

4. The 1940 or "pre-penicillin" edition of Cecil's *Textbook of Medicine* (W. B. Saunders Company, Philadelphia) gives the fatality rate in large city hospitals of Europe and America as in the neighborhood of 30 percent, in Bellevue Hospital ranging from 30 to almost 50 percent, and states: "The fatality rate in private practice is distinctly lower than that in hospitals. This is due of course to the fact that mild cases are treated at home, while severe ones are sent to hospitals." It was Cecil himself who made this statement, but I think the

differential mortality could also be interpreted according to the thesis offered in the text. Patients in private practice were obviously getting more personal attention than the patients in the corridors of Bellevue. The death rate of alcoholics was 56 percent. Cecil goes on to say that the patient's station in life is significant. "Patients in the higher walks of life, being well fed and clothed, and usually in good physical condition, are a better risk than those who are poor, underfed, and ill clothed." But the "well fed and clothed" patients are more likely to have and be allowed to receive visitors than the "underfed and ill clothed" patients lying in the corridors, so there is nothing here to challenge the internes' conviction that personal visitors increased the survival rate. But it was not fashionable in those days to make serious studies of such matters.

5. French, J. D.: "The Reticular Formation." *Scientific American* 196:54-60, May, 1957.

6. Brownfield, C. A.: *Isolation: Clinical and Experimental Approaches.* Random House, New York, 1965.

7. Barnes, R. B.: "Thermography of the Human Body." *Science* 140:870-877, May 24, 1963.

8. Heron, W.: "The Pathology of Boredom." *Scientific American* 196:52-56, January, 1957.

9. Kierkegaard, S.: *Fear and Trembling & Sickness Unto Death.* Anchor Books, New York, 1954.

10. According to the *United Nations Demographic Yearbook* for 1966, the infant mortality rate in Morocco and the Ryukyu Islands is 10 per 1,000 live births. In Canada and the United States, it is 23. In the Republic of South Africa, it is 29 for whites, and 136 for "colored," the highest in the "civilized" world except for India, where it is estimated at 146. For a further discussion of this ethical system, see my "manifesto" in *Transactional Analysis Bulletin* 8:7-8, January, 1969.

(In 1967 the lowest rate in the world was—surprisingly—in Papua [4.3, non-indigenous population]. The figure for the Ryukyu Islands excludes U.S. personnel stationed in the area, but is faulty because it also includes live-born infants dying before registration of birth. *U.N. Demographic Yearbook,* 1968.)

11. Senator, H., and Kaminer, S.: *Health and Disease in Relation to Marriage and the Married State.* Allied Book Company, New York, 1929. Two volumes, translated by J. Dulberg from the German original of 1904.

12. Kinsey et al. talk about health affecting sexual activity, but have little to say about the reverse. Senator and Kaminer have over 1,200 pages on the relationship between sex, marriage, and disease, but their conclusions, as noted, are prejudiced and unreliable. Most interesting are the statistics they give for mortality rates in Sweden, 1881-1890 (Vol. 1, p. 19). In almost every age group from 20 to 90, the death rate for single people of both sexes was significantly higher than for married people. At many levels it was almost double. The rate for widowed and divorced people was just about halfway between. In those days "single," especially for women, probably meant little or no sex, or at best, for a large population, infrequent and unsatisfactory sex; and widowed or divorced meant a period of regular sex, followed by infrequent or no sex. According to these assumptions, more sex meant more life, and less sex meant more death, sometimes twice as much, so that, broadly speaking, sexual abstinence was a fatal disease. (Just as a curiosity, the lowest death rate was 4.64/1000 for married men of 20, and the highest, 318.97/1000, was for bereft men of 90.)

In the absence, then, of hard research, we must fall back on soft clinical impressions for the ensuing discussion.

13. Berne, E.: *Transactional Analysis in Psychotherapy.*

14. For psychiatric aspects of urological phenomena see: Smith, D. R., and Auerbach, A.: "Functional Diseases," in *Encyclopedia of Urology*, Springer Verlag, Berlin, 1960, Volume XII.

15. Smith, D. R.: "Psychosomatic 'Cystitis.'" *Transactions of American Association of Genito-Urinary Surgeons* 53:113-116, 1961. This paper gives 18 references on the subject, including some on water and electrolyte excretion.

16. Freud, S.: *Complete Introductory Lectures on Psychoanalysis.* W. W. Norton and Company, New York, 1966. Chapter 25.

17. Symposium: "Sudden Death During Coitus—Fact or Fiction?" *Human Sexuality* 3:22-26, June, 1969.

18. Senator, H., and Kaminer, S.: op. cit.

19. Finkle, A. L.: "The Relationship of Sexual Habits to Benign Prostatic Hypertrophy." *Human Sexuality* 2:24-25, October, 1967.

20. *Time,* November 11, 1969.

PART III

Afterplay

7

QUESTIONS

A

QUESTIONS AND ANSWERS

Although the lectures upon which this book is based were open to the public, the people who came were mostly connected with the University of California. They included (roughly in order of age and sophistication) students from Berkeley and Santa Cruz, younger technicians from the medical school, medical students, graduate students in the social and medical sciences, secretaries, and faculty members from Berkeley, Santa Cruz, and the Medical School in San Francisco. They asked many questions after each lecture, some of which may also have occurred to the readers of this book. The answers given here are not always quite the same as the ones originally given.

QUESTION: What is the basic meaning of what you have said? What have you really told us?

ANSWER: I don't think there is any basic meaning. I'm used to thinking with a question in mind, and if there was such a thing as "the sexual question," I would try to answer it. But there isn't. The question in my mind was: "Is it possible to give five lectures about sex without merely repeating all the trivial or solemn or acrobatic or statistical things that many people say on such occasion?" I hope I've succeeded to some extent. I may have repeated some of them, but I don't think I've been hemmed in by them. What I've really told you are my thoughts about the subject after fifty-odd years of living and thirty-five years of practicing psychiatry, during which I've listened to several thousand people talking in detail about their sexual joys and sorrows. The main advantages I've had were my training in anatomy, physiology, psychiatry, and psychoanalysis, and the privilege of asking them any hardheaded questions that occurred to me.

Perhaps I would settle for calling these lectures instructive and thought-provoking essays rather than basic messages. But I wouldn't be entirely happy about it, since I prefer being basic. I think the most basic thing I said was that the feeling of autonomy is largely an illusion, and that if we do want to live our own lives, free of corruption, we should stop, look, and listen, and think.

QUESTION: When you speak on this subject, do you always find a predominance of women in the audience, the way it is here?

ANSWER: I've never spoken on the subject before, so I don't know. The way to test it would be to see what happened with a female lecturer. Margaret Mead gave these lectures some years ago. Did she have a predominance of men in the audience?

DR. LUCIA: It is possible that women are more fearful. Their information on the subject is more "amateur," and they would like to know more about safety. The men seem to be scot-free, while the women have to bear the burden of this sublime relationship.

QUESTION: How can you account for so many laughs from all of us on such a serious subject?

ANSWER: I'm sure I could have been so dismal about it that nobody would have dared to laugh without my permission. But since sex is supposed to be fun, I don't see why a lecture about it shouldn't be fun too.

QUESTION: What about perversions?

ANSWER: I'm not sure they should be called that unless they're very nasty and hurt or humiliate people, because that's a nasty word as it is commonly used by righteous people. Freud suggested "displacements," and the dictionary defines a perversion as an aberration, and I would prefer those words in most cases. Animals are full of aberrations, from paramecia up through porcupines and man, and they seem to be ready for anything any time, although most of them prefer to fertilize a heterosexual mate according to the standard operating procedure of their kind. So we should not suppose that human beings are different because they don't have a stereotyped sex life.

QUESTION: You imply that the real purpose of sex is impregnation. If so, what about immediate gratification and the "Wow"?

ANSWER: It's reassuring to know that it's there for procreation, but most human sex is done for the Wow, and animal sex, too, since animals probably don't know about impregnation. If human beings didn't make it more complicated than fertilization requires, there wouldn't be much to talk about. People would just do it for the immediate gratification, and impregnation would follow naturally when circumstances were right.

QUESTION: But that's why we have a population explosion —because some people don't know that sex leads to impregnation. So isn't necessary to discuss it with them?

ANSWER: I don't believe anybody is that stupid, really. Anthropologists used to say that some people didn't know the connection, but I've traveled in lots of countries, including New Guinea, and I just don't believe it. There's something else going on. As some people say: "If we could only send our bright young people over there to explain to them that sex has something to do with babies, they would use their contraceptives." But it doesn't work. It's not ignorance that keeps people from using contraceptives, and I don't believe it's poverty either, because even if you give contraceptives away, people won't use them if they're not inclined to. So it's neither ignorance nor poverty, it's something else, something more deep-seated. Maybe poor benighted people want to be immortal, too.

QUESTION: Do you think talking about sex is exploiting it?

ANSWER: Maybe, but it doesn't work too well. It isn't true that sex sells more products than anything else does. There are an awful lot of cornflakes sold nowadays without sex, and there are lots of other products sold without it too. I'm sure that they outnumber the products that sex does sell. Phony sex ads sell phony products, like chromy cars and soap operas. I think the answer to the question is that you can exploit phony people but you can't exploit real ones.

QUESTION: How do you link economics with sex? Sex is closely tied up with the family, and the family is an economic unit. Is this a true relationship, this economic sex?

ANSWER: I don't believe the family is an economic unit, although it can be used as one. I don't believe real people get married for economic reasons, although they may include them or get married in spite of them. I have a prejudice against the idea of the family as an economic unit; it is used by Engels, for one, as a false premise to lead to false conclusions and false actions. It's like the idea of culture, which to me is an academic term that has little value except to administrators, moneymakers, and economists, and to those who want research grants, but not to any living people. As far as the individual is concerned, culture is for jerks. The majority, which is 51 percent of people, can do pretty much as they like within the law, and if they choose to do as everybody else does, that's a good way to avoid responsibility, and that's what I mean by a jerk. And laws are not culture, because they can be made by politicians, or even by one politician, and reversed by politicians, or even by one politician. Culture in my estimation is just an old suit of clothes that can be changed overnight, as shown by Hitler and Stalin and Ataturk, and the people in Margaret Mead's village. I don't see any reason to take an old suit of clothes seriously just because most people look serious about it. Culture is the Emperor's old clothes, the perpetuated errors of previous generations.

QUESTION: Why are bedroom people winners and bathroom people losers?

ANSWER: Let's take the clearest possible situation, because what you see there can apply to other situations. The simplest way to study winners and losers is to play poker with them. There is no problem there in telling which is which, no questionnaires and no research and no doubts. You only have to know one thing: what they have in their pockets when they get outside the door. Now if you're an experienced poker player, you can tell within three hands usually whether a newcomer is a winner or a loser. He may win all three, but you still know he's a loser, or he may lose all three and you still know he's a winner. Here's how you tell a loser. First, he thinks poker is a game of luck. So if he gets bad cards he gets mad and says: "My luck's not with me tonight." Maybe he even slams his cards on the table. Secondly, he If Only's and I Shoulda's. "If only I had stayed in," "If only I had gone out," "I shoulda drawn three insteada two," and so forth. Thirdly, after the hand is finished he wants to do it over, and says: "Let me see the next card that I woulda got if only I'd got the next card insteada this card." The winners may say the same things to be good fellows, or to con the other players, but they don't really mean it. They know that if they lost the hand, they played it wrong or got bad cards, that's all there is to it, and cursing won't help. They can wait for the next hand to do better.

A winner is a person who sets out to do something he decides to do and gets it done if it's possible; if he doesn't get it right the first time, he gets it right the next time. He knows that everybody makes mistakes—except winners. He doesn't let his Child or his Parent impair his judgment. That's why poker is a man's game. If there's a woman in the game, all the men are in trouble from their Child or their Parent—if they have a Parent. What would your father say if he saw you winning money from a woman? Even worse, what would your psychiatrist say if you came and told him you had won from a woman? You would have to spend your winnings analyzing why you did it before you could relax. So only scoundrels who are not going to psychiatrists can win in a poker game with women.

Another mark of a probable loser is that he uses a lot of bathroom talk. A winner may use it occasionally, but not in every hand. The biggest loser I ever knew, who wanted to throw everything into the pot, including his wife and daughters and the family ranch, talked that way all through the game, although he was very proper at other times.

So a loser cries: "My luck is out, if only and I shoulda." A winner says, "I won't let that happen again," and doesn't. Of course a loser wins occasionally, but he makes sure not to keep it, and a winner loses occasionally but he makes sure he gets it back.

QUESTION: What's the difference between ego states and roles?

ANSWER: An ego state is a natural phenomenon, and a role is put on. A person can play many roles without changing his ego state. For example, a person in a Child ego state can play the role of either a parent, an adult, or a child. Children do that when they play house. One plays mother, one plays doctor, and the other plays the little girl, but all of them are in the Child ego state. Grownups can do that too when they play charades.

QUESTION: Can transactional analysis shed any light on the occurrence of great love with great antipathy?

ANSWER: Only to analyze which ego states are involved and how the transactions got started. Thus the Parent may have a great affection and the Child a great antipathy based on jealousy. Or the Child may love the Child in another person and hate the Parent. Or the Child ego state itself may alternate between the two, just as real children do. Transactionally, it starts with Mother's ambivalence: giving food and taking it away, pushing for bowel movements and throwing them away, kissing the child and pushing him away. There's an enormous psychoanalytic literature which tries to explain the origins in early life of such ambivalence.

QUESTION: How aware do you think most people are of which ego state they are in at any particular moment?

ANSWER: Unless they've had training or therapy in transactional analysis, or thought a great deal about it, they aren't aware at all. So there are about three billion people in the world who have no awareness of which ego state they are in, and maybe a half a million who have. If the three billion became aware overnight, then everything would get better tomorrow morning. An easy way to do it is to listen to what's going on in your head, and then you'll hear your three ego states talking to each other. If everybody did stop to listen to their own heads, they would all become beautiful people and spread the goodies around, and that would solve a great many of the world's problems right there.

Parent, Adult, and Child ego states were first systematically studied by transactional analysis, and they're its foundation stones and its mark. Whatever deals with ego states is transactional analysis, and whatever overlooks them is not. So that's why an acquaintance with that particular discipline is necessary in order to be aware of one's own ego states.

QUESTION: What about people who realize that they're playing a role?

ANSWER: Realizing that you are playing a role is itself a role. I hate that kind of talk, a paradox that swallows itself until it disappears, but in this case it's true.

QUESTION: How do you get over playing games?

ANSWER: The first rule is to spend your time spotting your own games instead of other people's. The second rule is to try not playing long enough so your favorite players will realize you have stopped and they may stop, too. Then see what happens. If things go well, you'll get your reward in good payoffs instead of bad ones. For instance, a couple who play Uproar and get their payoffs through anger may discover that sex is more fun than anger, which may be hard for them to believe until it actually happens.

QUESTION: How can you say that kids know more about human relations than grownups do when we're learning more and more about it all the time?

ANSWER: What you're learning is more and more words about it all the time, but kids can still spot a faker faster than a grownup can. Grownups don't have permission to look at people or talk straight to them, but kids do have up to a certain age. So they look right at you and you can't hide from them. Grownups never look at each other for more than a few seconds, except under special conditions such as playing I Can Outstare You, or when they're in love, or in certain professional situations such as psychotherapy. If you follow your own eye movements at any social gathering, or watch other people's eyes, you'll see that's true. But if you want to know about people you've got to look at them, and kids are still allowed to do that. That's one answer.

QUESTION: What did you mean by preventive intimacy?

ANSWER: Intimacy properly handled may prevent cervical collars, low back pain, stomach cancer, hemorrhoids, and dull eyes. That's what I meant.

QUESTION: How long does it take a spinal cord to shrivel up?

ANSWER: Quite a long time. At first there is a hunger for stroking, and that goes on and on: in a baby for weeks, in a grownup maybe for years. Then comes a point where the person gets irritable, and instead of receiving strokes gratefully, he tries to avoid them and won't receive them or "let them in." After that point is reached, he starts downhill, either naked on roller skates or fighting all the way.

QUESTION: What do you have to say about strong sexual mores and mental illness?

ANSWER: Let me tell you an anecdote about that. People go to Tahiti and say: "Isn't it nice, sexual freedom, and look how healthy they are." I know a very good reporter who went to Thailand and said the same thing. Well, if you want to know about mental health, you find out first about mental illness, and the mental hospital is the place to do that. Now, if you go down the street a mile from sexual freedom in Papeete, you'll find the mental hospital there. And in that hospital you'll find about the same percentage of mentally ill people and exactly the same mental illnesses as in any other place in the world, including New York and California. And if you stand in the dandy dance hall in Bangkok and look across the river, you'll see the mental hospital there. And in that hospital are the same percentage of mentally ill people suffering from exactly the same mental illnesses as anywhere else.

If you really want to be fooled, you can go to any small island in the Fijis, like Rotuma, and you'll find no mental illness there at all, and isn't that nice? But if you go to the mental hospital in Suva, you'll find all the mentally ill people from Rotuma, because that is where they were shipped. And the same goes for wild New Guinea and exuberant Africa and puritan Russia and China. So the answer to that question is that sexual mores in my experience have very little direct bearing on mental illness. Sexual conscience can get people upset, but that's an individual matter. As a matter of fact, the word "mores" I think only applies to very small societies such as villages, and is often misused, or at least used to avoid finding out what's really going on, which is individual parental programming.

QUESTION: If your spinal cord is going to shrivel up without sensory stimulation, why not use hallucinogenic drugs?

ANSWER: Because then you may shrivel up your brain instead of your spinal cord. Ovid knew that 2,000 years ago. Also the stimulation should come from outside. Many people who come down from a heavy marijuana habit will agree to that. Drugs are instead of people.

QUESTION: You described the satisfied female. What manifestations do you see in the satisfied male?

ANSWER: His step is springy, his eyes sparkle, and his children laugh merrily.

QUESTION: How about going to a chiropractor to keep your spinal cord from shriveling up?

ANSWER: I don't like chiropractors. H. L. Mencken said they should be encouraged, because in a welfare state the only method of natural selection left is chiropractors, so he favored letting the people who want to go to them.

QUESTION: How do you explain the bounce and spring of a man who doesn't have a girl friend?

ANSWER: I don't know, but imagine what he would be like if he did have a girl friend.

QUESTION: In most of what you say you must be kidding. Are you ever serious?

ANSWER: All my kidding is serious if you can read it right.

QUESTION: Aren't you rather arrogant?

ANSWER: I act arrogant only when I feel humble because I'm not sure what I'm talking about. It's more fun to be that way. It's more fun for me to come on arrogant than humble, and it's more fun for the listener, because then he feels free to criticize. After all, you can't criticize a humble man. You either bow your head or crucify him, and I'm not ready for either of those.

QUESTION: You "put down" a lot of books. What books do you recommend?

ANSWER: See the following section.

B

A SELECTED LIST OF BOOKS

Interestingly enough, the best sex book, as valid for San Francisco and London as for ancient Rome, was written 2,000 years ago. It deals not with special titillations but with practical problems of everyday life: where to go to meet girls, how to start a conversation with them, how to keep them interested, and how to get by with limited funds. And beyond that, it deals with something that may be even more important: how to fall out of love with them if you're rejected. It also has a section on how to be sociable rather than athletic in bed, and one for women on how to improve their appearance.

The Art of Love, by Publius Ovidius Naso (43 B.C.E.– 18 A.D.), called Ovid. Written 1 B.C.E. Translated by

Rolfe Humphries. Indiana University Press, Bloomington, 1957. Paperback.

Regarding drugs, Ovid says:

"Philters are senseless, too, and dangerous; girls have gone crazy, given a dose in disguise; philters can damage the brain. Let unholy things be taboo. If you want her to love you, be a lovable man; a face and figure won't do. . . . That's not enough, you will find; add some distinction of mind." Which seems like very sound advice.

Next in line are the works of Havelock Ellis, which tell in a readable and poignant way the many variations of sexual behavior and the different factors that affect it. His case histories, many of them autobiographical, are as touching as Victorian novels, and his comments are learned, fascinating, and reliable. He is human, not solemn or pedantic, and he has the added advantage of being educational and intellectually stimulating, since he cites many classical and medieval writers.

Studies in the Psychology of Sex, by Havelock Ellis. Written in 1898–1908. Seven volumes conveniently bound in two volumes by Random House, New York, 1940.

For those who are interested in the early development of the sexual instincts, Freud's book on this subject closely followed and drew from the work of Ellis, so that Freud's boldness set Europe in an uproar just as Ellis's had done to England. It is difficult reading, however, with words like "phylogenetic" and "ontogenetic," and the translations tend to be clumsy in their attempts to stick to the precise meaning and flavor of the original. But it is worth exploring to see what was going on in those days when sex and psychoanalysis were still unpopular subjects with most people.

Three Essays on the Theory of Sexuality, by Sigmund Freud. Written in 1905. Published as *Three Contributions to the Theory of Sex.* E. P. Dutton & Company, New York. Paperback.

In order to get a clearer idea of the psychoanalytic approach to sex, Ferenczi's essays are much easier reading.

Sex and Psycho-Analysis, by Sandor Ferenczi. Written

1906–1914. Dover Publications, New York, 1957. Paperback.

This book also contains papers on other psychoanalytic subjects, but the articles on impotence, masturbation, male homosexuality, and especially the one on obscene words, give a good view of psychoanalytic thinking on these matters.

So much for older works. Those who need reassurance or justification, or want to satisfy their curiosity about the habits of their betters or worsers, will want to look through the two chief works of Kinsey and his associates:

Sexual Behavior in the Human Male, by Alfred C. Kinsey, Wardell B. Pomeroy, and Clyde E. Martin. W. B. Saunders Company, Philadelphia and London, 1948, and *Sexual Behavior in the Human Female,* by the same authors plus Paul H. Gebhard, from the same publisher, 1953.

The most valuable and important parts of these books, however, are the first 153 pages (Part I) of the book on males and the first 97 pages (Part I) of the book on females. These sections describe the methods and problems involved in this type of research, and show how unreliable most numerical studies of sexual matters are. Kinsey's group interviewed 12,000 people and plans eventually to interview 88,000 more. They show clearly why statistical studies of smaller numbers are of little value, and help to nourish a healthy attitude of skepticism in the reader so that he will hopefully lose confidence in statistics about fewer than 1,000 people. This will keep him from entertaining erroneous beliefs which he might get from reading other statistics about sex based on small numbers of people.

But it should disillusion him only about overeager statisticians and their computers, however, and not about serious thinkers, who can deal very ably with smaller numbers or draw valid conclusions from a single case. In order to get a broader understanding of what is going on with sex nowadays, he might want to know about sexual customs and practices in various parts of the world and among higher animals, as well as the physiological factors that influence sexual behavior. For that he should read:

Patterns of Sexual Behavior, by Clellan S. Ford and Frank A. Beach. From lectures delivered in 1949. Harper & Brothers, New York, 1951.

This book deals with sexual behavior in 190 human societies and a large number of primate and other mammalian groups.

A fascinating book about the sex lives of animals all the way up the scale from the simplest cells through worms, insects, fish, birds, and us people, has been translated from the German.

The Sex Life of the Animals, by Herbert Wendt. Translated by Richard and Clara Winston. First published in 1962. Simon and Schuster, New York, 1965.

This is by far the most readable book on the subject, and here is where you will learn that although snails look dull, they have more fun than anybody because they are hermaphrodites and have simultaneous double sex (which may be called 138, 165, or 192, depending on how you look at it).

Then there is a book which summarizes a lot of the findings about human sex, together with a lot of other "scientifically established" facts about human social behavior and human behavior in general.

Human Behavior, an Inventory of Scientific Findings, by Bernard Berelson and Gary A. Steiner. Harcourt, Brace and World, New York, 1964.

Some of the findings are pretty dull, but there are a few surprises, and it is nice to have everything in one place.

The main thing about all these books is that they are reliable, and anyone who reads them can be as sure of his ground as it is possible to be in the present stage of our knowledge. They were all written by conscientious people of superior knowledge and intelligence, and some of them are quite lively.

The more clinical details of what happens during sexual intercourse should be of interest only to gynecologists, urologists, anatomists, physiologists, endocrinologists, zoologists, and psychiatrists, since they are the people best equipped to evaluate them. But a lot of other people would like to know about them too, for good or bad reasons. They are graphically described in:

Human Sexual Response, by William H. Masters and Virginia E. Johnson. Little, Brown & Company, Boston, 1966.

If you don't know what the origins and insertions of the Ischiocavernosus muscle are, or what a bilateral salpingo-oophorectomy is, you will not really understand what these authors are saying.

None of the above books, however, will really tell you what's happening to you sexually, or what you can or should do about it, if anything. What you need for that are some practical manuals. There are large numbers of these, many of them pretentious, sentimental, or sensational, and some of them inaccurate. The best plan is to choose books by reliable people, not all of whom may turn you on, but who will at least give you the correct answers where there are any. Starting with the sexual interests and development of childhood and adolescence, there are two good books: one about just sex, the other about how early sexuality fits into the life course of the individual in his society.

The Normal Sex Interests of Children, by Frances Bruce Strain. Appleton-Century-Crofts, New York, 1948.

This is a rather elementary book, mainly slanted toward schoolteachers.

Childhood and Society, by Erik H. Erikson. Published 1950. Revised edition, W. W. Norton & Company, New York, 1964.

This gives a revised theory of infantile sexuality that is more understandable and useful than that of Freud, who was the pioneer in this field. But Erikson goes much farther than infancy and shows how sexuality, among other items, fits into the sense of identity and the eight stages of psychological development in man, with particular emphasis on youth.

For girls, there is a very sensitive book by an experienced psychoanalyst:

The Psychology of Women, by Helene Deutsch. Volume I. *Girlhood.* Grune & Stratton, New York, 1944. Volume II, *Motherhood,* is equally valuable.

Unfortunately, there are no books of equal caliber for Boyhood and Fatherhood. Sorry about that. A book edited by Hanns Reich, *Children and Their Fathers* (Hill and Wang, New York, 1962), may be helpful, though.

Interestingly enough, there are more books about contract bridge than about contraception. Probably the best book on this subject is:

Birth Control and Love, by Alan Guttmacher. Revised edition. The Macmillan Company, New York, 1969.

Dr. Guttmacher is a man of impeccable qualifications in his specialty of obstetrics and gynecology (Johns Hopkins, Mount Sinai Hospital, Harvard), and from him you can be sure that you are getting the best and last word on the subject. He includes a section on impregnation and birth.

A marriage manual by a husband and wife who were concerned for many years about problems of fertility, contraception, and the enjoyment of marriage is called:

A Marriage Manual, by Hannah and Abraham Stone (revised edition). Simon and Schuster, New York, 1952.

This is recommended because the Stones are both reliable and experienced people of sound scientific background.

Square swingers can keep up with the latest developments in their fields through the girl's magazine, *Cosmopolitan,* and the boy's magazine, *Playboy.* Older people can find useful though slightly prissy information in:

Everything You Always Wanted to Know About Sex, by David Reuben, M.D. David McKay Company, New York, 1969.

If you have questions which are too far out to be answered by any of the titles given above, you may find what you want in Dr. Schoenfeld's interesting collection of questions and answers from the old *Berkeley Barb.*

Dr. Hip Pocrates, by Eugene Schoenfeld. Grove Press, New York, 1969.

Anyone who has read carefully this short list of fewer than 20 books can consider that he or she is exceptionally well informed in the field of sex—historically, theoretically, and practically.

And a final word, on the subject of pornography. This comes in three varieties.

(1) Literary realism (Joyce's *Ulysses,* Roth's *Portnoy's Complaint*). This includes books worth reading for themselves, which happen to contain sexual scenes.

(2) Erotica (found nowadays in reputable bookstores). These come as paperbacks with well-designed jackets and evocative titles. Their purpose is erotic stimulation of a reasonably healthy variety, buried with at least a pretense of style in some sort of plausible plot. *Evergreen* Magazine belongs about halfway (1) and (2).

(3) Filth (found in cigar stores that sell racing forms). This comes in paperbacks with plain covers and titles that are either common street slang or low-grade puns. They are often proctoscopic and are usually bummers.

8

A MAN
OF THE
WORLD

Both Cyprian St. Cyr, mentioned in the Foreword, and his friend Dr. Horseley pride themselves upon being men of the world. Some of their paragraphs and short sayings are worth recording here. But these are like after-dinner mints, to be taken a few at a time, and not all at once.

A

LOVE AND MARRIAGE

What happens is more interesting than how things are made, and how things grow is more interesting than what happens. Thus a mystery story tells how a plot is constructed, while a novel tells what really happened. But a Russian novel tells how people grow, and that is why Tolstoi and Dostoevski are the men to beat. In the same way, sexual intercourse is more interesting than sex organs, and the growth of an orgasm more gripping than sexual intercourse.

❦

Stendhal tells us of the crystallization of love in a French and romantic way, where men and women have no freedom from watchers, and deception is the order of the day. The Song of Solomon tells us how a king can love a slave. But in our times and places, where selection is the problem, and not deception or confinement, it goes differently. Let a man visit an art gallery every Sunday, and this is what will happen.

First, he sees her for the first time, standing and moving, and he thinks, "Maybe this is it." That feeling already makes life worthwhile, and if he has too many doubts he should go no farther than to glimpse her face, so that he can regret it sweetly for the rest of his life.

But if he dares the possible disappointment of talking to her, he may end up knowing, "This could be it."

After that, when he is alone, he starts to dream about seeing her again.

When he does see her again, he wants to be with her all the time.

He starts being with her all the time, and then he need no longer have dreams, for his life has become one.

Then come the first quarrels, the partings and reunions, for they cannot bear it long apart, and the only question is which will stop sulking first.

Then they move in with each other, married or unmarried, and between lovings they quarrel about money.

Twenty years later they are inseparable. Their love has been tamed into an affection that will unite them till the grave.

When at long last one goes to the grave, the other soon follows.

❦

¶ These, then, are the stages of sexual bliss.

¶ First, looking and hoping sweet hopes.

¶ Then seeing and testing in delicious anticipation.

¶ Then the conquest with its glorious sighs.

¶ After that comes certainty and confidence, with its smug feelings of superiority when other men throw her admiring glances, or even more perceptive strangers bow to her or tip their hats in her direction.

The final stage of paradise, unknown even to Dante, is when there is not only certainty, but a guarantee from what has gone on previously, of the highest possible degree of sensuousness, response, and surrender, the attainment of the unattainable. This guarantee gives such an ineffable splendor of anticipation to whatever goes before, the dinner, the concert, or the starlight by the sea, that even the admiring glances of other men become irrelevant, and the whole evening is like a warm and gentle flight toward the interior of a golden magnet where you will be borne high over the earth on blue flames of pleasure.

❦

Marriage is six days of excitement, and the world's record for sex.

Five more weeks of getting to know each other, fencing, lunging, and pulling back, finding each other's weaknesses, and then the games begin.

After six months, each one has made a decision. The honeymoon is over, and marriage or divorce begins—until further notice.

❦

When a man meets a married couple, he too often thinks, "What could she do for me?" instead of "What is she doing for him?" If they have love, why look for beauty, brains, or sex, or the sordid pleasantries of money?

❦

Middle-class husbands are like appliances. They come with a manual of instructions which you are supposed to read before you install them. They are guaranteed by the Church and *Good Housekeeping,* but the guarantee is void if you don't follow the instructions. There are maintenance manuals on every newsstand telling you how to keep them oiled properly. And when you have worn one out, madam, you can turn him in for a good price at the courthouse, after which you can stop worrying and send your clothes to the laundry. Then you will have plenty of free time on your hands, which you can use to sit around the house and bite your nails.

Middle-class wives are also like appliances. They come with a manual of instructions you are supposed to read before you install them. They are guaranteed by the Church and *Good Housekeeping,* but the guarantee is void if you don't follow the instructions. There are maintenance manuals on every newsstand, telling you how to keep them oiled properly. The difference is that instead of your wearing her out, sir, she wears you out, and instead of your turning her in and getting part of your money back, she turns you in and you have to keep up the payments. What kind of washing machine is that? No wonder some men prefer the laundromat.

❦

The best age for a bachelor is thirty-nine. He is neither too old for the interesting young ones, nor too young for the interesting old ones. It may come as a surprise—an unwelcome or even a distasteful one—to people under thirty to learn that some of the sexiest women are fifty. As anyone who reads a novel by an under-thirty can see, sex between people over forty is considered improper and in bad taste. But the over-forties know that the young are too cocky and forget that a mile run covers more ground than four 220-yard sprints.

❦

To every action there can be an equally happy reaction. Mr. Tolstoi had his roof built by Zenith Builders and his ceiling painted by Superior Paint Company, and used deodorants while listening to his hi-fi. Was he really happier than Mr. Shortstoi, who had his foundation laid by Nadir Concrete and his floor varnished by Inferior Paint Company, and used odorants while listening to his low-fi? Does a dwarf giant hamburger really taste better than a giant dwarf hamburger, as the industry would have us believe?

❧§§❧

What you agree on is easy. Find out what you disagree on, what his demands will be, and what he will do if you don't meet them. You don't really know him until you've seen him angry.

❧§§❧

In a divorce you are attending your own funeral with your lawyer officiating. There is really nothing you can do. Let him take charge, and play it cool like a good corpse should. It will be easier for you to come back to life after the wake is over.

❧§§❧

A woman sitting in a short skirt must perpetually classify men out of the corner of her eye, and that is her hell. These are those who avert their gazes when they talk to her. These are scared or hard to get. There are those who look boldly at her thighs, the frankly sexual; and those who steal looks slyly, the dirty young men. There are those who look only at her face, the ones who don't need her. Then there are the ones who look first at her face and then at her thighs, and for them she is a person first and a sexual object after that.

Those who look away can be seduced, the bold used, the sly humiliated, the respectful respected, and the last

loved. All this is noted by her and decided without a word
or even a glance in return, and she has known it all since
childhood if she is a real woman. If she puts her coat over
her knees, then she is waiting for something or somebody,
or trying to make up her mind about some trouble; in that
case she does not need nor want his glances, and the man
has known this since childhood if he is a real man.

～§§～

Women and their mysterious ways. Griping and nagging and then knitting you a sweater and cooking your
favorite chicken. Saying they will not stay with you another day, and then if you say, "My, you look beautiful
this morning!" they will stay with you forever. But once
you are truly bound together by children, all this is less
important, and then what?

～§§～

The most common game played by women runs as follows:
"Do you promise not to kiss me?"
"I promise."
She wins either way. If he kisses her, he has broken his
word and is no better than all the others. If he doesn't she
can say to herself: "That wishy-washy eunuch didn't even
try to kiss me."

～§§～

The man who is loved by a woman is lucky indeed, but
the one to be envied is he who loves, however little he gets
in return. How much greater is Dante gazing at Beatrice
than Beatrice walking by him in apparent disdain.

～§§～

If all else fails, here is a cantrap that will always work.

"The thrice multiplied panegyrics of all the lovers of eternity would but half describe your charms. The ten thousand joys of a thousand perfumed nights rolled into a doeskin bag would be but a mulberry compared to the Arcadian pomegranate of pleasure which could be kissed in one fleeting moment from your lips."

If she doesn't appreciate that, she won't appreciate anything else you have to offer, and you are better off without her. If she laughs (appreciatively) you are at least halfway there. But then the other half is up to you, and you will have to come up with something better for an encore. That is the way it is with all cantraps.

❦

An orgasm is like a rocket ride. First the ascent, then the blackout, and after that the burst of light as the golden apple turns into the golden sun and azure skies with a slow parachute until the earth appears below, streams and meadows or a city street. You slowly touch and bounce up again, invisible to the tranquil cattle by the stream or the busy passersby. Then you slowly touch once more, and then the afterglow and the deep refreshing sleep. It is Maireja the nectar of ecstasy that comes from Adhumbla or Sabala, the magic cow that gives you everything you want, which bursts into your mind like Tchintamani, the glowing jewel of all wishes. But, say the elders, all this is for us, since you might appreciate it too much.

B

SHORT SAYINGS

The sooner you make new friends, the sooner you'll have old ones.

❦

The obstetricians say that menstruation is the weeping of a disappointed uterus.*

❧§❧

Knowing that Santa Claus is just Father is the beginning of wisdom. Knowing that your husband is just Santa Claus, so that you don't expect him to be real or there every night, is the end.

❧§❧

Real apples have worms, so you want golden ones. Well, do you like golden worms?

❧§❧

Your body is your friend. Don't treat it like an enemy.

❧§❧

If you can't see what's in front of your eyes, find out what's behind them, as Amaryllis used to say.

❧§❧

If you take away the big words and the solemn face, there is still plenty left, so there is no need to be scared.

❧§❧

Be willing to happen to somebody, and somebody will happen to you.

❧§❧

The trouble with a disagreeable wife is that she makes

_____
* EW: Garbage!

you angry. The trouble with an agreeable wife is that she makes you think instead.

෴

With drugs you experience everything and understand nothing.

෴

Some people look for anxiety like pigs look for truffles.

෴

His mind was filled with hate and sex because he had no love.

෴

There are no problems, only indecisions.

෴

It is harder to give up failure than success.

෴

The pube is the eternal triangle.

෴

If you don't know which girl to choose, let someone else choose, and then choose the same one.

෴

He tied a bunch of carrots to his head so he would have

something to look forward to. He always did the right thing: he was even born on Labor Day.

☙§§❧

According to the words of Bhagavant, women enchain men in eight ways: Dancing, Singing, Playing, Laughing, Weeping, and by their Appearance, their Touch, and their Questions.

☙§§❧

Venereal disease is sordid because it is always second-hand. There is no such thing as a brand-new crab. Even if you acquire it in the highest quarters, and wear it like a badge of honor, its genealogy will soon disillusion you as it plunges to the most ignoble depths.

☙§§❧

Whoever has had his soul turned to stone by Medusa's head will be Medusa's slave for life.

☙§§❧

Women look at the trees, and men look at the forest. Men build, and women furnish.

☙§§❧

Where there is a hare and a tortoise, it is best to be a winning hare.

☙§§❧

The most disastrous attitude for a woman is: I need a man, but you're not good enough. Either don't be that anxious, or take what comes.

☙§§❧

It is easy to tell the courting couple from the married one. The courting couple keep their faces taut while they listen to each other, and answer "You . . ." The married couple are relaxed, and answer "I . . ." not from ego but from uneasiness or ease.

❧§❧

Filial obedience. Her mother told her to be careful and wear her rubbers so she wouldn't get her feet wet. She also told her to drop dead. So like a good girl, she wore her rubbers when she dropped off the bridge.

❧§❧

Freud knew the answers. If you don't understand something about sex, don't say it's awful or mysterious. Look it up in Freud.

❧§❧

The reason so much is written about sex is that it was invented to happen and not to be described. Thus you can safely remember what went before, but in remembering an orgasm you spoil it. Those who want to remember don't really have one. A remembered orgasm is like a pie with a slice out of it, which someone has put aside to take home for a souvenir.

❧§❧

No man is a hero to his wife's psychiatrist.

❧§❧

Men like to be more masculine than the person they are with. So do some women.

❧§❧

Dating bureaus offer dehydrated friendships. Add a little moisture and you have plastic sex. Manufactured sex is not as good as the home-made variety.

❧ ❧ ❧

Here are some colors of different people's orgasms: champagne, all colors and white and gray afterward, red and blue, green, beige and blue, red, blue and gold. Some people never make it because they are trying for plaid.

❧ ❧ ❧

Some men are like snowmen. You build up an image of them and then it melts away.

❧ ❧ ❧

Since fighting and sex didn't mix too well, they gave up sex.

❧ ❧ ❧

Both are in trouble if she interrupts love-making to pull some hairs out of his chest and tell him her troubles. She is neurotic, and he has married one.

❧ ❧ ❧

"I'd like to lay her" (with the implication that she wouldn't let him) is blaming her for his own unattractiveness or impotence.

❧ ❧ ❧

Uneasy women treat life like a boxing match. They lead with their breasts, their bottoms, their vaginas, or their brains, and always they feint.

❧ ❧ ❧

A man's working effectiveness often depends on the phases of his wife's menstrual cycle.

❧⤜§⤛❧

In a car you remember incidents. On foot, you are part of them. A car is passing through; walking is being there. That is the difference between sex and loving.

❧⤜§⤛❧

Havelock Ellis confirmed: If you want to know next year's styles in women's clothes, look at this year's prostitutes.

❧⤜§⤛❧

Something not all women know about clothes and men. When a skirt conceals two or more different colors, such as stockings, legs, and other things, sex begins where the color changes, and grows where it changes again.

❧⤜§⤛❧

Unadorned spaghetti tastes pretty much the same all over. It's the sauce that makes the difference.

❧⤜§⤛❧

Romance is when a woman has woman-power over a man, and to the delight of both of them, becomes more important to him than other things.

❧⤜§⤛❧

Never return early, because goodbye is a promise that you won't.

❧⤜§⤛❧

Some men become impotent because they are overwhelmed by sheer overwork; others, because they are underwhelmed by sheer underwork.

❧§❧

One sign that a man's youth is going is hair growing out of his ears. A more reliable one is when he talks about money instead of women at the lunch table.

❧§❧

. Sex should be a treat for all the senses: sight, sound, smell, taste, temperature, and touch. Don't knock it until you try it. It's like money. If you don't have it, you're likely to be unhappy until you do. But once you have it, what you do with it is much more important than how much you have, and how you use it reveals what kind of person you are.

C

THE SAD ONES

Men drifted into her vagina and out again, without her getting to know them or them her.

After her trip to Kinseyland, she settled down on the Island of Monogamy.

Alive, millions claimed her every day. Dead, her body lay in the morgue unclaimed for many days.

❧§❧

Life is simple. All you have to do is figure out the most probable outcomes of various courses of conduct, and then pick the most attractive or the least troublesome. Only if you want certainty does it become difficult, because that you cannot have. Sometimes it amounts to deciding which of the things you don't want to do you should go ahead with. For example, each day a man may have to decide whether he would rather have his testicles cut off or his brain washed.

❦

It is easier to sell people death than life, hence insurance salesmen can be more honest than those who sell encyclopedias.

❦

What to do about death? Finish everything and then wait for it like a rotting log? Or leave some things unfinished and die with regrets? The art of living is to walk the earth like a prince, scattering apples wherever you go. The art of dying is to finish your own apple just at the right moment to say, "I am content, the rest are for you to enjoy at my wake."

D

FINAL RAP

Irresponsible love is an ego trip. If you love mankind but don't dig real cats and chicks, you're loving from your own container. Loving responsibility is real rapping. You've got to get out of the love bag and torque in to the real world of loving. There's plenty of balling on a violence trip, but it doesn't cancel out. If you're freaked out, a groovy smile is only a toothpaste ad. You've got to flip in to look and love what's really there, and that's what's beautiful. What you do after the ball is over is what counts.

A star is the glowing light inside the other person, distantly seen, brave soul's tiny flame, too bright to approach without great courage and integrity. Each person lives alone in inner space, and intimacy is out there. Intimacy is outer space, and if that's where you are, you don't say "Cuff you!" to a star.

APPENDIX: THE CLASSIFICATION OF HUMAN RELATIONSHIPS

A

INTRODUCTION

Structural analysis—the analysis of the human personality into Parent, Adult, and Child ego states— offers a consistent theoretical basis for classifying human relationships, both logically and empirically.

Psychoanalytic theory deals with mechanisms and drives and clarifies the nature of transference relationships, but it does not offer a systematic classification which can be applied outside of the treatment situation. Anthropological classifications deal with formal, contractual, and blood relations within the clan, gens, or tribe. The legal classification is a pragmatic one, designed to clarify matters of rights, injunctions, and sanctions. None of these offers a consistent, convincing, or comprehensive classification of informal relations as they occur in daily living, nor is any of them psychologically cogent and precise enough to have predictive value in such situations. Prediction is one of the chief aims and values of the structural and transactional approach.

In the text of this book (Chapter 4), we have dealt reductively with observed phenomena, reducing complex sets of observations to simple diagrams. An *a priori* logical approach enables us to set up a consistent and systematic set of models with which living transactions can be compared. The discussion here will be confined to dyadic relationships, those between two people, although the theory is amply generous enough to include more if desired. When the number of individuals involved is great enough to form a party, group, or organization, new elements appear, and such social aggregations (strictly speaking, aggregations of more than two people) have been dealt with in a previous work.* The present classification, therefore, is intended to fill in the gap between individual psychology and the psychology of groups by dealing with two-handed relationships.

B

TYPES OF RELATIONSHIPS

I. *Simple Direct Relationships.* Simple direct relationships are those which involve only one active ego state in each person. An inspection of Figure 15 (which is the same as Figure 2) shows that there are nine such relationships possible, and that they are of two types: those in which the vectors go straight across, and those in which they are slanted.

A relationship in which the vectors go straight across is called a *Symmetrical Relationship.* Here each party ex-

* *The Structure and Dynamics of Organizations and Groups.* J. B. Lippincott Company, Philadelphia, 1963, and Grove Press, New York, 1966. This has also been published in German by Rowohlt Verlag, Hamburg, 1969.

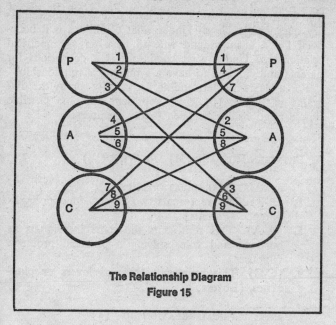

The Relationship Diagram
Figure 15

hibits the same ego state, so that they are on an equal basis, with a bilaterally reciprocal contract.

One in which the vectors are slanted is called an *Asymmetrical Relationship*. Here each party exhibits a different ego state, so that they are not on an equal basis, and the contract is skewed. It is evident from the diagram that there are three possible symmetrical relationships (1, 5, 9) and six possible asymmetrical ones (2, 3, 4, 6, 7, 8).

A family offers easily understood illustrations of both types. Schematically at least, the two parents are in a symmetrical relationship with each other, and in an asymmetrical relationship with their children. This statement offers an immediate yield in the hypothesis that if both clauses are not true in a given case, "something is wrong," and it supplies a basic position from which to pursue investigation. Note that the equality is not a social or occupational one, but a psychological or transactional one.

The same position can also be used to investigate secondary questions, such as: Under what conditions is it beneficial for a husband and wife to have an asymmetrical relationship? Under what conditions is it deleterious for parents and children to have a symmetrical relationship?

For a clearer understanding, let us now survey the diagrams in Figure 16, which represent the nine possible simple relationships between family members.

A. BETWEEN HUSBAND (H) AND WIFE (W)

SYMMETRICAL RELATIONSHIPS (S)

1. (P-P). This represents two parents functioning as parents. (Parents)
5. (A-A). This represents the same individuals as husband and wife, solving a practical problem. (Spouses)
9. (C-C). This represents them as lovers or playmates. (Lovers)

ASYMMETRICAL RELATIONSHIPS (A)

2. (P-A). This represents the husband encouraging the wife in a practical task. (Bolster-Worker)
3. (P-C). This represents the husband comforting the wife. (Comforter-Bothered)
6. (A-C). This represents the husband teaching the wife a new task which she is afraid of or resents. (Teacher-Pupil)
   The remaining three vectors (4, 7, 8) are the inverses of these.

B. BETWEEN PARENTS (P) AND OFFSPRING (O)

SYMMETRICAL RELATIONSHIPS (S)

5. (A-A). This represents a child and a parent working as equals. (Co-workers)
9. (C-C). This represents a parent playing with a child at the child's level. (Playmates)

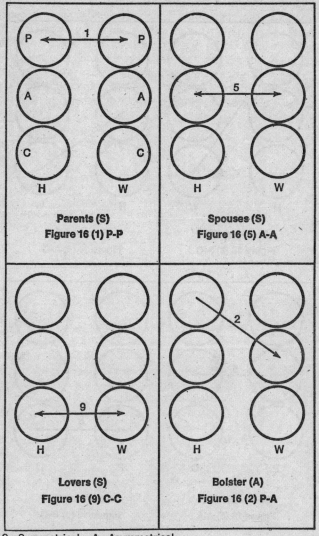

Parents (S)
Figure 16 (1) P-P

Spouses (S)
Figure 16 (5) A-A

Lovers (S)
Figure 16 (9) C-C

Bolster (A)
Figure 16 (2) P-A

S=Symmetrical   A=Asymmetrical

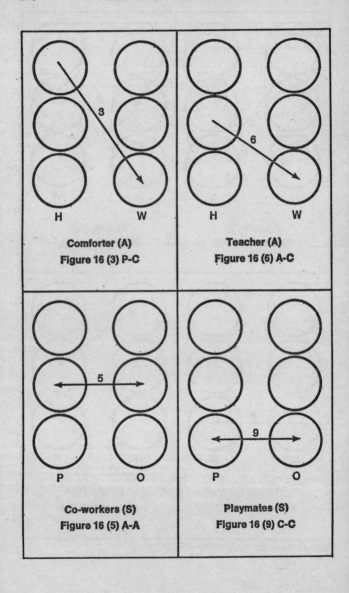

Comforter (A)
Figure 16 (3) P-C

Teacher (A)
Figure 16 (6) A-C

Co-workers (S)
Figure 16 (5) A-A

Playmates (S)
Figure 16 (9) C-C

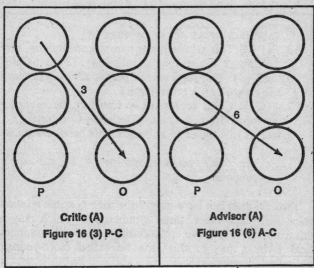

Critic (A)
Figure 16 (3) P-C

Advisor (A)
Figure 16 (6) A-C

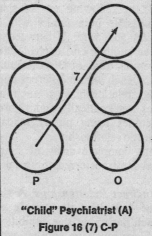

"Child" Psychiatrist (A)
Figure 16 (7) C-P

1. (P-P). May also occur, as in families where the oldest child replaces an absent parent.

ASYMMETRICAL RELATIONSHIPS (A)

3. (P-C).This represents a parent encouraging, criticizing, or disciplining an offspring. (Parent-Child)

6. (A-C). This represents a parent advising or teaching a child. (Teacher-Pupil)

7. (C-P). This represents a troubled parent asking comfort from a child. (Bothered-Comforter)

2. (P-A). Is the same as between husband and wife.

The other two relationships (4, 8) are rare or anomalous.

Two children can have any of the nine possible relationships with each other, three symmetrical (which may in this case be called twin relationships) and six asymmetrical (which may in this case be called older-younger sibling relationships).

Thus, in all, the following sets of simple dyadic relationships are possible in a family with two children: 9 between husband and wife; 9 between father and each child; 9 between mother and each child; and 9 between the two children; a total of 36 possibilities, each easily recognizable, and each with a different implication. Triadic or three-handed relationships in such a family can be analyzed just as systematically and rigorously and profitably, the difficulties being purely schematic. The same applies to quadratic relationships.

This gives the complete array of simple relationships, which can be easily transferred to social relations outside the family.

II. *Simple Indirect Relationships.* A simple indirect relationship is one in which only a single active ego state is exhibited by each party, but this exhibition is preceded by an internal dialogue involving another ego state. Examples of this have been given in the text under Respect, Admiration, and Lechery. In respect, there is first an internal dialogue between the Child and Adult before the Adult behavior is released; in admiration, there is a consultation between the Adult and the Child before the Child is released; and in lechery, a head transaction between Parent and Child, bypassing the Adult and urging the Child to go ahead. These are represented in the diagrams in Figure 17. Such situations are technically called "programming." Figure 17A represents a Child-programmed Adult, Figure 17B an Adult-programmed Child, and Figure 17C a Parent-programmed Child.

III. *Compound Relationships.* A compound relationship is one which requires more than two active ego states to sustain it. These are the more intimate and enduring relations of human living. Family relationships must be compound if they are to survive. In the family analysis given above, we have broken down what are actually, over any long period, compound relationships into a series of simple ones which might exist for brief periods.

Companionship, friendship, and intimacy are compound relationships which have been described in the text. The ego states of the two parties will shift under the impact of varying circumstances, so that in the long run all six of them will be exhibited at one or another. Compound relationships may also be direct, or indirect with internal consultation.

C

DISCUSSION

To illustrate the value of this classification, two examples of predictive statements can be offered.

A. Simple relationships, both direct and indirect, tend to proceed smoothly until exhausted. People at parties can deplore together (P-P,1), compare together (A-A,5), flirt together (C-C,9), or console (P-C,3). They can do any of these smoothly and indefinitely until the active ego states are exhausted, and then the participants separate. Over a longer period, people can work together in an

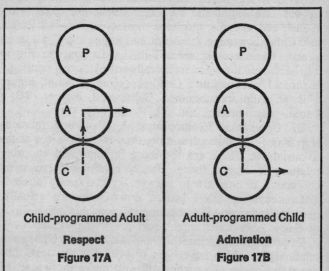

Child-programmed Adult

Respect

Figure 17A

Adult-programmed Child

Admiration

Figure 17B

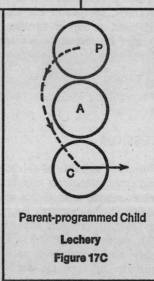

Parent-programmed Child

Lechery

Figure 17C

office (A-A,5) smoothly and without incident, year after year, but they are usually glad each evening when quitting time comes. Incidents occur only when the relationship becomes compound by the intrusion of some ego state other than the contractual Adult-Adult ones.

The following example is instructive. A "leaderless group" met weekly for well-motivated intellectual discussion. Things went smoothly for about a year, but then the members began to get restive, although they wanted the meetings to continue. The transactional consultant they came to saw little possibility of the group surviving under the current simple Adult-to-Adult contract. He first recommended that they find a strong leader, but they didn't want to do that. He then suggested that they turn it into an "encounter" group, which meant changing the contract so as to permit exhibitions of Parental and Child ego states. This changed the relationships of the members from simple to compound, and the group survived for another year until new types of difficulties arose from the "encounters," as anticipated. These finally convinced the members that a strong leader was needed.

The basic transactional principle here may be stated as follows: In a simple relationship there is no possibility of crossed or ulterior transactions, since those require more than two active ego states. Hence communication will proceed smoothly and indefinitely unless and until exhaustion occurs. Exhaustion can be prevented by permitting the participation of fresh ego states to form a compound relationship. But that usually leads to games, which must then be dealt with.

B. Compound relationships tend to create misunderstandings, crossed transactions, and games, all resulting in "incidents," but they survive better because there are more gratifications than in simple relationships. The transactional principle is: In a compound relationship, communication may be disturbed repeatedly, but it is usually resumed because of the many payoffs available.

To recapitulate, a simple direct relationship involves only two active ego states. A simple indirect relationship involves in addition one or more latent ego states. Either of these may be either symmetrical or asymmetrical. A compound relationship involves more than two active ego states, and may also be symmetrical or asymmetrical. For example, companionship and friendship are compound symmetrical relationships, while the Roger-Susan relation described on page 145 was a compound asymmetrical relationship. The variables, then are:

Simple	Symmetrical	Direct
Compound	Asymmetrical	Indirect

A simple, symmetrical, direct relationship is the simplest and straightest. A compound, asymmetrical, indirect relationship is the most complex and offers the most opportunities for games and other forms of ulterior transactions.

INDEX

INDEX

257

Invest $8.95 in a better marriage.

Every year, one half million American marriages break up. Very often because of sexual ignorance, frustration, boredom, and apathy.

It doesn't have to happen. Not to you.

You can enjoy more sexual satisfaction. You can know the secret of woman's "cycle of desire."

You can enjoy more sexual freedom.

A Marriage Manual is a tactful, illustrated guide that delves into every aspect of the art of marriage from the first sex act to Vatsyayana's Kama Sutra. It has already sold three-quarters of a million copies.

▼ **AT YOUR BOOKSTORE OR MAIL THIS COUPON NOW FOR FREE 30-DAY TRIAL** ▼